HIT 'EM HARD

HIT 'EM HARD
JACK SPOT, KING OF THE UNDERWORLD

WENSLEY CLARKSON

HarperCollins*Entertainment*
An Imprint of HarperCollinsPublishers

HarperCollins*Entertainment*
An Imprint of HarperCollins*Publishers*
77–85 Fulham Palace Road,
Hammersmith, London W6 8JB

www.**fire**and**water**.com

Published by HarperCollins*Entertainment* 2002
1 3 5 7 9 8 6 4 2

Copyright © Wensley Clarkson 2002

A catalogue record for this book is
available from the British Library

ISBN 0 00 712440 6

Set in Photina by
Rowland Phototypesetting Ltd,
Bury St Edmunds, Suffolk

Printed and bound in Great Britain by
Clays Ltd, St Ives plc

CONTENTS

'This was more than a mob fight. It was a victory over the Nazis. I don't want to swank, but that night I was the hero of the East End.'

Jack Spot, after the Cable Street riots of 1936

AUTHOR'S NOTE

The central figure in this story, Jack Spot, changed his last name many times during his lifetime. In an effort to avoid confusion, throughout this book, he is referred to as Spot. Some of the dialogue represented was sourced from available documents, some was drawn from tape-recorded testimony and some was reconstructed from the memories of participants. I've had to make some informed deductions for dramatic purposes, but the actual facts are as they occurred. References to the cost of items, such as clothes and food, are as they were at the time.

In Jack Spot's era, gambling was the equivalent of the drug trade in today's society. Fortunes were made and lost with alarming regularity. Some villains paid for their mistakes with their lives. I encountered a few of the survivors and many of the reporters mentioned in this book during my childhood, through my father, a Fleet Street tabloid journalist. Now I hope to share this reckless, yet exciting world with you . . .

ACKNOWLEDGMENTS

I cannot begin to express the depth of my feelings for the many individuals who've made this book possible. I owe them my deepest and most heartfelt gratitude.

To my commissioning editor at HarperCollins, Val Hudson, I say many, many thanks. Without her and the superb editing skills of Monica Chakraverty this book would never have been possible. Their support and guidance has been very much appreciated. Then there is John Glatt, Jo Holt, Bob Duffield, Fran Pearce, John Irvin, Oein McCann, Jimmy Smithers, Evzen Kolar, Frank Page and many, many more friends and associates of Jack Spot.

Also, a final tribute to the memory of so many great Fleet Street reporters including the gentlemanly Victor Sims and the legendary Duncan Webb, plus Spot's ghostwriter Steve Francis, whose white-washed villa in Rosas, on the Costa Blanca, marked the beginning of my love affair with Spain.

PROLOGUE
The Fight That Never Was

12 August 1955

'KING' SPOT IS STABBED

By the *Daily Express* Crime Bureau: Percy Hoskins, Geoffrey Dowling, John Lambert, Keith Morfett

London may be on the brink of a new gang war.

The knives are out.

And this morning three men – one of them the No.1 gang boss, forty-three-year-old Jack Spot, who once said he has a thousand men to back him – are in hospital.

Three men, all savagely stabbed.

It all started as the hands of the clock above the Italia Espresso coffee bar, in Soho, pointed to 12 midday. Mob king Jack Spot, in a forty-guinea suit, was about to be stiletto slashed in a dozen places.

Mambo music was blaring from the jukeboxes. Men in slouch hats and draped suits were taking the air on the corner. Two men were standing beneath the clock. One was Jack Spot, a big cigar jutting out from between his lips.

Everybody on the street knew him. Many gave him a polite 'Good morning' as they passed the King of Soho. But few knew the identity of the other man under the clock.

Suddenly the smile was wiped from Jack Spot's face. A scuffle started. The eyes of the man on the corner focused on the pair. A woman passing by screamed when she saw the stiletto flashing in the sunlight. Blood splattered on the pavement beside a barrow-boy's pitch. The barrow boy had gone for a convenient stroll.

The two men continued struggling along the roadway to the corner of Old Compton Street. The doorways of Frith Street became crowded with men who had been standing on the corner just a few seconds earlier. A box of grapes – priced at 2s. 6d. a lb – squashed on the pavement as the men lurched against the Continental Fruit Shop on the corner.

Then – just as fifty-year-old shop proprietor Harry Hyams was weighing tomatoes – the fight swung inside the shop. The stiletto rose and plunged swiftly as the two men fought. Trays of plump melons, and plums and peaches toppled down as customers fled.

At that moment thirteen-stone Mrs Sophie Hyams went into action. She picked up a heavy metal scoop from a weighing machine and began beating the fighting men over the head with it. The two men weaved to get out of the way. The stiletto kept flashing but forty-five-year-old Mrs Hyams kept on banging the scoop on the men as blood splashed over her white overall.

Soon Jack Spot lay on the floor bleeding. The other man limped out of the shop clutching a wound in his stomach. The stranger started crawling out into the street.

Jack Spot struggled to his feet and began staggering down the street, alone, as the jukeboxes blared. He slumped into the scarlet-and-cream salon of a hairdressing shop.

'Fix me up,' he whispered. 'Clean me up, please,' added the man with the six-guinea shirt and £15-a-pair shoes.

An ambulance was called. Jack Spot was taken to Charing Cross Hospital. Police drove up. They cordoned off the street and started asking questions. But nobody in Frith Street seemed to know anything.

'Listen, mister,' said one bystander. 'If I see a chiv fight, I look the other way. It's healthier that way.'

Jack Spot's condition was said to be critical. He had deep stab wounds in his neck, stomach, and lungs and surgery was carried out.

It was to become known on the streets of Soho as 'the fight that never was'. And it marked the beginning of the end for Jack Spot. But what a life he'd led . . .

1

THE BAD OLD DAYS

To outsiders, the East End in the first half of the twentieth century seemed a world apart from the rest of London. Visitors to the area were taken to see the dosshouses on the old Ratcliffe Highway then down to the East India Docks before a pint in Charlie Brown's pub, which had been turned into a licensed museum.

Over in Limehouse, the Chinese played fan-tan with cards and ran illegal Puk-a-pu joints where you betted on numbers in the street and a kimonoed character hoisted the betting slips in a forked stick up to a first-floor croupier. In Cable Street, dark-skinned people strolled the pavements and opium dens, rat-holes of dirty divans and sackcloth curtains, where the Chinese quietly smoked their beloved narcotic.

In Sidney Street there was the famous spot where Peter the Painter had held a siege and shot two policemen. Rookie constable Ted Greeno later recalled how it was also the place where he challenged a huge West Indian who lived on the fat of the sea, rolling drunken sailors for their payrolls. Greeno explained: 'It was 11.30, very dark and he'd knocked out a seaman and was rifling his pockets when I grabbed him by the arm.' Up went his arm and up went Greeno. Up and down, like a monkey on a string. It took four coppers to get the West Indian into a van. Next morning when he should have been in court, the man was in Vallance Road Infirmary complaining of stomach pains and wrongful assault. That was the way it was.

In nearby Wapping, visitors were advised never to enter the area after dark. In those days it was an island full of violent, drunken Irishmen. As Ted Greeno remembered: 'On Corpus Christi day it was beautiful with children marching in white, and clean curtains and shrines at every window. On Corpus Christi night only the sober stayed indoors and only policemen tried to stay out of fights.'

Suicides were commonplace in the East End. And the nearby Thames was the favourite location for a dramatic exit. To some it was a happier prospect than a life of poverty and violence.

In Shoreditch, for four shillings and sixpence return, you could escape the poverty for a day at the Newmarket races. 'If you got there with your wallet intact you were lucky,' Ted Greeno recalled.

Then there was the district of Hoxton, renowned for the shop-lifters who swooped through to the West End. Greeno explains: 'I remember following three women from Hoxton to Walthamstow who went into a draper's like sylphs and came out like heavyweights. Then they went down the "Ladies" and came out slim again, carrying carrier bags. We took them back to the draper, who was amazed that three women could steal so much so quickly. So was I. In four minutes they had rifled the shop of socks, coats, dresses.'

Police and villains spent their precious days off-duty at places like Greenford trotting-track. Thoroughbred horses in feather-weight sulkies made a pretty picture and the sport was keen – and wide open. If a trotter broke into a gallop it was disqualified and a crooked jockey could 'throw' a race by 'accidentally' speed-ing up their horse. When the 'wrong' horse was leading, spectators by the rails would throw their jackets over its head. The horse would then break into a gallop and be disqualified.

It was into this chaotic and dangerous world that Jack Spot was born.

ƒ   ƒ   ƒ

John Colmore, better known as Jack Comer, but best known as Jack Spot, was born Jacob Comacho, at 38 Myrdle Street,

Whitechapel, on 12 April 1912. 'Jackie', as he was known from the time he could walk, was the youngest of four children. His dad was a poorly paid Jewish tailor's machinist who'd moved to London with his wife from Lodz, Poland, in 1893. Number thirty-eight Myrdle Street was on the fifth floor of a crumbling tenement building called Fieldgate Mansions. In an effort to blend in more easily with the local population, the family changed their last name three times – from Comacho to Colmore to Comer – but still they faced deep-rooted anti-Semitism.

Before Jackie had reached three years of age, the world was at war. The effects of the slaughter in the trenches of France and Belgium soon reached the East End as detachments of wounded soldiers were sent to local hospitals. One Sunday evening, on 30 August 1914, the London Hospital in Whitechapel received more than a hundred soldiers, who were transported from Waterloo Station in vans provided by well-known food manufacturer J. Lyons. The lucky ones were provided with taxicabs.

But many others in the East End had gone out of their way to avoid being called-up for duty. Numerous Russian and Polish Jews such as Jackie's father – who'd been granted British nationality – refused to obey calls to colours by claiming to be conscientious objectors. Some even used local solicitors to provide forged certificates that lied about their ages, or faked some disease. Young Jackie's dad was happy to let British soldiers fight for him while he stuck to his 'soft job' in the East End rag trade.

During the war, wholesale pilfering down at the East End docks was organised by older dockers who'd hadn't been called up because of their age. They used young boys like Jackie, some only five or six years old, to deliver rum and port stolen through a variety of methods including 'sucking the monkey', the insertion of a metal pipe with a rubber tubing, which the thief then sucked until the liquor started to flow, and 'spiking the cask', which involved boring holes in the barrel.

But when little Jackie wasn't up to mischief, he could be found sitting on the damp, warm ridges of a draining board, swinging his legs and listening to the sound of his mother talking and laughing over the din of doing the weekly laundry in the communal washhouse under their low-rise home. All the women had aprons on and sleeves rolled up above their elbows. They scrubbed collars and cuffs on the rubbing boards, their hands chapped red from the hot, sudsy water in the big butler sinks round the washroom. But still they managed a smile and a joke.

Jackie grew up in a true ghetto street: Jews down one side of Myrdle Street, Irish down the other. Yet Spot later remembered the Irish womenfolk with particular respect. 'They fought better than men, them women,' he said.

Like a lot of East End kids, young Jackie had no garden or park to play in. With few toys, and none of today's high-tech games, he and his pals used their imagination and inventiveness to entertain themselves. They'd fashion a cricket bat out of a piece of wood and play in the middle of the street outside their home using a manhole cover for a wicket. Others drew three lines across the street and made that into a tennis court. They'd use their hands for bats. In the winter many played football in the middle of the road, marbles in the gutter and hopscotch on the pavement.

Jackie was particularly keen on the marbles he stole from Woolworth's. They were all made by hand and every one was different. Each glass sphere was a tiny world filled with a beautiful, streaky coloured eye. Tin-can stilts were another favourite game, where two empty cocoa tins had holes punched in the ends to put string through. The cans were then turned upside down, with the strings held in hands, and used simply to walk up and down on, clanking and clonking until the child tumbled to the ground.

Each game and pastime had its specific season in the year. There were cigarette-card seasons, marble seasons, peg-top seasons and, in the autumn, the conker season. Jackie and his young friends would soak their conkers in brine or vinegar and bake them to make them last longer and hit harder.

But Jackie's favourite pastime of all was making a complete nuisance of himself. He was dead keen on Knock Down Ginger, which meant tying a piece of string to the front door knocker of a house, trailing it around the corner out of sight and then pulling as hard as he could. As one neighbour who remembered him well later recalled: 'The owner of the house would do their nut after Jackie did it five or six times. He loved causing aggro.'

The council rubbish dump over at Hackney Marshes often doubled up as a popular playground for Jackie and his pals. They'd use homemade skates or a wooden box cart to rush through the streets. He and his pals would then spend all day searching amongst the rubbish for anything of value.

Back at home, few parents worried about what their kids were up to. By today's standards, Jackie and his mates stayed out until very late at night. A visit to the local picture house to watch a silent film was often a rowdy affair with the audience constantly cracking peanuts, noshing on sweets, rustling newspapers filled with fish and chips and talking non-stop to the screen. Punch-ups were also two a penny at the flicks.

Sometimes Jackie found himself waiting outside the local pub while his mum and dad were inside supping a few pints. Other times he was sent down to the local bottle and jug, or off-licence, to get a jug of beer for them to drink indoors.

But as the world headed towards the Great Depression, life became even harder for those in the East End. Jackie's dad was frequently out of work and there was no unemployment benefit to keep the family going. The Comers, along with many other families, were issued with coupons from the doctor for a bowl of soup, which was usually collected from a basin in the local school. But it didn't go far.

Jackie and his pals always had holes in their shoes because there was no money to buy new ones or repair them. Every family made its own particular sacrifice. Wedding rings were pawned and much else besides. Some schools provided kids with boots, but they'd have a hole punched in the side as a mark so they couldn't be pawned.

In those days, many roads were surfaced with tar-covered wooden blocks, which were stolen to use on the fire at home to keep warm. Jackie's family were so hard up, they went for an interview with the Relieving Officer, who assessed families for public assistance. They were given extra tickets for food, made out for a week's supply and exchangeable at the local shop.

Inevitably, many in the East End were driven to crime. When the father of one of Jackie's best pals was nicked for stealing a radio from a shop, he got three months hard labour in Brixton Prison. Families considered it wrong, but necessary, to steal in order to survive. Heavyweight organised crime was non-existent in those days. As one East Ender later recalled: 'To start with, people didn't steal from their own. They took from people who had money and were well insured. Not from people who had nothing and couldn't cover their loss. But everything was done on spec.'

Sharp-eyed Jackie learned at an early age never to leave a trail after once watching the dad of a school pal get nicked by the police. They'd followed the trail of sweets left by a penny-in-the-slot machine, which he'd ripped off a wall a few minutes earlier. Over in Petticoat Lane, Jackie and his pals began stealing purses from market shoppers.

Down at the Thames, dockers queued in the despondent hope of half-a-day's casual work, while women stretched their meagre budgets to feed their husbands, then their children, and often went without themselves. Many families were destitute because the man of the house had died in World War One. A frequent meal was boiled rice, with a spoon of jam if they had a few bob that day. Many families were often so short of food they ate starlings and killed neighbours' racing pigeons to put in a pie.

Jackie and his pals decided at a young age that they wanted to earn good money whatever it took. They knew only too well how hard it was for their parents. Unlike many others in the hard-working, law-abiding, Jewish East-End community, young Jackie already felt restless and frustrated by his family's poverty.

ƒ   ƒ   ƒ

By the age of seven, Jackie had joined a local gang of kids often involved in pitch battles with other youngsters. The kids at one end of Jackie's street fought their rivals from the other end of the street. At other times, mobs of kids from a few streets away tried to invade the 'opposition's' pitch. Membership of the gangs usually depended on precisely where a child lived and whether he was a Jew or a Christian, since there was still much inbred prejudice against the Jews who'd moved into the area over the previous thirty years.

Young Jackie then started being nicknamed 'Spotty' because he had a big, black mole on his left cheek. As he later recalled: 'I resented the nickname at first, but at that age you don't resent anything for too long. At least it was better than being called "Comer the Jew Boy".'

Spotty – already with broad shoulders and strong arms – was renowned as a snappy puncher who could also soak up some heavy punishment. At just eight years of age he was elevated to leader of his own street gang even though there were many other bigger kids in the gang. Naturally some of those older children resented being ordered around by a 'tiddler' but Spotty stood up to them all. As he later recalled: 'I was without fear. I took on anybody, no matter what their size. But sometimes, if it was two or three of them, I'd call on my best pals.'

These close friends were Morris Goldstein, a.k.a. 'Moisha Blueball' and Bernard 'Sonny the Yank' Schack. As Spotty later explained: 'Moisha was a snotty-nosed, spaniel-eyed kid with his hair cropped down to the skull.' He'd got his nickname because he'd had a blue testicle. (The name was later changed to Blueboy for reasons of decorum although Spot always called him Blueball.) Sonny the Yank was short even though he was a couple of years older than his two pals. But he was tough and only spoke for a good reason. When he did, it was with a strange nasal sound giving him almost an American accent. Other boys ridiculed him. 'Sonny had to be tough to prove to other kids he didn't like being laughed at,' Spot later said.

One night, Spot and his mob went to the nearby market place after it had closed down, to arm itself for a street battle. They collected discarded vegetables such as overripe tomatoes that mashed up into a gooey mess if not held carefully. There was also brown and pulpy fruit that smelled sickly sweet, old mouldy potatoes and banana stalks that could be used as clubs if too heavy to throw. Soon every kid was armed for imminent battle.

Spot's gang greeted the opposition with a fusillade of rotten food. As Spot later explained: 'Then it was every kid for himself, fighting as hard as we knew and often rolling in the dust under the weight of two or three assailants.' The rival gang carried wooden swords and shields made from cardboard, just to add some colour to the occasion. Spotty's gang also had homemade bows and arrows and let loose awful, blood-curdling yells. But during hand-to-hand combat, these theatrical weapons were abandoned and knuckles always took their place.

That day, Spot's enemy mob were under so much fire they took cover, pressing themselves against walls, behind dustbins and lamp-posts as Spot and his pals chanted what seemed like a never-ending battle-cry. Then thirty more of their rivals turned the corner and Spot realised that his mob was seriously outnumbered.

'The leader of the opposing gang was a tall kid wearing a ragged jersey and cut-down corduroy trousers,' Spot later recalled. 'He'd got Titchy Barrow's head under his arm and was pasting hell out of him. I ran at Jersey, pulled him away from Titch and rolled with him into the gutter. But Jersey was a strong boy and every time I managed to get astride his chest he rolled me off again. I got a firm grip on his wrist and started twisting. Jersey kept punching me hard in the belly until I let go. We kept on fighting, wrestling, punching, rolling over and over in the dust and once rolling right through a mound of horse droppings. We forgot this was a mob fight. This became a personal battle between us two, with neither of us willing to concede supremacy to the other. Then finally I got a grip on his wrist again and twisted hard until he screamed.'

'Give in?' panted Spotty to his opponent.

He sat astride the other boy twisting his wrist.

His archenemy breathed hard but said nothing.

'Give in?' gritted Spotty as he twisted the wrist even tighter.

The boy screamed again, but when Spotty eased the pressure he clamped his lips together in defiance.

Spotty squeezed even tighter a third time and his archenemy's voice was shrill and thin with pain. 'Give in,' he shrieked. 'Give in.'

'Louder,' gloated Spotty. 'Louder.'

'Give in,' the other boy whimpered.

Spotty climbed to his feet, still breathing hard and brushed the dust and filth off his ragged clothes. The other boy sat up moaning, holding his wrist and pretending he was more hurt than he really was. It was only then that Spot turned around and realised that all the rest of his gang had retreated at least 100 yards back and were shouting insults and defiance at their opposition. He was completely isolated.

'I wasn't really afraid,' he explained. 'I was ready to take on all of them together, counting on my own mob to come running to my assistance.' Spot then calmly began walking in the opposite direction from where his mob waited, intending to completely circle around the block and rejoin them.

But Spot had only covered about twenty yards when the boy he'd beaten a few moments earlier came running towards him. Spotty turned and saw the look of spite in his red-rimmed eyes. He hit Spot hard, splitting his lip. Blood streamed from Spot's nostrils.

Spot gritted his teeth and fought back at the other boy furiously. Then the rest of his enemy's mob surrounded them, cheering the other boy, spurring him on and giving him more strength. He was raining blows into Spot as his shoulders pressed up against the wall. He struggled to protect his face behind his forearms. The cheers of his friends urged him to victory.

Spot knew he had to get away. He later explained: 'When a kid has to escape, he doesn't think about the harm he does to others. He just strikes out blindly all around. So I kicked out wildly and savagely. It was a bad kick in a bad place. He doubled up much more quickly than anyone might have expected.' Spotty kicked the boy again as he doubled up, and his toecap caught him flush in the mouth.

An ominous silence followed as it became clear the other boy was seriously hurt and Spotty hotfooted it, with thirty boys on his tail. He kept ahead of them by sprinting whenever they got close. Spot tried to double back around the block to get closer to his home. But they were waiting for him and cornered Spot in a cul-de-sac surrounded by three high walls. He later explained: 'A hundred arms twined around me, a thousand fists pounding, the flagstones bruising my knees and the awful weight of them. I was suffocating. I opened my mouth and my compressed lungs tried to suck in air. I wanted to scream that I was dying.'

Spot was eventually left lying in the gutter, sobbing with blood flowing from numerous wounds. As he struggled through the streets to find his home he started brooding about what had happened. When he reached a railway line he noticed his arch enemy down by the tracks.

Spot explained: 'He'd placed a halfpenny on the line and was waiting for a train to pass so that the halfpenny would be flattened and enlarged enough to fit into a penny-in-the-slot machine.' Spot glanced around to ensure the coast was clear and then rushed the boy from behind. Spot beat him severely before turning and running home along the top of the railway embankment. He'd learned a lesson that day. It was a lesson he carried into later life. As he recalled: 'I discovered that I had to be patient to exact a full toll of vengeance. That fight taught me the desperation of being hounded, and for the first time it taught me fear. Terrible, gibbering fear!'

♪   ♪   ♪

Away from the violent gang clashes, there was a real sense of pulling together whenever one of Spot's young pals was up against it. Moisha Blueball's sister was taken seriously ill when their father was in prison and his mother was scraping a living as an office cleaner. Most of the family's furniture had been sold since the old man went away and their doctor said the only way Moisha's sister would get better was if she started eating proper, nourishing food. He suggested chicken.

Moisha, Spotty and Sonny the Yank licked their lips at the very thought of it. Then Sonny said dolefully in his strange American-style accent: 'Maybe we could go round the houses collectin' jam-jars?' But Jack Spot had already devised a much bigger plan. 'If we had some old bits of lead we could sell them,' Spot pointed out. The boys said they'd never get up on the high roofs where most lead was, so Spot suggested they raid the yard of local rag-and-bone merchant Jack Reeves. Over the years his business had prospered and he owned an open-air yard crammed with all kinds of junk, from iron bedsteads to old motorcars. Spot was sure they could get away with it.

Within days, Spotty and his pals had stolen enough lead from old-man Reeves' yard to sell it back to him for half a crown. Spot and his gang spent an entire morning flattening the lead with bricks to make sure it was unrecognizable. 'He didn't have a clue it'd come right out of his own yard,' Spot recalled.

The following night Moisha Blueball explained in mouth-watering detail to his pals what a chicken looked like when it was roasted, how his sister had eaten half of it at one sitting, and how she could hardly wait until tomorrow to eat some more. His mother even pointed out the wishbone and let Moisha break it with his sister. The boys naturally concluded they could buy themselves a chicken every day if they stole some more lead from old-man Reeves' yard and sold it back to him like before. But on their third raid of the scrap yard they encountered the local law. Spot got away, but Sonny panicked, fell awkwardly, cutting his arm badly and was arrested. 'But Sonny never told on us,' Spot later recalled. 'They kept on at him and made all kinds of threats but he stuck at it that he worked alone and that he alone had stolen the lead he sold to Reeves.'

Sonny ended up in reformatory school for a year, but the bond had been firmly sealed between Spot, Moisha and Sonny. And Spot even learned something from it. He later recalled: 'Robbing old-man Reeves' junk yard taught me never to go to the same well twice. And, what's more, it taught me the importance of being able to rely on the man who bought from me. A good and reliable fence is worth his weight in gold.'

*   *   *

Spot and his mob of young tearaways soon graduated to more grown-up games. One was called 'Undercover'. East Ender Jimmy Hall remembers how it went: 'There was a crowd of girls and a crowd of boys. Some of one lot would get under a load of old coats, while the other lot went away. Then they came back and guessed who was under the coats by touching. It was all a bit saucy.'

When Spot was just ten years old, he encountered a fifteen-year-old neighbour called Betty Smith, a fat, sweaty girl well known because she was always panting as if she'd been running. She'd once got a mob of smaller kids to go down a mews with her and then charged them a penny each to look at her knickers. After a few minutes she laughed at the boys scornfully, shook her skirts straight and danced off with all their pennies clutched tightly in her sweaty palm. Betty got money off older boys for more intimate acts and before she reached sixteen she was taken off to have a baby, never to be seen again.

Meanwhile, scrapping remained the key to Jack Spot's survival. He recalled: 'When I was a kid, and for years afterwards, a fight was better than a good dinner for me. We all lived, slept and dreamed fighting. We fought with our fists. And all of us were up against bullies in one way or another.'

Spot later used these experiences to explain his attitude to life: 'One thing I have proved in my life. The geezers who are the biggest bullies are yellow. Hit 'em hard enough and they scarper.

They don't come back for more.' 'Hit 'em hard' was to become Spot's philosophy on life.

♪   ♪   ♪

Back in the Spot household, Jack's older brother had become a tailor under the watchful eye of their father. One sister was working as dressmaker to the court of St James, for the Royal Family no less. The other sister was already working shifts in an East End sweatshop. But all were lowly paid and had to continue living in Myrdle Street because they couldn't afford places of their own.

At fourteen, Spot left school and registered at the local labour exchange. Every day he joined the jobless queue in the hope of something turning up, but he soon got so bored, he didn't bother. Then his father managed to get him a job in a nearby tailor's shop, earning fifteen bob a week. His main duties were to sweep the floor and make the manager cups of tea. Spot hated it but knew it made his dad happy so he stuck at it. Spot gave thirteen shillings of his salary to his mother each week, and kept a couple of bob for spending money. But he particularly hated the way the older people at work treated youths like him. One day he had a row with his bullying foreman and knocked him out with one punch, grabbed his jacket and walked out.

Then Spot got himself a job in a caff in Whitechapel, working twelve-hour shifts that started at eight in the morning. Many local villains met up at the caff: thieves, pickpockets, safe crackers. Spotty soon got to know them all. The only problems at work came from tearaways, teenage bullies who came in the caff, ate their food and refused to pay. But Spot, now a broadly built six-footer who looked at least three years older than his age, sorted them out. Customers quickly learned to steer clear of any trouble with Spot.

Eventually he got tired of the long hours and became a lather boy in the local barber's shop. Then he switched to selling newspapers on street corners – anything was worth a try if it meant he could earn enough money to pay his keep.

§   §   §

One sunny spring afternoon, Jack Spot, now fifteen years of age, found himself sitting alone on his doorstep dreaming of the day he could afford to buy himself some new clothes and start dating girls. He was desperate for a pair of proper, long trousers, as he'd had to make do with his father's ill-fitting cast-offs since turning thirteen.

The warm weather at the time meant local girls dressed in thin frocks, which showed off the contours of their bodies. Spot soon noticed his neighbour Maggie Klaut walking along the street. Maggie had been obliged to sell her body 'Up West' until she'd got a regular job three months earlier. She was wearing a thin, flowery frock that caught Spot's attention. He no longer saw her as a grown-up woman but as a provocative, sexy female. He admired the way her thighs pressed against her thin dress, how she held her shoulders well back and the way her chest jogged up and down as she walked in her high heels.

Spot recalled: 'Maggie had a nice smile: a warm, affectionate, all-embracing smile. I kept looking at her. It was as though in that moment the full significance of being adult and male had hit me a powerful, atomic blow in the belly.'

The two of them exchanged polite conversation on the doorstep and Maggie offered the teenager a cup of tea. He sheepishly followed her up the steps into her house. Her two kids were at school. Maggie served him bread and butter with jam and then revealed she'd heard Spot and his pals discussing her as they sat on the doorstep a few night's previously.

'I go with men for just one reason,' she told the nervous teenager. 'To get what I can out of them. Most women are the same. Never trust a woman. You're just a meal ticket to them. They don't care what happens to you and they'll take all they can get, even if it leaves you starving.'

Jack Spot never forgot those words. He felt instinctively that Maggie was right. Men were supposed to be stronger than women, but they were really much weaker than them. When a woman wanted something, she could make a man do exactly what she desired. Then Jack Spot asked Maggie what sex was really like. Minutes later he was making love for the first time in his life.

ℬ   ℬ   ℬ

Over the next few years, Spot kept returning to the caff where he'd previously worked. One of the other regulars was a boy in his late teens, called Jumbo, who went up and down Petticoat Lane on Sunday mornings, blackmailing the stallholders for protection money. At first, Spot was appalled by the way Jumbo would beat them up. As he later explained: 'It used to make my blood boil. And my mates didn't like it, either. We couldn't understand what he was up to.'

Spot's main 'henchmen' at the time were Moisha and Sonny plus two other kids called Turk and Little Hymie. All five stuck together like glue. One day, tearaway Jumbo asked Spot if he and his gang wanted to join his mob. Spot later recalled: 'I still didn't like him but I suppose I was flattered. He was the big noise and I was a kid. I still hadn't tumbled to his racket at that time. All I knew was that he got into a lot of fights. If a stallholder didn't pay up, Jumbo would always start a row.' Jack Spot and his cronies forgot their earlier objections to blackmail, and were soon steaming in with all fists flying.

But once Spot realised he was making Jumbo a lot of money, he had a showdown with him, telling him he objected to doing his dirty work. 'I smacked him on the chin. He was a big fellow, weighed twelve stone. His mob was with him and they just stood and gaped when I hit him. It was a fair cop, we mixed it hard for a quarter of an hour. I was showin' a few bruises, but his face was a fair pulp when I got in a final clip under the jaw and knocked him out cold.' Jumbo's gang fell apart and, soon afterwards, Spot crowned himself the king of Aldgate's youth. He was just sixteen years old.

By now Jack Spot, as he was already known to all in the East End, was a strong, well-built fellow with a good-tempered face and an inexhaustible number of comical Jewish stories, mostly with the laugh against himself. His favourite method of talking business was to think of a good idea, seek out the opinion of his pals, homing in on the right man to make it happen and then say: 'Well, let's do it, then!'

By now, Spot was hanging around the local gyms and boxing clubs where all the East End tearaways congregated. He'd adopted a style of life very different from his hard-working parents, brothers and sisters, all still trying to earn a crust in the tailoring and dressmaking trade. Spot's fearsome reputation as a scrapper soon prompted requests from Jewish businessmen, bookies, promoters and shopkeepers who felt themselves increasingly vulnerable to anti-Semitism and intimidation. The profession of violence was beckoning.

2
DEN OF RASCALS

East End crime was on the increase. Nimble street Arabs known as 'van draggers' trailed behind horse-drawn vans until the driver got down and then they pounced. They would dive through the fly-sheets and run off like greyhounds with a chest of tea or a box of soap. They often hid out in open railway drays where they stashed their loot.

Then there were the street walkers near Spot's family home in Whitechapel, who'd nip out for a bottle of beer or go out to curb crawl, only to come back to find their boyfriend (and pimp) had made off with their handbag or the coin-box from the gas meter. The only incentive for the bobbies on the beat was that the Commercial Gas Company paid a reward of £1 for every meter thief jailed. With policemen averaging £3.50 a week it was a useful addition to their income. The only other crime-catching perk available to the police at the time was a ten-bob reward, from magistrates or the commissioner, for a commendation.

Many young bobbies were promoted to the Met's 'winter patrol' which meant they could wear plain clothes but were not officially in the CID. They could also work any hours they chose, provided they were not less than eighteen hours a day. Each afternoon the young policemen were supposed to attend classes at Scotland Yard. Then it was back on duty in the late afternoon followed by a few hours sleep in the station section house dormitory. Then they'd be off to hitch a horse to a wagon, to comb the streets of the East End for any early birds of crime.

♭   ♭   ♭

Young Jack Spot had already concluded there was life beyond the East End so he ventured west to the sleazy neon lights of Soho – a place where few respectable citizens dared to venture after dark. In those days, the streets of Soho were the wickedest area in the nation. Many called it the 'square mile of vice'. Scotland Yard's Ted Greeno recalled: 'You could buy anything and see everything – and in the right circumstances you could get your throat slit more promptly than in a pirate boat on the China Seas.'

The teenage Jack Spot was hooked on Soho from the first moment he clapped eyes on it. On the street corners were the faces of young girls with over-painted lips, leaning provocatively against walls. Suddenly, out of the shadows, would come their beady-eyed protectors, who'd try to introduce the girls to Spot and his pals before explaining their prices. A few more paces up the street and a glint of light from a cellar showed that yet another illegal club had opened up. The streets of Soho were constantly changing, winking in and out like the neon lights.

At the notorious 43 Club, in Gerrard Street, manageress Kate Meyrick ran one of the wildest nightspots in the land. There was even a back exit through a courtyard beyond the outside toilets and past an unlocked door into an adjoining shop. Kate was a neat, stern-faced woman always dressed in black, who presided over the 43 Club from a small desk built into the draught-proof cashier's box by the entrance.

A few doors away was the Big Apple, one of the best-known coloured clubs in London. Heavyweight boxer John Margot from Senegal kept guard on the door with quiet efficiency. Customers at the Big Apple soon learned about the boogie-woogie and calypso from the regulars. In nearby Ham Yard was a club run by legendary East Ender Freddie Ford, renowned for serving the finest champagne and caviar. Ford looked like an officer from the Royal Guards with his vast military moustache, ruddy complexion, oxen shoulders and straight back. He was known to flout the licensing laws but he never complained when he was fined by the cozzers.

Next door to the Big Apple was The Hell Club – a nightclub known as the favourite haunt of Soho legend Sam Henry who at one time was head waiter at the Shim-Sham Club in Wardour Street. The Hell Club was installed with concealed lighting that changed colour slowly from pink to deep red, throwing ghastly, purple, flickering shadows across customers' faces. The invention of the bottle party in Soho made Sam Henry his real fortune. His chain of off-licences provided all the booze.

Young Jack Spot also heard rumours about the Nest Club, in Kingly Street, where the regulars smoked cannabis reefers. In the Twilight Club, at the back of Gerrard Street, the customers were also greeted by the prickly whiff of marijuana, which hung in the air like the taste of sin. Sipping coffee in the corner, not talking much, were the real villains, the pimps – white men usually – who sat and watched the young girls dancing. When the reefers burned out, it was the pimps who offered fresh supplies. As one senior Scotland Yard detective said at the time: 'Of all forms of drug-taking and dope-peddling that have infiltrated into London, this new marijuana menace is becoming the worst and most diabolical in the history of Metropolitan crime.'

But young Spot wasn't interested in drugs; he preferred the billiard hall in Wardour Street, where you could see a brilliant punch-up any night of the week. By the end of the 1920s, there were 295 registered clubs within one mile of the statue of Eros in Piccadilly Circus. But, just behind Leicester Square, were at least fifteen more unregistered premises known to the police. At the headquarters of Scotland Yard's Vice Squad there was even a well-thumbed big black book called 'The Clubs Book' which was the bobby's guide to London nightlife.

Spot was also fascinated by gambling premises – known as

spielers – where card sharps ruled. These men could, by a slight movement of their foot under the table, operate a device called a 'hold-out' and whisk a chosen card from the deck out of sight up their sleeve, at a speed the eye couldn't possibly follow. When they played this stolen card, they moved their foot, and the card was flipped into the sharp's hand.

But marked cards weren't used in big games. Police and experienced gamblers detected them by a method known as 'The £100 Secret'. The pack was picked up and rifled with the thumb, then back the other way. Any slight variation of the pattern and it was immediately spotted under the naked eye.

Marked cards could be bought at a conjurer's shop, but the big-money cheats actually marked the cards whilst in play. It was done by a smear of 'daub' which was a crayon-like paste made by mixing a little printer's ink with stearine and wax to which was added a few drops of turpentine. One West End card sharp was known to conceal the daub on his waxed moustache, which he fingered thoughtfully throughout play.

The nearest place for a legitimate punt with a bookie was White City dog track, but that was five miles to the West. Soho seemed a much more attractive proposition to Jack Spot: a nether world that he was determined to become a part of.

*   *   *

One day a character called Larry Soper turned up on Jack Spot's doorstep in Myrdle Street, Whitechapel. They exchanged pleasantries and a little local banter before Soper got down to business. He wanted Spot to work for his association, the 'Stall Trader's Fund', formed to keep new traders from setting up stalls so that the existing members could get through the depression.

Soper told Spot: 'All my traders pay up regularly. They're pleased to. But recently one or two have been dropping behind with their subs and some reckon there's no need for the association no more. But if they don't cough up then the others will soon follow suit and the association will close down. Then word will get out and new stalls will start being set up. The older members want the association to continue and everyone to pay up.'

Soper offered Spot the job as his collector.

'You mean . . . just collect the dough?' asked Spot.

'That's right,' said Soper, looking the tall, well-built youth up and down as if he was inspecting a prize fighter. 'Collect the dough. But make sure you collect it.'

'And if they don't want to pay?'

Soper's smile disappeared. 'You wouldn't let them talk tough to you, would you Spotty?'

'When do I start?' asked Spot.

Collecting time was Saturday night after the stalls had closed down. Spot checked out the books and realised there were only two or three serious 'backsliders' to deal with. The worst offender was a character called Stiltson. Spot stepped up to him just as he was about to wheel his barrow away into the market mews.

'I've come from Larry Soper,' Spot told him. 'You owe six pound ten shillings' in subs. But we'll make it easy for you. You can pay off the arrears at a quid a week in addition to the weekly.'

Stiltson tilted his head back and looked Spot straight in the eyes. 'How many more fuckin' times do I have to tell Larry I ain't a member no more?'

'You ain't got no choice,' Spot told him reasonably. 'It's in your interests to keep the others out.'

'Listen mate,' said Stiltson, tapping Spot on the shoulder. 'I'm alright, see? I ain't afraid of competition. And I ain't payin' no blood money to no association. Understand?'

'It's five bob this week,' Spot told him. 'With a pound off the arrears, that makes twenty-five bob. I'll take it now.'

'Fuck off. Don't come botherin' me again,' Stiltson told Spot.

Spot pulled out a razor blade and drew the point of it down Stiltson's cheek to the peak of his jaw. Stiltson collapsed in the gutter with his face buried in his hands. It was just a surface wound but Spot had managed to cut both Stiltson's cheeks. He overturned Stiltson's barrow and trampled on all his vegetables. Stiltson's shoulders slumped as he moaned to himself in the gutter. Blood ran through his fingers over the backs of his hands and some of it dropped onto the cobblestones. As Spot later recalled: 'In a way, I felt a bit bad about doin' it, but it was his own fault. I couldn't help it if he was set on fightin' the whole wide world. Mind you, if I'd used a knife it would have left an ugly scar for him to worry about. But it's inside where he really hurt. It's amazing what a difference a couple of quick cuts make to a man. He can be as perky as a gamecock, full of fight and spirit and ready to slug it out with the big 'uns. But cold steel is something that takes all the corpuscles out of a man's blood. A nick from a razor breaks a man's spirit.'

When Spot returned to Stiltson's stall the following Saturday, Stiltson was wearing a long strip of plaster down both cheeks. As soon as he saw Spot he dug his hand into his pocket and paid his arrears without a murmur. Spot explained: 'He wasn't cheeky no more. He'd lost all that boisterous cockiness. He wouldn't even look me straight in the eye.'

Word soon got round about the new, keen young collector. Spot's new status pleased him: 'I liked the way I was building myself a reputation. When I went into a pub, men would stop talking, nudge their companions and nod towards me. I knew what they were saying: "That's Jack Spot."'

Jack Spot's attitude to life was that, even though he knew the difference between right and wrong, his priority was to look after number one. That's why it didn't bother him that he'd started making a small fortune leaning on stallholders to pay up protection money.

Next came a brief spell as a lookout and minder to a local housebreaker. However this came to an abrupt end when he was arrested and made an appearance at Middlesex Quarter Sessions. For some reason, known only to him, the young Spot then coughed up to forty other offences but, astonishingly, was only bound over to keep the peace. Spot was soon thinking about his next move, away from the riskier street elements of crime. Racetracks were the place to be.

§   §   §

Spot's first move on to racecourses came when he started working a classic fairground scam called 'Take a Pick'. Punters would happily shell out sixpence to pull a straw with a winning number from a cup. Most of the time they won nothing more than a prize worth just tuppence, while Spot would later boast of clearing between £30 and £40 a day. He also began pulling the same scam back on Petticoat Lane, where he could clear £50 in a good morning. But he had his eyes firmly focused on the bookies at the racecourses. These men regularly 'welshed' on punters by fleeing the track before paying out on the last race, and it was a racket Spot dreamed of making his mark on.

Horse racing had been attracting villains for years. The only form of betting allowed at that time was through the bookmakers at each track and there was incredible competition – and intimidation – for each bookies' pitch (the piece of ground where he worked from). Hundreds of pounds could be made in one day at the races, so it was hardly surprising that gangsters had long since realised there was a rake-off in it for them. That's when the charges for so-called 'protection' came into play.

Shortly after World War One, a gang of racetrack thugs emerged from Little Italy, in the Clerkenwell Road. Five Italian brothers called Joe, Darby, Charlie, Young Harry and Fred Sabini took on and beat gangs who'd been in complete control of the protection rackets for bookmakers on the courses.

'It's the Sabini boys!' went up the terrified cry as these uncrowned kings of the turf, backed up by gangs of 'cosh boys', strolled onto a racecourse. Any resistance to the Sabinis was met with violence; bookies' stands were wrecked. The Sabinis soon spawned a number of pale imitators. War was waged relentlessly between the gangs for almost twenty years and many men died or were horribly mutilated. The prize was tens of thousands of pounds of protection money paid out by the bookmakers.

It was during this period that the razor slashers became the expert marksmen of the gangs. They knew exactly where to strike to maim and disfigure their victims without killing them. The slasher didn't simply walk around with an open razor clutched in his hand for everyone to see. More often it was strapped to his palm, in a piece of cork held in place by string, which did not show in a clenched fist. From the cork, there protruded about one-eighth of an inch of blade that would not penetrate deep enough to cause serious injury but would slice a face open with one deft movement.

It was a common sight on racetracks for a razor slasher to walk up to his victim, seize him by the shoulder in a friendly way and then whisper these few fateful words: 'On your way.'

'Who the hell are you talkin' to?' would be the perfectly natural response.

Then the hand would leave the shoulder and would whisk across the victim's face, slashing up and down. In the confusion that followed, the attacker would melt into the crowd; naturally, nobody would have seen what happened.

At razor-slasher school, they taught a second technique, which was just as effective but a tad clumsier. The slasher would wear an ordinary cloth cap that contained a blade. Once again, the cutting edge would protrude slightly and the assailant would snatch off his cap and strike his victim with its peak, thus laying his face open.

By the mid-1920s, the Sabini gang found themselves competing with the 'Brummagen Boys', a gang from Birmingham who called themselves 'the Loonies'. Armed with guns, razors and iron bars, the Sabinis went spoiling for the fight of their lives with the Brummies at the Greenford Park racecourse, on the outskirts of London. The Birmingham gang's thugs were doing their rounds, collecting protection money from bookies who knew better than not to pay. Then one of the Sabinis butted into the Loonies, and words were exchanged. The Sabini boy pulled out a revolver but, before anything could happen, the police nicked him and he was hauled before a local magistrate who bound him over to keep the peace. The revolver never even got a mention and the battle never took place, but a more lasting war was declared instead.

Days later, there was a ruckus on London Bridge Station before the Sabini mob got on the trains for Plumpton racecourse. A number of men were taken to Guy's Hospital for treatment. At Plumpton itself there were further flare-ups. By the end of the day, the Sabinis proclaimed themselves outright victors. The truce that followed lasted just a few hours, when the ringleader of the Loonies was found shot outside a club.

The victorious Sabinis and their soldiers pulled in vast sums of cash which bought them luxury flats, flashy clobber, diamond rings and fancy women. They were known in London as the 'easy-come, easy-go boys'. For the first time in British history, criminals were living better lives than most ordinary citizens. But then the Sabini Gang's henchmen began demanding better pay and conditions. Rival factions sprung up from the Sabinis, and four brothers named Cortesi – later known as 'the Frenchies' – acted as unofficial shop stewards for some of the gang's discontented followers.

Meanwhile another group, primarily Jewish in origin, sprang up and became known as 'the Yiddishers'. Relations between the Jewish community in Whitechapel and the Italians in Clerkenwell seemed amicable enough, and the Yiddisher gang initially sided with the Sabini boys to cut out the Cortesi crowd. The all-powerful Sabinis continued recruiting Jewish heavies who then 'protected' many Jewish bookies and other 'businessmen'.

Meanwhile, new gangs moved from their shabby hideouts, often in the London suburbs, into Soho, where they began taking over the smaller clubs and spielers so as to spread themselves and make their presence felt throughout the manor. Territorial rights were being fought over as savagely as they were across the Atlantic in Chicago. But the Sabinis reigned supreme until the mid-1930s.

*   *   *

Betting was like a second job to many villains. For people who worked the way Jack Spot did – hit and run, on and off – there would be a lot of free time to fill between jobs. And that's how villains got even more immersed in the gee-gees. Spot knew that, if he prepped it carefully by studying the form, then he'd make an even bigger killing placing bets.

Young Spot went racing with an Aldgate villain called Mad Mick, who asked Spot to accompany him to Epsom on Derby Day. Spot jumped at the chance. Mick carried a small attaché case, which the young Spot presumed had money in it. 'We set up our pitch on the Hill and Mick started making a book on the Derby,' Spot later explained. 'It was the only race we were betting on and the money came rolling in.'

Just before the 'Off', Mick closed the book and told Spot: 'While this race is being run, I want you to fetch the tea.' Spot headed off to the tea tent. He was just walking back when he saw Mick opening his little case. But it wasn't cash he was carrying – it was a disguise.

Mick pulled out a false moustache, a cap and an old tweed coat. Off came his panama hat and his pricey alpaca jacket. Within a few seconds Mick was sliding off with a bag full of loot. Spot quickly cottoned on and scarpered while the crowd was still watching the race. A few days later he bumped into Mick in Aldgate who gave Spot ten bob – a fortune in those days.

Spot soon became a regular racegoer observing all the shenanigans. He watched Darby Sabini and his brothers hard at work and did more and more part-time business for some of the characters on the courses. 'I made myself generally handy to the bookies I knew.'

ƒ   ƒ   ƒ

Throughout this time, Spot proved he was certainly never afraid of a punch-up. He was frequently set upon by other East End

toughs, who considered him to be a 'lippy Jew boy'. Jews still
weren't liked by certain other East Enders and Spot relished
being known as a protector to many Jewish businesses. There
wasn't another East End Jew – straight or crooked – who didn't
know Spot. Often Jewish stallholders would descend on Spot's
favourite haunt, Ziggy's Cafe in Petticoat Lane, asking in their
Eastern European accents: 'Is Jack Spot in there?' They'd
then queue up to give him money for keeping them safe and
healthy.

Not surprisingly, young Spot's reputation attracted the attention of certain other local criminals back in the East End. One
well-known face called Darky Mulley was introduced to Spot by
his bookie Jack Scarp. Mulley represented a group of villains who'd
bought pitches from the gypsies at racetracks across the country.
Gypsies had long since made their presence felt at racecourses,
where they pulled off all sorts of cons and deals. They even sent
in teams of pickpockets to then fleece punters of their remaining
cash. Darky Mulley had lined up dozens of new bookies to move
onto the pitches, before he came up against one big snag: the
other bookies who already worked the racecourses. They had to
be 'removed'.

As Mulley told Spot one night over a pint: 'They're not goin'
to like new bookies movin' in and takin' their trade. They've got
friends and they've got an organisation. They won't stand by and
see the stands go up without a fight.'

Mulley offered Spot big money to organise protection for his
team of bookies. Spot feared the job might be too big for him and
his boys to handle but Mulley was very persuasive. Spot recalled:
'So we clinched a deal right there in the boozer. I was going up
the ladder fast. Only nineteen, yet already my qualities of leadership had been recognised and were being paid for. I had been
placed in a position of trust and appointed to select an organised
mob.'

Spot looked on his new appointment as a natural elevation
from being an eight-year-old gang leader on the streets of the East

End. Now he was moving his mob off the manor. He'd take Moisha, naturally, and Sonny the Yank plus Little Hymie and a couple of dozen others he knew were useful scrappers.

ƒ   ƒ   ƒ

With the Depression's strikes, lockouts, mass unemployment and poverty, criminals had no trouble recruiting to their ranks. Even the bookies discovered to their delight that, the more desperately poor the punter, the more they wanted to gamble away their last few remaining pennies.

By now Soho was firmly established as the headquarters of 'race gangs' such as the Sabinis. As well as their involvement with the racetracks, the hoods owned 'joints' – small underground drinking dens – in which they installed their fancy women as hostesses or manageresses. Strangers were not welcome to open such businesses in Soho. The gangsters knew that their clubs would be patronised by the 'get-rich-quick' boys, who'd graduated directly from Soho's own academy of crime. Many gangsters ran the protection rackets that still exist in Soho to this day mainly so they could always have some cash available to cover overheads and travelling. And Jack Spot soon learned all sorts of tricks pulled to 'persuade' businesses that they needed protection.

One day, he and half a dozen of his boys entered and sat in a cluster around a darkened table in a club that Darky Mulley said he was 'having a few problems with'. Spot and his mob started shouting for drinks. The owner, a Spaniard called Tony, refused to serve them. A fight ensued and the other customers fled. Then Spot and his troublemakers began jostling the club band and snatching their instruments from them. Soon tables and chairs are overturned. Spot and his boys scarpered, leaving the owner with more than £100 worth of damage and the fear that his regular customers might never return. The following day another of Darky's boys visited Tony the club owner. He looked around the wrecked club with a sympathetic eye. 'What about a fiver a week and everything will be alright in the future?' he asked Tony, who nodded his head in agreement.

In the illegal gambling spielers of Soho, thousands of pounds were changing hands each and every evening over games of faro and chemin-de-fer. The gangs even added a little cosmopolitan flavour by opening casinos with roulette tables and employing expert croupiers. Between the wars, illegal gambling was estimated to have an annual turnover of £450 million, more than any other industry apart from the building trade. But these casinos were run from behind locked and heavily guarded doors. Drinking was naturally encouraged and, outside, commissionaires in uniform stood ready to press the alarm buzzer if the boys in blue appeared.

♪   ♪   ♪

In early 1935, Spot met a young East End woman called Mollie Simpson. The couple were introduced through their families and a relationship was encouraged because they were both Jewish. Spot and Mollie went out on a number of dates together. At first, Mollie seemed like a breath of fresh air. She was an unpretentious, well-mannered girl of just eighteen whom he did not have to impress. The relationship progressed well because Spot liked the fact he didn't have to put on any airs and graces in front of Mollie.

Then Mollie became pregnant, prompting a marriage ceremony attended by only a handful of relatives and friends in Essex. The couple moved into a tiny rented flat in Aldgate and, in early 1936, Mollie gave birth to a son called John. 'I never even realised Spotty was married at the time. He kept it so quiet,' one old East End lag later recalled. Spot never even told his childhood pals Sonny the Yank and Moisha Blueball what it was like to be a father or whether he was excited by the baby's birth. Many years later, he said he felt under so much pressure to provide for his young family that he simply didn't have time to think about the emotional aspects of being a father. No doubt Spot thought that, if it was known he was married with a child, it would cramp his style as a respected young tearaway.

Mollie knew all along what her husband was up to, but was given little choice in the matter. She stayed at home and brought up their child, as all mothers did in those days. Mollie always called her husband 'Jackie', and later recalled with deep regret: 'I gave Jackie a lot of freedom because I thought it was what he needed.' Spot was away much of the time, hanging out at late-night spielers, running contraband and working the tracks. Molly soon began resenting the nights when her husband didn't make an appearance.

Meanwhile, Jack Spot learned the art of splitting his life into two sections. By all accounts, he still enjoyed the company of numerous other women in the clubs and gambling joints that were already dominating his life. Marriage and children really were just a bit of an inconvenience to him.

ƒ   ƒ   ƒ

In the early 1930s, many of the local Italian boys began making Fascist-sponsored visits to their homeland, where they were encouraged to be anti-Semitic. A feeling of resentment soon spread through London's Italian community. By 1936, the Yiddisher gang were so concerned by this new wave of hatred that they broke away from the Italian gang and Soho was marked off into districts run by the Jews and Italians.

An uneasy peace existed between the factions until June 1936, when open warfare on Lewes Racecourse, in Sussex, broke out after a large gang of Hoxton and Islington Jewish tearaways set upon a Jewish, Sabini-protected, bookie called Alf Solomons and his sidekick as they were setting up for the races. When the Sabini boys arrived, the ringleader of the north-London thugs shouted, 'Here they are, boys. Get your tools ready!' Then he pulled a hatchet out from under his coat. The entire mob ran at the two Sabini men, brandishing hammers, knuckledusters and two-foot iron bars. One man had a length of inch-square rubber and another man's club looked like the half-shaft of a car wrapped in a newspaper. Bookie Alf Solomons was smashed over the head. He took three or four blows and then ran like a hare. Solomons escaped with minor injuries, but his clerk, Mark Frater, was surrounded and would have been chopped to pieces if the police hadn't steamed in. The Battle of Lewes was seen as a benchmark for the racecourse gangs.

Gangsters from both sides were eventually imprisoned for a total of forty-three-and-a-half years, and the judge, Mr Justice Hilbery, summed up: 'Gang violence in this country will meet no mercy. Let that be understood by each one of you and by your many friends who have congregated at this Assize. Gang violence exercises terror on its victims. I have not the least doubt that you thought that the man who was attacked would not dare, for fear of you, to identify any of you and you would thus make your escape.'

Jack Spot played no role in the Battle of Lewes, but he was already feared and respected by many of the racetrack villains. As 'Elephant and Castle' gang member, Brian McDonald, recalled: 'Spot was already a big feller with a punch like a mule's kick and a dexterity with a razor that was legendary: a stripe down the cheek or under the chin, or from one cheek, under the chin, and up the other, delivered to order.' Spot was also credited with encouraging the practice of striping a razor down the side of a leg and around the buttocks so the victim feared to sit down in case the stitches came open. It was soon to become his most frightening calling card.

3

THREE GOOD BLADES

Unemployment and the worldwide depression continued to haunt the nation. Virtually every week, firms laid off their workforces. The queues grew longer and longer outside the labour exchanges. Clothes were threadbare, food scarce and a full-time job remained a rarity. Across the Atlantic, the depression hit even harder and sparked bloody riots in many US cities. In Europe, the sound of Nazi jackboots sparked a flood of Jewish refugees fleeing from Germany.

The depression undoubtedly helped fuel membership of the Communist Party, which warned that capitalism was the root cause of the misery. Meanwhile, the Fascists claimed the world needed to be rid of the 'menace of the Jews planning to enslave mankind'. In England, Fascists led by Sir Oswald Mosley held meetings and planned provocative, noisy demonstrations through the very heart of working-class districts. Many of the unemployed were infuriated by the fascists' plans and swore not to let them pass.

In the East End, Jack Spot and his pals heard that fascist supremo Mosley planned a massive demo through their streets on 4 October 1936. Word spread through the community, sparking deep anger and resentment.

ƃ   ƃ   ƃ

'It's announced. It's to be next Sunday.'

'They're mad if they try it. They won't get through.'

'They've got the cops on their side. The cops will get them through.'

'You'll see. They won't get through. Everyone's coming out.'

'The docker's union, too?'

'Everyone. I've heard they're planning to rip up the paving-stones in front of Jenner's Store. The barrow boys will be there. And their barrows! There'll be barricades built clean across the streets. The cops won't get them through that!'

'What about the Jews?'

'They'll be there. You can stake your life on it. That big bastard Spot's getting a mob together!'

        §   *§*   *§*

On the day before the procession, Spot went to a cabinet-maker in Aldgate and asked him to make him a weapon. He'd usually fought with his bare fists until, a few months earlier, he'd been beaten up in a West End club by a gang armed with iron bars. Spot's head had been split open and he'd had eleven stitches. 'After that, I knew there were times when I would have to carry a weapon. And I knew this was certainly one of them,' he later recalled. The cabinet-maker produced a short, turned, sofa leg and filled the top with lead. Spot slipped it into a carrier bag and left the shop.

Communists, socialists and local tearaways like Jack Spot and his boys were well prepared that October Sunday, when Mosley's neatly dressed squads of Blackshirts began assembling near Tower Hill. Thousands of demonstrators were out to stop the march at all costs.

At 3.30 p.m. precisely, Mosley swept up to the Royal Mint in an open car to a salute of raised hands and shouts of 'The Yids, the Yids, we must get rid of the Yids.'

The angry crowd retorted: 'Go to Germany' and 'Down with Fascism'.

To Spot and many of the men gathered to oppose the Fascists, it really was more than just another mob fight. As Spot explained: 'They were the pale-faced, narrow-lipped tormentors who called us bloody Jews, and who accused us of trying to rule the world!'

Tempers flared as police tried to clear the crowds for Mosley and his 2500 troops. They were met by a hail of bottles, sticks and paving stones. 'For the first time Gentiles and Jews were fighting shoulder-to-shoulder against the Blackshirts,' said eyewitness George Shaw, a twenty-year-old, East End lorry driver.

Mosley then halted his march for hurried consultations with Sir Philip Game, the Metropolitan Police Commissioner. Mosley was prepared to pull every string in the book to get his demo through. With the route blocked, the Met chief offered the only alternative: a march along the Embankment and right into Cable Street, in the heart of the East End.

Spot recalled: 'I'd made my plan. The main attack was going to be on Mosley's bodyguards. They were the strong-arm boys the Blackshirts thought were unbeatable. Bash the bullies first, show that they are yellow, and the rest would bunk. That was my idea.'

Spot issued orders to his mob and then stood back in a side road as the procession approached. Moisha, Sonny, Turk and Little Hymie had to wait until Spot gave the signal.

Spot relished telling the story: 'Sir Oswald Mosley was standing upright on the seat of an open car in his black shirt. He had one hand on his belt and the right hand stuck up in the air in the Fascist salute, just like Hitler.'

Walking on each side of the car were half a dozen all-in wrestlers: Mosley's personal minders. They were followed by another mob of Blackshirts, headed by more strong-arm boys, and were surrounded by police.

Spot and his men waited patiently in the side street that opened up onto the main thoroughfare. The pavements were filled with soft caps, ragged overcoats, angry-eyed youths and aggressive looking men. They'd been there for more than two hours, jammed together shoulder to shoulder, stamping their feet against the cold and shouting their protests until they were hoarse.

Spot believed the Fascists would get through because the police were obliged to guard them. The local union leaders, the Communists, the left-wingers and the militants were left to shout their heads off. As Spot explained: 'The Fascists had plenty of opposition: thousands and thousands of workers. But all they did was stand still and merely shout a protest. It was all highly explosive powder without a fuse.' Spot intended to spark his own fuse.

Spot glanced over his shoulder. Moisha was right behind him, his big head hunched down into his massive shoulders, black eyes glittering, and his hand stuffed into his jacket pocket caressing a length of bicycle chain he was planning to lash across a Fascists' face. Behind were the rest of Spot's thirty-strong gang, all grim-faced and waiting. Some had knuckledusters; many had coshes. Others were armed with old-fashioned, cutthroat razors with a hollow-ground blade that sliced through flesh like butter.

Sonny the Yank was stationed further along the street on a rooftop with ammunition painstakingly prepared; ten pounds of King Edward spuds, each with two or three razor blades inserted for maximum damage. Further along the main street, a murmur among the crowd soon became a roar as word passed down the ranks like lightning.

'They're coming. They're coming!'

Spot glanced over his shoulder again and nodded towards his men. 'Wait 'til I give the word,' he ordered, 'then we go straight in. And go in yelling. We've got to fire this crowd and get them fighting with us.'

The mounted coppers on their horses passed first, their heads showing clearly above the crowds. Then came the banners and the microphone vans, followed by the parade itself.

'Hold it,' warned Spot. 'Hold it!'

Spot waited until half the parade of fascists had passed. He intended to split the column into two sections.

Spot glanced over his shoulder once again and nodded vigorously. 'Down with the Fascist bastards,' he yelled. 'Down with Fascism!'

The mob charged towards the parade, screaming at the top of their voices. The startled crowd on the pavement immediately split to allow Spot and his boys to find a route to the Fascists. A few coppers and a lot of startled, white faces above the black shirts. Spot sized it all up then gave the word to one of his henchmen, a champion boxer called George. His job was to create a diversion. He ran in amongst the mounted police, shouting and waving his arms. One bobby fell off his horse as the mounted police prepared to charge. In the commotion, Spot coolly walked towards the Mosley bodyguards. The leading minder was a big, meaty wrestler called Roughneck.

' 'Ello, Roughneck,' said Spot before pulling the sofa leg out of his bag and smashing it across the other man's head. Roughneck buckled at the knees, pitched forward on his face and went out like a light. Spot later explained: 'But he must have been tough because my lead-lined sofa leg split like a matchbox.'

When Moisha saw Roughneck go down he gave a shout to Turk and Little Hymie to lead their mob from the other side of the road. Soon hundreds of ordinary East Enders were joining in. It was a complete free for all. On the overlooking roof, Sonny let rip with his special recipe: razor-filled spuds.

Mosley strong-arm merchant Tommy Moran, a Royal Navy boxing champ, was waylaid by the mob, and newsreel at the time showed him picking his attackers off one by one with straight lefts and rights, until they lay around him in a circle. A blow to the head from a chair wrapped in barbed wire finally saw him collapse in a pool of his own blood.

Meanwhile the cowardly Sir Oswald Mosley dived under the seat of his car. Cozzers tried to seize charge of the situation by ordering the crowd to disperse. The Blackshirts picked up their wounded and retreated.

Back on the ground, Spot struck out again and again. Blood spurted, while horrifying shrieks pierced above the noise of the crowd. Spot continued hitting out mercilessly. Suddenly, breathing hard, he found himself standing virtually alone. He glanced around to see groups of fighting men milling all across the roadway while others on the pavements stood and stared. 'Hit 'em hard,' Spot yelled aloud. 'Get those Fascist bastards.' Then he brought his arm over his head, urging his troops to mount a fresh attack.

Just then a baton smashed down on Spot's hand, pulping his knuckles and sending pain screaming up through his elbow. More blue uniforms looked over Spot as he dodged another baton before another one scraped the side of his face and thudded into his shoulder at the base of his neck.

Spot went in low to try and stop the assault. He butted one copper in the belly, wrapped his arms around another policeman's thighs and lifted him bodily into the air and threw him clean over his shoulders. But as he went down, the copper grabbed Spot's waist and the two men fell to the tarmac. As Spot later recalled: 'At that moment I hated that copper every bit as much as I hated those Fascists. I could only use one hand because my other hand was sending shafts of splintering pain into my brain. I pounded at him, smashed at him, used my knees and my head, and all at once there were more blue figures charging towards me.'

A baton split open the back of Spot's head and he toppled sideways as the weight of at least three officers fell upon him: 'My lungs compressed inside my chest and I tried to breathe and couldn't. I knew I was suffocating, and the panic reared up inside me, gibbering, and I was fighting desperately to get the weight off me.'

A red mist descended in front of Spot's eyes at that moment. His limbs couldn't move. Then his head snapped around savagely and his lips encountered something moving, so he sunk his teeth into flesh. This was followed by another thump from a police baton across the temple. Then everything went black.

ℓ   ℓ   ℓ

Spot remembered nothing more until he woke up in a hospital bed with a uniformed bobby sitting beside him. 'You're nicked, son.' Spot couldn't afford a lawyer so the local communists supplied Spot with a 'legal advisor'.

But nothing could dampen the sense of satisfaction he felt. 'I don't want to swank, but that was the night I was the hero of the East End,' Spot recalled. He planned to visit the cabinet-maker and show him the remains of the sofa leg and demand the £2 back that he'd paid for it.

Newspaper accounts of the battle of Cable Street shocked the nation. Between 200 and 300 people were injured and 84 arrests were made amongst the estimated 10,000 people who took part. Political repercussions were so great on Stanley Baldwin's weak government that, within a year, all demonstrations by Mosley and his supporters were banned by law.

Meanwhile Spot was taken from his hospital bed to a prison cell, to await trial for assault. He wasn't allowed bail and his young wife, Mollie, only got to hear about his arrest when a policeman turned up on her doorstep three days after the Cable Street riots. She was virtually penniless, with a baby son and no visible means of support. Mollie burst into tears when the PC told her the news. He felt so sorry for her that he promised to inform the Discharged Prisoners' Aid Society, who would help her with furniture and life-insurance arrears, and keep up any other payments. Later that same day, Mollie tried to see Spot in prison, but the police told her she'd have to wait another five days until the next official visiting time came around.

Two days later, Spot appeared in court where he admitted the charge of GBH. His Communist 'legal advisor' was more interested in talking to reporters than to the judge. 'He raved on about the deliberate provocation by the Fascists marching through our streets and urged that the Police Commissioner ban Fascist demonstrations,' said Spot. 'But he didn't do me any favours.' When the Communist finally finished his closing speech, the judge simply said: 'Six months' hard labour.'

Spot later reflected: 'Now ain't that screwy? They send me down for six months for being anti-Fascist. Yet a few years later they were giving everyone guns and telling them to go out and kill Fascists. Just because I was a little quicker off the mark than the Government and was doing what they wanted before they were ready themselves, they sent me to jail!'

Spot didn't mind it in prison, even though he was locked up in the notoriously grim Wormwood Scrubs. As he later pointed out: 'Some of us inside had never had it so good. We were eating regularly and not having to worry where the next meal came from.' Many inmates looked up to Spot who was considered a villain with a bright future and a bit of a martyr, thanks to Cable Street. He explained: 'All the boys inside reckoned I'd had a raw deal. But then, we Jews always get a raw deal.'

Going to jail was a turning point in Jack Spot's life. He recalled: 'I had a head on my shoulders and I knew how to use it. I found myself mixing with blokes who were specialists; artists at their work who'd served an apprenticeship at their trade with unflagging zeal.'

Inside Wormwood Scrubs, inmates were assigned details in various parts of the prison. Spot was sent to the tailor's shop – a stinking, crowded loft where a lot of the prison toughies worked. As one inmate later recalled: 'They didn't operate sewing machines to cut smart suits of clothes. Instead they sat side by side in rows, to patch and stitch filthy, smelly convict clothes. We breathed a compound of granite dust, charcoal fumes and stinking fluff.' Each morning after breakfast inmates were herded into the workroom where they sat on low wooden stools, sewing mailbags and clothing while the warders walked up and down each side of the prisoners, ready to crack a baton over the shoulder of anyone who dared to speak out of turn.

On Spot's first day in the tailor's shop a safe-breaker called Legsy told him about all the different makes of safe and how to open them. Spot's brain buzzed with calculations of how much could be made from this type of villainous work. He certainly didn't consider himself a big shot compared to many of his fellow inmates: 'Alongside them I was a cheap chiseller, a no-account petty crook. I pretty soon realised that, if I was going to gain the respect of these men, I'd have to keep my mouth shut, my ears open and learn as quickly as I could.'

Another new friend, a car thief, had stolen fifteen vehicles before being nicked, having made a staggering profit of £1500. He told Spot that the way to make the really big money was to 'work with the mob'. As Spot later recalled: 'When he said that I suddenly saw myself as nothing more than a no-account petty thief, stealing a bike and repainting it to sell up the lane, or knocking off some valuable left in a car parked in a deserted street. For the first time I was in the swim with the real underworld, rubbing shoulders with craftsmen who were also experienced criminals. My six months would have been completely wasted if I hadn't taken advantage of the grand opportunities it offered me.'

Spot managed to play the prison game cleverly and eventually wangled himself an easier job as a gardener in the grounds. At mealtimes he forged numerous friendships with other petty criminals, many of who had equally big ideas for the future. He found that time inside prison 'passed like wildfire', he was learning so much. His car-thief friend drilled him about all the ways to steal a car. Counterfeiter Rube Tarson practised his skill in his cell every night and promised to provide Spot with anything from a passport to a printed invitation to the next opening of Parliament. Then there was Johnny Zind, the confidence trickster. He wouldn't reveal the tricks of his trade, but he was such a charming, courteous character that he convinced Spot he was capable of talking anyone into doing anything.

Spot also picked up a few tips from the prison toughs. These were the men who got what they wanted through sheer force. It was important to understand their 'skills' as well. Spot recalled: 'One fact became increasingly obvious to me. No one man is capable of possessing all the various skills that the perfect criminal needs. But to achieve perfect robberies, beautifully executed and with no fear of failure, the separate skills of all these men should be welded together into one concentrated effort.' Spot believed he could one day create an organisation, each man playing his own specialised part with the job he knew best. 'Then perfection in crime could be achieved,' Spot said.

While Spot was in prison, the Discharged Prisoners' Aid Society helped his wife Mollie keep up various household payments. They also found her a cheaper home to rent. The PC who had originally informed her of Spot's predicament even persuaded his colleagues at Aldgate police station to make a donation to her living fund. Many of the officers felt that Spot's imprisonment had been harsh considering his role in defence of his people.

Mollie was by all accounts a proud woman. She didn't like taking charity from anyone and she also feared Jack would be offended if he found out. Her visits to see her husband in the Scrubs were not easy. She often started sobbing, which left Spot wondering how they ever came to be married in the first place. 'We weren't very compatible,' he later recalled.

At 8.00 a.m. on a cold day, exactly four months after he'd been sentenced, the imposing gates of Wormwood Scrubs opened, and Jack Spot stepped out. He'd earned all his good conduct remission. He was a 'ticket-of-leave man', a convict on licence. He'd put on weight in prison. It's strange how many men did. His old suit wouldn't fit him, and the Discharged Prisoner's Aid Society fitted him up with a new, tailor-made one 'in accordance with his previous station in life', as they put it. It was a reasonable suit, although Jack Spot promised himself he'd buy a decent one once he'd earned a few bob. As he departed, he was given a copy of the rules, and a stamped envelope. All he had to do was report in writing once a month to the Central After-Care Association.

The old days, when a man left prison wearing a brown or grey herringbone suit that every copper would spot a street away, had gone. Spot didn't even have to carry his 'ticket of leave' on him the whole time. Nor was he ordered to stay out of pubs and cinemas, or banned from going to the races. He also didn't have to report to the police. (This was only done if a man broke parole with the Central After-Care Association.) The Discharged

Prisoners' Aid people gave him £3, and the local Labour Exchange gave him as much help as they could. But there was nothing around for a fellow just out of prison.

Back at their small, one-bedroom flat in Aldgate, Mollie seemed distracted when Jack Spot turned up on the doorstep. Within hours, she told him she'd fallen in love with another man. Even worse, he was another villain called Alf Lucy, one of the guv'nors of West Ham. Spot bowed his head and walked quietly out of the flat without saying a word.

In the back of his mind were the words of his first lover, his neighbour Maggie Klaut. 'Most women are the same. Never trust a woman. You're just a meal ticket for them. They don't care what happens to you and they'll take all they can get, even if it leaves you starving.' Spot swore he wouldn't trust a woman again. He rarely spoke about Mollie ever again.

He moved back to his parents' flat in the crumbling, low-rise, redbrick block in Myrdle Street, Whitechapel. 'From now on I'm just going to use women,' Spot thought to himself. 'I don't want to give them anything that they can hurt me back with.' Spot's domestic problems also made him even more focused on his criminal career. Before, he'd dreamed of settling down with his wife and children. Even trying to get a straight job. But now there was no wife and no family so he threw himself into the underworld.

Within a couple of days, Spot was at the dog track, drunk and in bad company. After spending so much time inside, the alcohol went straight to his head. And as an ex-con, he had few friends – except other villains. Jack Spot knew exactly which direction he was heading in and then he heard on the grapevine that Darky Mulley wanted Spot back on his team.

ℬ   ℬ   ℬ

At every racecourse, the bookies needed a printed list of runners to pin on their blackboards, with the fluctuating odds chalked alongside. They cost a farthing each to print but the bookies had to pay half a crown per set as part of Darky Mulley's protection racket. While bets were being laid on one race, another man would dash between the bookies, bawling the official runners for the next race. The list would then be issued by the stewards of the meeting, but none of the money the bookies paid went to the Jockey Club. This was part of the ring to which the 'water boys', 'chalks' and other racecourse pests belonged. And to ensure there was no backsliding, strong-arm boys like Jack Spot paraded around, leaning on anyone who got in their way.

Even the police had a slice of the action. Arthur Harding, an East End hard man employed by bookies to protect them, explained: 'In every division the police had these two men whose job it was to take the bookies in. They didn't have to hide in a cart or anything like that, they'd come round quite polite and say: "Stick a man up tomorrow, we're having a raid." Well all we had to do was find a man who was hard up – any Tom, Dick or Harry – and say: "Here's a chance to earn yourself a couple of quid," and they'd say: "Oh, blimey, yes." They'd stand in the street, and then the plain-clothes man would take them in and charge them with illegal betting . . . it was all part of the game.'

Sometimes a bookie would show some independence by refusing to pay Spot or any other tearaway, but they usually paid with a razor slash across the face. Or someone with a hammer poking out of his pocket would nudge the bookie when he was surrounded by a big crowd and suggest he lend them a tenner. At other times, ruffians would start an affray near the bookie until people began taking their business elsewhere. Arguments would often be started by 'punters', claiming a winning bet, which the bookie could not then trace in his book.

Then there was the 'broadsmen': the pickpockets, card sharps and three-card tricksters and prick-the-garter merchants, who operated with the full backing of people like Darky Mulley. This hard core of race gangs had the country divided into their own zones. Sonny the Yank's favourite weapon: razor-blade studded potatoes were particularly popular if anyone encroached on another gang's turf.

ƒ   ƒ   ƒ

At Kempton Park on Boxing Day; the course infested with pests of all colours, shapes and sizes; pickpockets amongst every crowd of more than six people. Jack Spot was in his element.

Word soon spread about Spot's racetrack achievements and tearaways from rival gangs began joining his outfit, working under the umbrella of Darky Mulley's mob. Spot explained: 'It was a good sign. After the second week on my first course we had no more trouble.' Spot and his mob quickly moved onto tracks across the south, on behalf of Mulley.

'I was learning all the time,' Spot recalled. 'And there was plenty to learn. As each new track opened, I had to adopt new tactics. We learned what weapons were handiest to use at close quarters, the quickest way to cripple a man, how to defend ourselves, and the art of feinting. I learned, too, the wisdom of being subtle, and avoiding publicity. Everything was on our side as long as the mobs were left to fight it out amongst themselves.'

In those days, even the bushes on the edge of Epsom racecourse were filled with 'spinners', who'd pick up their spinning boards and their tables and scarper whenever a lookout shouted a warning as coppers appeared on the horizon. At Ascot, there was even a police court under the stands and some villains, especially pickpockets, begged to be dealt with instantly because it never meant more than fourteen days in jail.

Spot accomplished his mission for Darky Mulley by safely establishing new bookies with their stands and, as he later pointed out, 'I made money,' which meant, 'Darky Mulley and his organisation made money, too.'

Then the newshounds of Fleet Street got to hear about what was happening on the racetracks and headlines screamed out about gangs violating the law. They revealed that the Jockey

Club's gatekeepers at each course were bribed to let these teara-ways in, and decent, law-abiding citizens were afraid to say what they'd seen unless they wanted a chivving.

There were a series of appalling incidents, including the beating up of a Cardiff bookmaker in his office; the murder of a Sheffied man in the street; the killing of another man in a Tottenham Court Road fight; brawling on trains to the races; and even razor battles in Brixton, Brighton and over in the East End.

Home Secretary Sir William Joynson Hicks put pressure on the nation's police to smash the gangs. Realistically, the only way the police could stamp out the gangs was to trail them, night and day. But, since the nation's police forces were reckoned to be at least 10,000 men under strength at the time, this was highly unlikely to happen. London was overrun by petty criminals, yet the Metropolitan Police had only 1400 detectives out of a force of 20,000 men. Public attention focused on the more glamorous activities of those small, elite teams employed in the Special Branch and the Flying Squad. But only 400 of these men were actually based at Scotland Yard.

Back then, in 1938, a police constable's pay was sixty-two shillings a week, with six shilling's rent allowance and one shil-ling's boot allowance. Decent digs cost around thirty shillings, and the only alternative was the grim police-section house. Bobbies on the beat were still regarded with outright hostility by the poor, and it was hardly surprising that many policemen were susceptible to bribery and made free use of 'Johnny Wood' – their truncheon – when not getting a slice of profit from a crime.

Up-and-coming Scotland Yard detective Ted Greeno reckoned there was only one way to handle the hoodlums: 'You had to be as tough as they were; tougher in fact because the race gangster is toughest with his pals around him and a weapon in his hand. The policeman was usually alone and unarmed.'

Up until then, the closest tearaways like Jack Spot got to real detectives was through films such as Hitchcock's early classic *Blackmail*. Screen detectives tended to be hard working, orderly, respectable and marked by a certain flinty integrity. But police detectives were only really as good as their network of informers – 'snouts' or 'grasses' – if they had any.

As maverick Scotland Yard detective John Gosling explained: 'Like the respectable professions, the criminal world is a small one in which "shop" is talked constantly. Almost everyone knows everyone else, either in person or by repute. A good job is discussed by those who did not do it as lawyers will discuss a QC's brilliant defence line, or a journalist a good scoop. They will discuss these things, even with a policeman, when the policeman has won their confidence.'

The police worked hard at containing the problems on the racetracks for a while. Spot and his mob of hoodlums even found themselves hanging around courses, 'with our hands in our pockets and drawing dough for nothing', thanks to the increased police presence. But that's when Spot began to get uneasy. He explained: 'We were all earning good dough, buying snazzy suits and putting on the dog. But we were standing still. And nobody gets anywhere by standing still. You either go up or down.' Spot knew full well that soon his boss Darky Mulley would decide he was paying Spot and his boys good money for nothing.

Spot urged Darky Mulley to take over *all* the established bookies' stands. He explained: 'We'd form an association and make all bookmakers members. Every bookmaker would have to keep in line then, and we wouldn't have any more trouble with the cops or have mobs fighting each other.'

Mulley gave young Spot's plan the green light. Now he had to make sure all the established bookies joined his 'association'. As the number of policemen at racecourses once again declined, it gave Spot and his mob the space to 'canvass' the bookies. Spot explained: 'We did it persuasively and without threats and had good results. Indeed, far more bookies joined voluntarily than we'd hoped.'

The few who did stand up to Spot and his gang were approached away from the racetracks, in their offices, clubs or sometimes even at their homes. Spot explained: 'It's surprising how quickly the word gets around. My mob didn't have to cut more than one or two bookies before the rest of them joined our association solid.'

Spot soon reckoned he was doing the police's work for them. 'I accomplished what the cops never could accomplish. I cleaned up the racetracks. I restored peace and order where previously there had been riots and mob fights. After that, the bookies could work with complete confidence and safety, knowing that never again would they go in peril of personal injury. And, as the man who was the promoter and leader of their association, I was naturally looked up to by them and respected.' Spot was also raking in a huge 'salary'.

Then Sir Oswald Mosley's friend, Adolf Hitler, sparked World War Two.

4
THE BOOM YEARS

Race thugs and villains had made a handsome living until the outbreak of war in 1939. Then the tracks were shut down virtually overnight and it was presumed the gangs would disband. Nothing could have been further from the truth. Many gangsters moved onto point-to-point racing where police control was almost non-existent. As war fever took over and the black market came to prominence, morals loosened and many once honest people began buying their goods 'off the back of a lorry'. The attitude of millions changed drastically. Normal home life ceased to exist and criminals reaped a golden harvest.

The blackouts in the big cities provided excellent cover and the dark alleyways of Soho became even darker. With everyday activities restricted by the Government, many turned to other forms of entertainment. Spielers opened by the score, shady nightclubs crowded with prostitutes did a roaring business and phoney whisky at exorbitant prices was available everywhere. Touts invaded the West End and stood about on street corners offering a wide range of services to newcomers by directing mugs to basement dives. Soldiers from Canada, France, Holland, Poland and Norway turned London into the wildest, most cosmopolitan capital in the world. Women offered themselves in West End streets in broad daylight; at night, they used torches to sell their bodies. Many operated in dingy rooms in Soho's Lisle Street, Gerrard Street, Frith Street, or in the area's dingy alleyways.

The other war, between gangs like the Yiddisher Boys and the Italians, grew even more ferocious. Spielers were at the centre of the fiercest battles. Groups of men would enter the club of a rival gang, beat up the occupants and wreck the premises. The police would then arrive on the scene and close the place down, leaving more business for a rival firm. Out on the blacked-out streets, fights with chivs were commonplace. Fists were a weapon of the past.

When Italian fascist leader Mussolini declared war on Great Britain, Soho really felt the full impact. Scores of Italians were interned and the streets of the West End were wiped clean of half the gangsters who ruled the roost. Italian premises were stoned by vicious mobs. Many attacks were encouraged by the Yiddisher Boys, who immediately moved their people into the Italian territory, killing off any hope that the underworld might collapse.

*   *   *

Jack Spot had his own opinion on the war: 'A few years earlier, if the Government had given me and my mob a few rifles, we'd have cleaned up the Fascists once and for all. But no. The Government had to put me in jail and then wait a few years before following the lead I'd given them. Lining up against the Fascists was poor comfort for me. There isn't a Jew alive who won't fight Fascism in one way or another until he draws his last breath.' But Spot was a Jew with a prison record. 'That meant the Government ignored my qualities of leadership. It meant nothing to authority that I was famous in my neighbourhood for my uncompromising resistance to Fascism.'

Spot had desperately wanted to be a commissioned officer. He believed he was capable of 'gaining a position that would enable me to put my real ability to its best use'. In reality he knew he'd be called up for squaddie duty so he didn't exactly rush off and volunteer.

In June 1940, Spot was dragooned into the army after police raided a spieler in Aldgate. Spot didn't object to fighting the Fascists, but he wasn't happy doing drill in an ill-fitting uniform at Norton Manor Barracks, in Taunton, Somerset, where he occasionally manned anti-aircraft guns. He later admitted that he spent much of his time cowering in a bomb shelter. 'I seethe with anger every time I think about it. I was compelled to shine boots and buttons to satisfy a loud-mouthed sergeant's hawk-eyed inspection and obediently take orders from pasty-faced little runts with officers' pips. Me, being ordered around just like any other common soldier!'

On a more practical note, Spot's call-up completely interrupted his criminal career. His old boss Darky Mulley was, in the words of Spot, 'the really smart boy. He paid a half-blind bloke of his own age two hundred nicker to present himself at Darky Mulley's medical examination.' Darky also had the good sense to move into spielers and the black market when he realised the racetrack game was falling apart.

In the middle of all this, Spot received a telegram informing him that his father had been killed during the Nazi blitz of the East End. Spot's Jew-baiting corporal saw this as highly amusing, so it was hardly surprising when Spot knocked him out with a flurry of punches. Spot – now marked down as a troublemaker – was locked up in a cell in the barracks for a month, and missed his father's funeral. It was a cruel fate and Spot would never forgive the army. He became even more isolated from most of his comrades, constantly moaning and groaning about the poor pay and bad food. He'd become such a non-stop headache for authorities that, after three years in the army, he was discharged as mentally unstable, in the autumn of 1943.

One wet afternoon a few days later, Spot visited his old East End haunts. Moisha Blueball, Turk, Little Hymie, Sonny the Yank and all the rest of his boys were all still in the services. He returned to the Blitz-devastated area, with his father dead and most of his pals dispersed. Spot was a mummy's boy and found her still living in the same tenement building in Myrdle Street, Whitechapel, where he'd been born. Somehow Hitler's bombs had missed the block. After seeing his mother, Spot wandered around the old manor aimlessly. His brother and sisters had all moved on and now had families of their own. The girls still had their jobs in the rag trade. His brother had joined the RAF. Spot's siblings occupied a different, more honest world than the one he belonged to. He felt extremely alone. He couldn't even contact his ex-wife and son because they'd been evacuated to the Gloucester countryside and he'd lost their address. Spot had nothing and no one to share his life with.

*   *   *

A few days later, Spot found himself sitting in a half-empty spieler on the Edgware Road arguing with a character called Edgware Road Sam, who'd been abusing the club's Jewish barman. Spot got so angry he punched Edgware Road Sam in the face. Sam pulled a knife on Spot but Spot managed to wrestle it from him and ended up giving Sam a severe beating before his opponent stumbled out of the club nursing a sore head. Spot later recalled: 'His two mates just sat there gaping. They were surprised at my nerve in tackling this geezer.'

The two men warned Spot that Sam had probably gone to get a gun before they hotfooted it out of the spieler. Spot didn't believe them and stayed put. Half an hour later he looked out of the window and spotted Sam getting out of a police car with his head bandaged. As Spot later explained: 'He'd gone and squealed to the cozzers so I slipped quietly out the back door.'

Spot was determined to avoid prison. 'There were plenty of witnesses in the club and I was frightened they'd stitch me up, so I did a bunk. I had to clear out of London.'

At nearby King's Cross Station, Spot bought a train ticket north. He'd heard that Leeds had become a hotspot full of duckers and divers since the outbreak of war. Many said it was the black-market capital of the north. 'So I took my chances and headed up there.'

ϑ   ϑ   ϑ

Leeds was a bustling community dominated by the rag trade, which was predominantly run by Jews. It therefore felt like familiar territory to Jack Spot, who later called it the East End of the north. There were four main gambling spielers in Leeds when Spot arrived. Black-marketeers made up most of the customers who played faro, chemmy and rummy. Spot later explained: 'The big boys with a load of money in Leeds would wander from one club to the other.'

Gambling sessions tended to be in specific shifts. One club called the Regal went on all night and it was Spot's first port of call after his arrival in Leeds. He sat down in a corner and got chatting to another East Ender who'd come to the city to avoid the Blitz. Spot bought the man a drink just as a big fellow walked into the club and started an argument with the owner. Spot recalled: 'As soon as he started talking everything went quiet. All the play stopped and the men at the tables just sat watching the big bloke and the boss, who was obviously scared to the seat of his pants. His eyes were popping out of his head and the big bloke was doing all the talking. Not very nice talking, either.'

When Spot stood up, his East End pal warned him to be careful because the other man was a toughie known as 'Liverpool Jack'. The name meant nothing to Spot so he walked across to the two men.

'I could feel all the men in the room watching me. It was like a film,' Spot later recalled.

'What the bloody hell's your problem?' asked Liverpool Jack.

'You're out of order,' said Spot.

'Who the hell're you?'

'Just leave it out.'

'Fuck off.'

Spot caught Liverpool Jack with a quick-fire flurry of punches and he went down like a bag of coal. When he tried to get up again, Spot crashed a billiard cue over his head and then tore into him with his boots. Moments later Liverpool Jack stumbled out of the club.

Other customers reckoned he'd probably be back with his boys for a battle. It turned out Liverpool Jack was the leader of one of the toughest gangs in the north. But Jack did not return and the guv'nor of the Regal was so delighted by Spot's intervention he asked him to take charge of security at the club.

Not long afterwards, Spot encountered two Polish brothers who allegedly ran Leeds' underworld at the time. He refused to let them lean on the Regal's guv'nor for protection money. There was a dramatic face-off, but the Poles refused to be drawn into having a fight. 'Jack stood up so close to one of them, he pressed his nose against the other man's face. They'd never encountered such bravado before,' one old northern villain recalled many years later. The Poles had heard rumours from other villains down south that Spot always carried a blade on him and he wouldn't hesitate to use it. Many concluded that the Poles were so surprised to be challenged on their own turf that they feared they might lose a showdown and backed off.

One day a slimy character called Milky, who hung round at the Regal, asked Spot: 'How come you're not frightened of 'em?'

'Why should I be frightened of them?' asked Spot.

'You mean you'd stick around and face them if it came to a real showdown?'

'Yeah, if that's what they want.'

While in Leeds, Spot got a tip-off from London that Edgware Road Sam had been jailed for working a 'tweedie' and there was a good chance the prosecution against Spot would collapse. A tweedie was when a villain took a genuine diamond ring into a jeweller or pawnbroker and asked how much he would pay for it. Then the villain would refuse the first valuation and put the ring back in his pocket. Then, as an afterthought, the villain accepts the valuation after all. That's when he gives the dealer back another, fake, ring, takes the money and scarpers.

Edgware Road Sam was doing two years inside for this stunt when Jack Spot decided to return to London and give himself up to police. But Sam insisted on going through with the prosecution and gave evidence in court with a prison guard either side of him. Luckily Spot came up with enough witnesses to prove he'd fought Sam in self-defence in the Edgware Road club. Spot was acquitted and opted to stay on in London.

Soon afterwards, Spot got a message from a contact in Manchester. A bunch of club and billiard-hall owners wanted Spot to see off a character called Cockney Jim and his gang, who were causing a lot of aggro. Spot travelled up north and sorted them out. His name was spreading across the country's underworld. Soon afterwards, Spot went to Liverpool to handle more troublemakers. Similar trips to Birmingham, Nottingham and Newcastle followed before he headed back to London.

*   *   *

By 1944, the East End's docks, railways and high-density population had taken a pounding from Hitler's bombers since air raids began almost four years earlier. Some days there had been as many as 400 German aircraft overhead. A further 250 returned each night in wave after wave. But, beyond the chaos, Jack Spot believed there were some opportunities to be had.

Deserters had become much better organised and many now held fake identity cards. All kinds of coupons were stolen and then reproduced in huge, well-organised rackets. Few villains needed ration books because they tended to eat in caffs. Poles, Czechs and French-Canadians joined up with British villains on the run, and many used guns. When one man was refused admission to a West End restaurant, he pulled out a pistol and was only captured after a chase by Flying Squad officers.

Teams of gangsters were doping greyhounds at various tracks

up and down the country. Businessmen were lured to houses with the promise of big deals only to find themselves bound, gagged and robbed. Country housebreakers targeted properties on virtually a nightly basis. With German bombs dropping everywhere, looting was rife. The War definitely shifted the balance of power even more in favour of the criminals. The black market helped the underworld focus in on the community at large. Opportunities for new crimes were an everyday occurrence.

As one old villain later explained: 'Money? It was coming at us like pieces of paper. I rarely went out with less than a monkey (£500) or a grand in my pocket. That was spending stuff. Emergency funds in case I got nicked, or in case the bite was put on me.' Stick-up men reckoned they took an average £3000 a week. Even when they were sent down for at least two years after being caught in a getaway car following a robbery, it didn't deter others from following in their footsteps.

Spot and numerous other villains centred their activities in the once-quiet London suburb of Romford, which had become the black-market centre of the South East. Clothes, meat and millions of eggs were sold to wholesalers signing themselves 'Neville Chamberlain' and 'Winston Churchill'. The capital's seriously undermanned police force could do little to stamp it out.

Six hundred thousand supplementary clothes coupons and 100,000 ration books were stolen from the Romford Food Office. They were worth half a million pounds on the black market. It was the most lucrative haul until the Great Train Robbery in 1963. The thieves were never caught and none of the ration books were ever recovered. Later, 14,000 ration books were then stolen from a government office in Hertfordshire. And so it went on.

During the blackout hours, many premises were easy to break into and damaged buildings proved ideal for hiding stolen goods. Shortages of all food and clothing made it easy for Spot to dispose of stolen property that before the war might not have been worth taking. Large-scale crimes, such as bank robberies, were financed by big-time, black-market operators; entire lorry loads of goods also regularly went missing.

As Arthur Helliwell, well-known columnist on the *Sunday People* newspaper, pointed out: 'We've developed into a nation of bribers. Everyone is on the game, from the big shot who buys the motor dealer's wife a fur coat and gets delivery of a new car in a week, to the housewife who slips to the fishmonger a packet of cigarettes after the queue has gone. The butcher runs a car, but he can't get much petrol – slip him a couple of coupons and get an extra steak for yourself. The coal merchant can't get eggs – send him a couple of dozen and there's a ton of coal in your cellar. A page of clothing coupons to your tobacconist – and there'll always be a packet of twenty under the counter for you.'

The war saw the introduction of the spiv into British society. Jack Spot already qualified as one. But he was also developing a capacity for organising groups of villains and an ability to get hold of inside information. So, when the end of the war finally came, it was time for Jack Spot to put all those experiences to the test.

5
A NEW ERA

On VE Day in May 1945, Jack Spot hit the East End. People were in a frenzy preparing street parties. Everyone dragged out timber they'd been saving for a huge bonfire. Many residents were up ladders hanging out bunting and Union Jacks. In Spot's old street, a piano had been pushed out in front of the terraced houses and low-rise redbrick blocks of flats. Bells rang out and, as it got dark, the streetlights came on for the first time since the Blitz had begun five years earlier; over at the local town hall, fireworks exploded in the sky above as searchlights danced in the moonlight. People sat in the street or stood over bonfires as effigies of Hitler roasted. The war was over. And now new opportunities beckoned for a smart operator like Jack Spot.

⚡ ⚡ ⚡

With new weapons and their old, ruthless methods, the gangs quickly re-established a grip on the newly reopened racecourses. The real war had even encouraged the introduction of the Italian 'springer' knife in place of the open razor. The springer knife was a blade concealed in a metal or leather handle, which was released by the touch of a knob. It then sprang out, a thin, double-edged stiletto.

In Soho, protection rackets flourished. Soldiers of all nations crowded into the capital after VE Day with money to spend. Over at Spot's beloved Cable Street, E1, the area had become known as the 'coloured man's village' after the war. Africans, West Indian and Indian seamen were the most regular customers in the pubs and clubs. Many tried to get work ashore. But there was a severe shortage of rooms. Few landladies would take them in and hostels were all overcrowded. Local residents even put together a petition demanding that the area be cleaned up.

But Jack Spot had bigger fish to fry. He hooked up with a bunch of Italians called the Carlino Gang, who'd devised an ingenious way of stealing cars. One of the Carlinos had seduced a pretty blonde clerk at the Petroleum Office, in London. When car owners sent in petrol coupons she managed to 'mislay' their logbooks, for which the Carlinos paid her £20 a piece. Then they went out and stole cars that closely matched the descriptions in the logbooks. They fixed false number plates, suitably bleached and over-printed the logbook entry before selling the cars openly at market price.

Spot helped finance their work and quickly made up to £250 a week. But then the Carlino gang were nicked by the police after the tax-disc details on one car didn't match up in the log book. Spot – as the 'financier' – was so far removed from the actual crimes, he got away without any problems. Avoiding direct involvement in crime was paramount if he was going to start building an empire.

After the war, a lot of London crooks returned to their former trades such as smash-and-grab robberies, safe breaking, car stealing and just about every petty crime imaginable. More violent armed robberies soon began occurring on a regular basis. Petty criminals used loaded weapons and the police feared London was turning into the Chicago of the thirties.

In December 1945, 2000 Metropolitan Police officers swamped Soho, checking the papers of everyone they came across in pubs, caffs, dancehalls and gambling clubs. The following month, check-points were set up on all major roads leading in and out of London, plus all the Thames crossings between Tower Bridge and Hammersmith. Police hoped to round up some of the 20,000 deserters reckoned to still be on the run. All it really did was flush out a few small-timers, while the big-time villains like Spot continued climbing the ranks of the underworld.

Spot then connected up again with his old boss Darky Mulley, now well established in the Midlands running three spielers and making a fortune from the black market. A bunch of tearaways were trying to muscle in on his clubs so Mulley, keen to avoid any problems with the police, asked Spot to run the spielers for him. Spot agreed on condition that his old pals Moisha Blueball and Sonny the Yank – both just out of the army and in desperate need of money – could join the team. Spot prided himself on his loyalty to old friends.

Spot, Moisha and Sonny ran one spieler each and shared out the spoils at the end of each week. The clubs were packed each night with black-marketeers from London, Liverpool, Manchester and other big cities. They played recklessly for high stakes, knowing only too well that the days of easy money were coming to an end, and trying to double their cash before it was too late.

Spot quickly got to know his regulars, many of whom were genuine big-time crooks who'd think nothing of nicking a large consignment of rationed goods that needed half-a-dozen lorries to shift them. Spot also encountered fences: men who'd amassed a fortune by handling and then selling on stolen goods. Spot believed they had the most important role of all.

Practically every commodity was still in short supply: printing paper, pepper, ice-cream powder, paraffin, meat, textiles, cigarettes, petrol – you name it. But food yielded the highest profit. The Government's rationing system restricted the use of certain food in the home, but not in restaurants. Owning a restaurant was virtually a licence to print money – if you could get the goods.

Black-marketeers scoured the countryside, buying up broken-down horses which would later be served up as choice rump steaks in high-class establishments. As one old lag explained: 'Even the toughest of meat, if pounded long enough by a hefty table-tennis bat studded with gramophone needles could be served up tender as lamb.'

Spot, Moisha and Sonny soon came up with what they believed would be a real money-spinner. Employing two or three of their old pals, they clinched a deal with a black-marketeer to supply ponies from the New Forest, in Hampshire. Spot and his boys also invested in consignments of cigarettes. They bought two vans, employed their own labour and bribed truck-drivers to look the other way while their vehicles were stolen as they sat supping a cup of tea in a pre-agreed caff. Then the load would be transferred to one of Spot's vehicles. Later the trucks were found abandoned and empty.

But Spot and his pals had no contingency plans for a rainy day. When rationing began to ease, they simply presumed they'd have to work a little harder to make the same money. When the takings in the Midlands spielers began dropping off, Darky Mulley announced he was pulling out and retiring while he still had a packet of cash under his mattress. He offered the clubs to Spot, but warned him, 'If you're as smart as I think, you won't take them. Just keeping the clubs open is going to cost money from now on.'

Spot – along with Moisha and Sonny – couldn't resist taking the risk. However, within a couple of weeks, he and his pals were struggling to afford to keep the spielers open. With Darky's doom-laden prophecy ringing in their ears, they pooled what little cash they had left and headed back down to London. Spot soon linked up with a well-known Jewish 'businessman' who wanted to finance the opening of a new spieler. Within weeks Spot was fronting the Buttolph Club, in Aldgate. As he later explained: 'It was a private club, open for drinking, talking and gambling.' Spot hoped the Buttolph would be his springboard to a new level of criminality, for, while spielers outside the capital were dropping like stones, London remained a boomtown.

Soon, Spot later claimed, the club was taking in at least £3000 a week, tax-free, and Spot now saw himself as a Jewish 'godfather':

'I didn't have to buy nothing. Every Jewish businessman in London made me clothes, gave me money, food, drink, everything. I was what they called a legend to the Jews. Some crook goes into a Jewish shop, says gimme clothes and a few quid, the local rabbis say, "Go and find Jack Spot. Get Jack, he'll know what to do." So they did and I'd end up chining a few bastards. The Robin Hood of the East End, a couple of taxi drivers once told me. "You helped everyone," they said.'

ƒ   ƒ   ƒ

Behind the bravado, Jack Spot was exploiting a huge opening for anyone with the brains and initiative to organise crime. He never forgot what he'd learned in prison and the contacts he'd made. As he later recalled: 'That judge who sent me away never knew what a great favour he did me.'

At the Buttolph Club, Spot met up with familiar faces such as Rube Tarson the counterfeiter, Johnnie Zind the confidence man, Soapy Brucker the expert safebreaker and dozens of others. The Aldgate club rapidly became a favourite rendezvous for professional criminals. Spot and Moisha served drinks over the counter to an assortment of cat burglars, pickpockets, car thieves and hold-up men. And Spot told them how much easier things would be if they would only get properly *organised*.

ƒ   ƒ   ƒ

Jack Spot shouldered his bulk vigorously through the crowded streets of the East End. He visited pubs, clubs, caffs and restaurants. He talked briefly to dozens of men and women. They listened, nodded – he and his men were on the hunt for the people in the know. They leaned on bar counters, drank tea in all-night caffs, consumed two-bob orangeades in near-beer joints, swore at the diluted whiskies in nightclubs and gambled in other spielers besides the Buttolph. Spot and his mob, who were all in their twenties or early thirties, looked like prosperous businessmen in their sharp suits. The women – mostly brasses – talked, laughed, drank, told dirty stories, swore like troopers and even squabbled over men. The word was out that Jack Spot was putting a team together. As he later explained: 'I was one of the first to realise that criminals could be organised, each crook becoming a small part of a master plan in which every cog and spindle operated perfectly. I aimed to be the planner and the mastermind.'

A couple of weeks later, Spot's team entered a bank through the front door, thanks to the expertise of a cat burglar who'd made wax impressions of all the locks and keys on a previous visit through a high window. The robbers knew all about the alarm system thanks to background information supplied by a confidence man. Then an alarms specialist had disconnected everything. The safe was opened quickly and expertly thanks to three safe breakers. The getaway was equally well planned. Three new, fast cars had been stolen simultaneously the previous night; one was abandoned just five hundred yards from the bank; the other two cars were changeover vehicles found by police two days later. The gang's haul was £5000 in small currency. Naturally, when the cozzers pulled in all the experts on their books everyone had the perfect alibi.

Two weeks later, Spot's men pulled off another daring raid. This time a consignment of fur coats was driven away from a warehouse at eleven o'clock at night. It wasn't until five hours later that the alarm was raised. After a couple of days, the police swooped on every known suspect, looking for the fur coats. But they found nothing. As Spot later explained proudly: 'The streets had long ago taught me an important lesson. Before one steals, one must always have a buyer lined up.'

Just six months after arriving back in his old home town, Spot had money, power and influence and was boss to dozens of people. He explained: 'It wasn't a complete walk-over. We met with opposition and we had our difficulties. But once you grow strong, it's easy to grow stronger.'

And Spot's Aldgate spieler, the Buttolph, was run with military precision: At five o'clock every afternoon, the clerks of the Aldgate Fruit Exchange would leave their office and Jack Spot's 'scene-shifters' walked in. The blinds would be pulled down, the desks dragged across the room into a side area. Long tables were then set up and chairs placed around the room. In the corner, the snack bar was set up. The Aldgate Fruit Exchange had, in minutes, been turned into the biggest gambling club in London. Spot explained: 'There was so much money about that we could hardly take it fast enough. We were clearing thousands of quid a week profit, and I was on a percentage so I didn't exactly starve.'

Jack Spot's wealthy backer at the Buttolph wanted it run purely on straight lines. This meant only three games were played regularly; baccarat (chemin-de-fer), faro and rummy. Chemin-de-fer was a game in which the players bet on being dealt better cards than the banker held. Faro was an old-fashioned Viennese gambling game with players betting on which order cards would be drawn from a shuffled pack. Both were games of pure chance, the only skill being a swift calculation of the odds at each stage of the deal. Rummy, of course, gave the player an opportunity to exercise a certain amount of ingenuity, and when hard money was on the table it became a very serious game. Such card games provided plenty of opportunities for cheating, particularly in manipulating the deal. But Jack Spot insisted: 'There wasn't any need to fiddle, with the house taking a cut of two bob in the pound on the bets and the kitties running into the thousands.'

And it wasn't just local flyboys who turned up at the Buttolph. Bigwigs from 'Up West' drove to Aldgate, parked their cars a few streets away and walked in for a night's amusement. As Spot later explained: 'We had a rum mixture: there were big businessmen; there were bookmakers with pockets full of sucker money; there were spivs and screwsmen from the underworld getting rid of cash they'd picked up for the gear they'd stolen.'

A heavyweight called Arthur Skurry was the main doorman at the Buttolph, but there were always at least three other doormen and bouncers around. Many of them were 'punchers', men who could be relied upon to stand up and fight, although they were careful to avoid damaging the so-called 'faces'. Every Friday afternoon, one of Spot's boys was dispatched to Waterloo station with a carrier bag full of daffodils and five-pound notes to keep their favourite City of London policemen happy. The bribery of cozzers was an accepted part of life for a criminal like Spot.

In the Buttolph, Spot usually drank lemonade instead of alcohol, which provoked derisive comments from his enemies, but he liked to be in control at all times. One young tearaway called Johnnie Warren, a cousin of the notorious White family from King's Cross, was followed into the toilet of a West End club by Spot and given a severe beating one night for daring to suggest Spot was a 'poof' because he didn't drink. Spot proudly explained: 'I used to knock 'em out in the lavatory that was my surgery. Go in the toilet and bomp! Leave 'em in the piss.'

The Buttolph was also frequented by villains from areas across the river such as Walworth Road, Old Kent Road, Kennington, Lambeth, Waterloo, Blackfriars, Peckham, Camberwell and the Borough. Spot's place was always filled with blue smoke from cigarettes angled in the corners of mouths, curling past hooded lights. It echoed with the clink and rustle of money; the whispers and yells of success and failure, which all combined to produce an atmosphere guaranteed to quicken the punters' blood and lead them to rash judgements in the heat and excitement of concentrated gambling.

Most of the money changed hands in small bets, but a bucketful could be won and lost in an evening. The croupiers, provided by the club, would take something out of the pot from every winning run, or winners would 'see the croupier' by tossing him a portion of their winnings. Players knew instinctively what to give and it seemed to work smoothly most of the time. Now and again cheapskates would be 'rowed' out of a game and not asked back – a severe black mark against any face. Spot also made a tidy profit from drinks and sandwiches.

But the Buttolph was also a useful staging post for Spot to

recruit new talent. When he heard that legendary razor man Johnny Carter was about to be released from a five-year stretch for cutting up a rival, Spot picked him up in a limo at the prison gates and gave him full-time membership of his firm, dealing out broken arms and decorated faces to order. Carter was a legendary expert with the chiv, and had literally carved up a bunch of hard men in a battle over illegal bookie pitches. He was held in such high esteem that he was even given his own share of lucrative protection rackets, soaking up money from scores of Soho clubs, boozers and clip joints.

Spot's favourite regular customer at the Buttolph was a cat burglar known as the Shepherd's Bush Kid. Spot rated him as the finest thief in the business. As he explained: 'Climb! Talk about Mount Everest – that's nothing to what the Kid can do on a drainpipe. He's a big-built fellow, too, but as fit as any athlete and in his crepe-soled shoes he can go up the side of a house like a fly.'

The Kid concentrated on big jobs, which yielded a high return: minks, diamonds and other such valuables to the tune of £500,000 during his career. But the Kid could never hold onto his money. Some nights he'd visit Spot's spieler and blow £5000 in one session. As Spot later explained: 'Sometimes the crowd round the faro table was so big, the Kid couldn't get near it to see the play, or place his bets. So he'd roll up a bunch of fivers and throw 'em over players' heads, and wherever the money landed on the layout would be the card he'd back.'

Another regular in the Buttolph was Tall Mick, one of the best pickpockets in London. He worked alone and was always immaculately dressed like the perfect gentleman. Mick's speciality was the 'coat and newspaper lark'. He'd stand on a train with a coat over his arm reading a newspaper, looking as if both his hands were occupied. In fact, one was exploring the hip pocket of the person next to him. Mick was also renowned in busy theatre crowds for pushing through foyers in the crush. Women's diamond brooches would disappear from the front of their dresses before they'd noticed a thing.

Spot genuinely believed that the Buttolph was a 'classy joint' compared to other spielers. And, as he later explained, 'the great thing was that play was so quiet that the police never came nosing around'. At the Buttolph, one punter lost £10,000 playing faro (£120,000 today). Spot later recalled: 'He strolled out that night with a nod to me. Three days later he shot himself. Of course, he may have had other troubles . . .'

The club closed at six each morning, when Spot's furniture shifters got to work, so that by the time the respectable people of Aldgate got up for work they had no idea what had been going on just a few hours earlier.

But Fleet Street was outraged at these illegal gambling emporiums. As the *Sunday People*'s columnist Arthur Helliwell told his readers: 'I watched gin rummy being played for £1 a point. I saw a Slippery Sam school where the kitty averaged between £200 and £250 a hand. I drank a glass of champagne with a suave, silver-haired, slickly tailored character who takes a rake-off on a £15,000 to £20,000 turnover every time he runs a chemmy [chemin-de-fer] party. I visited a poker game where you couldn't see the green baize for fivers and I rounded off my tour watching a Negro dice game that shifts its rendezvous and changes its entrance password every night. "I'm driving a Ford V8" was the open sesame the night I called. There were three other white men in the dingy, smoke-filled room. The rest were zoot-suited, sombrero-hatted, jazzily necktied, coloured boys. A chocolate-coloured dandy in a long, black overcoat with an astrakan collar had the dice.'

§   §   §

It was around this time, in 1946, that Jack Spot decided he wanted to make a push back onto the racetracks. Spot knew that, in the North of England, local mobsters ran the newly reopened courses at a profit in a similar way to the Sabinis in earlier years. Track officials were even dishing out pitches themselves to bookies.

Spot travelled up north to meet one racecourse official, an ex-copper. Spot suggested helping the official in the tricky business of allotting pitches. As he later put it: 'I made sure there was no trouble and he was grateful.'

Back down south, Spot and his pals focused on the royal race meeting at Ascot where one of his most hated enemies, Little Jimmy and his Islington gang, were trying to take over the hallowed turf. They'd already grabbed all the best pitches on the free side at Ascot and threatened to clear Spot and his team off if they made any attempt to move in. 'So my pals and I decided to do the clearing instead,' Spot later explained.

Spot completely saw off Little Jimmy and his Islington boys from the racetracks by early 1947. Then, with his own boys and the considerable support of his allies in the Upton Park and Ilford gangs, Spot decided to widen his power base by spreading his net across the entire nation's racecourses.

But first Spot had to deal with the King's Cross gang, led by bookie Harry White, a curious, round-faced fellow. White sent his two daughters to Roedean, England's most expensive school for girls, yet was renowned for cutting anyone who dared get in his way. Besides a big presence at the races, White and his mob were also trying to move into the West End club scene. Spot then heard that a bunch of the King's Cross boys had been mouthing off about him in one Mayfair Club. Back at the Buttolph, he assembled Sonny, Moisha and Little Hymie to discuss the situation. He later claimed he held his henchmen back at first because he wanted to find out if the King's Cross boys were really looking for trouble. Spot ventured into enemy territory and began asking around until he found Harry White and three of his boys in a pub in King's Cross. Just as Spot was asking White what was going on, one of his minders – a fellow called Big Bill – leaned across and told Spot: 'Mind your own fuckin' business.'

Spot swallowed hard and kept his cool. As he later explained: 'After all, I was single-handed against four, the landlord was a pal of theirs, and the pub was in their territory.' Spot walked out without saying another word. But he saw their attitude as a clear declaration of war. 'I was hoppin' mad. I knew that Harry had a really terrible mob, but I was ready to settle this argument in one battle.'

The following day Spot sent a couple of scouts out to King's Cross, to see what Harry White was up to. They reported back that White had surrounded himself with even more minders than usual and was heading into the West End later that day. Spot, accompanied by Sonny, Moisha and Little Hymie headed west in Spot's newly acquired white Cadillac. They eventually found White in a club in Sackville Street, off Piccadilly. White was standing at the bar, drinking with racehorse trainer Tim O'Sullivan and White's mouthy minder, Big Bill.

Spot walked up to White and said: 'You're Yiddified' – meaning he was anti-Jewish. White denied it: 'I have Jewish people amongst my best friends.' That was the signal for Spot and his men to steam in at high speed. As Spot later recalled, 'There wasn't any politeness. They knew what I'd come for. And I sailed right in.' Spot lashed out at White and then hit him over the head with a bottle. White collapsed into a fireplace and the seat of his trousers caught fire. Spot later said: 'He hollered, but though he was burned he wasn't badly hurt.'

One of Spot's men then attacked O'Sullivan, who was beaten unconscious. Big Bill was slashed with razors and stabbed in the stomach. Spot recalled: 'The King's Cross boys couldn't stand up to it. Harry scarpered. You couldn't see the seat of his trousers for dust. They all ran – except Big Bill. He had guts and he made a fight of it. Unluckily that meant he got the worst of it.' By the end of it, Big Bill was lying on the floor bleeding profusely from a deep knife wound. Spot got the barman to phone for an ambulance before he and his mob disappeared.

Within days, Harry White let it be known he was planning a return battle and began assembling troops in King's Cross. White reckoned he'd wipe Spot off the map for good. Spot got together a private army of at least a thousand men. They were armed with Sten guns, hand grenades, service revolvers and automatic German Luger pistols. And they had plenty of ammo to spare. Tension built up across Soho, the East End and North London. Business in the dives and the spielers dipped because people didn't want to get caught in the crossfire. Even the police were on alert.

But no one knew when or where the battle would commence. Each side continued to send out scouts and put out cautious feelers as to the strength and whereabouts of their opponents. Then Jack Spot took the initiative and phoned Harry White to find out where the battle would take place. White, suspecting Spot was trying to set him up, slammed the phone down and vanished within hours, even clearing his family out of their home. He left behind his gang, ready for battle, under the command of a character called Terrible Mike.

Spot put the word out that he'd stood down his troops. In fact, he left Moisha and Little Hymie to hold the fort while he and his toughest henchmen went looking for his opponents. After four nights of searching, they found two of the King's Cross boys in a pub in Camden Town. One of them ran away and the other was given a good hiding and sent back with a message to his pals. 'Put up or shut up.'

Spot believed that, with Harry White out of the way, the entire gang would quickly crumble. Scotland Yard thought otherwise. The police turned up on Spot's doorstep in Aldgate early one morning. Spot feared that if the cops searched the premises they'd find his arsenal of weapons. So he agreed to be driven to Savile Row police station 'for a chat'. There he was greeted by some old, familiar faces, including Chief Superintendent Peter Beveridge, Divisional Detective Inspector Bob Higgins and a couple of other heavyweights from the Yard. They offered Spot a chair and then gave him 'a right royal rocketing'.

As Spot later recalled: 'It wasn't like any normal business talk I have had with the police. This was straight talk. They told me they were not going to have any gang warfare in London. They said that if there was any outbreak of violence they would hold me responsible, and that they would make quite certain that I went inside for a long, long time. Only a mug would ignore a warning like that. I know nearly all there is to know about fighting, and I know you can't fight the police.'

Spot's chief 'advisor', a legendary old-time villain called Wal McDonald, told Spot to keep the cops happy and stop smashing up clubs and handing out beatings. Meanwhile, White's team retreated back to their stronghold of King's Cross and Islington. When Spot got back to Aldgate, he called together his heavy mob and told them to 'pack it up and get rid of the ironmongery'. Spot later explained: 'So we collected all the Stens, the grenades, revolvers, pistols and ammunition, loaded them into a lorry after dark and dumped the whole lot in the Thames.'

Spot's 'victory' over Harry White meant he could now claim the title of the king of the underworld. He expected utter loyalty and respect from other villains. Instead, he got a ticking-off from businessmen and bookies he was associated with who were angry with him for taking on the Whites in the first place. Spot was even persuaded to go to the Essex seaside resort of Southend to cool his heels for a while and let the dust settle following his clash with the Whites. That January of 1947 turned out to be the coldest January for more than a hundred years.

On 13 January, newspaper columnist Arthur Helliwell in the *Sunday People* reported seeing 'the notorious missing gang boss [Spot] who ducked out of London a week or two ago when the heat was on'. And Helliwell warned that 'carloads of cosh-and-razor-armed thugs have been searching Soho to carve him up'. Spot laughed off the article. He knew he'd be back in Soho within a couple of weeks.

§   §   §

A month after the battle, Harry White was at Lord Roseberry's point-to-point meeting at Bletchley, in Buckinghamshire. At 10 a.m., just as the bookies were erecting their stands, a coach drove onto the field. Out climbed Jack Spot, fedora hat down over his eyes, followed by thirty of his gang. Within moments, Spot's boys stood around Harry White's clerk and tic-tac man. Spot told him: 'I want a twenty-five per cent cut out of your business from today Harry.' Spot's mob stood laughing as White meekily replied: 'Okay, Spot.'

Harry White later recalled: 'He had done what no other man had ever been able to do in twenty years' racing – he'd frightened me to death.' Spot then stood alongside White as his thirty men moved amongst the other bookmakers, demanding protection money. Those who wouldn't pay were thrown off the course. Then Spot and his gang piled into the big marquee tents to enjoy cocktails and jellied eels at the buffet. Harry White later recalled: 'The bookies' stands were being ground underfoot by Spot's mob, and their umbrellas flew through the air. I had to tell them it would all blow over in a few days. But they thought I was in with Spot.'

By the time the actual racing began, Spot was smiling gleefully at customers as they rolled up to place their bets. And at the end of that day, Spot held out his hand for twenty-five per cent of Harry White's winnings. From that moment on, Jack Spot made White accompany him to just about every racecourse he ever visited. White explained: 'When there was more than one race meeting in a day and I sent two or three betting teams to courses, Spot made sure that his men went along to jot down the winnings. He was only interested in the winnings. If I lost money, Spot would turn to me and say: "You've got to be more careful in future, Harry."' And he always took his cut out of the cash. Any debts at the end of the day always came out of White's share.

Spot later insisted that when the King's Cross boys broke up it marked the end of the race gangs and that he went out of his way to make sure it stayed that way. Spot paid £300 for a piece of ground at a racecourse. Then each bookie got his pitch for £25 for the meeting. There were hundreds of pitches at each racecourse so Spot's profits were vast.

Yet Spot always claimed: 'The only advantage I took was that my pals and I got the best pitches. After that it was every man for himself to make a profit. And if you know how to make a book and use your loaf it isn't often you can lose on a race.'

The smartest men on the racecourses were the bookies' clerks, who thought like accountants but at twice the speed. A clerk entering bets and balancing the books at the same time could make £40 or £50 a day with a big bookie. But clerks with the ordinary, small firms managed just £3 or £4 a day. The outside man, who held the bag, got about £3 a day, and the tic-tac blokes, who were paid by bookies, were on about the same rate.

Spot later claimed one of the biggest bookies in racing had come to him personally and said: 'You've made racing a pleasure, Jack. We no longer go in terror of our lives.' But there were still race-track flare-ups. Spot explained: 'Two men I'd once helped started putting it about they were "taking over from Jack Spot". I called together a few of my close pals and asked what they knew about it. All they had was gloomy looks and shut traps, so I knew the tip I'd got was right.' Spot eventually traced one of the two men to an East End billiard hall and confronted him. The fight that followed was, in the words of Spot, 'one of the worst I've ever been in. It nearly ended in tragedy.' Spot claimed he had to carry his opponent to his car and drop him at the nearest hospital.

His propensity for violence knew no bounds.

6

BILLY THE KID

The London underworld in those post-war days was an ever-shifting nucleus of people moving backwards and forwards across the capital. The West End thrived because there was a need to enjoy oneself, even after wartime. But now drugs, blackmail and classic long-firm scams – where old ladies with money were conned into investing in fake businesses – could be added to an already potent mix.

Jack Spot knew that, if he was to maintain his reputation as the king of the underworld, he needed to watch his back. He also had to get a few important villains on his side. One of them was a classic smash 'n' grab merchant called Billy Hill. He was a real West Ender, born in 1911 at Seven Dials on the Holborn side of Leicester Square, which then resembled a Dickensian scene, filled with poverty and street beggars, and just a stone's throw from the vice dens of Soho.

Hill's mother was a 'buyer of bent gear' and his father 'had five or six cons for belting cozzers'. His first job as a grocer's delivery boy came with an attractive sideline feeding his brother-in-law information about likely targets for burglaries. Then he did his own break-ins and quickly became an expert at 'drumming', the speedy ransacking of a house in its owner's absence. Hill then turned to more lucrative targets such as vaults and safes of banks, building societies, cinemas and restaurants.

At nineteen years of age, Hill got out of borstal as, in his own words, 'a tough and bitter young thug, ready to do anything except go straight. The first thing I did was to buy a couple of smart new suits and a first-class set of burglar's tools. Then I got together my first gang. Not that I wanted to stay an ordinary screwsman for long.'

During the war, Hill became a notorious smash 'n' grab merchant – specialising in throwing bricks into jewellery shop windows and grabbing everything in sight. Then he got banged up yet again. From his cell in Dartmoor Prison he sent a letter to Jack Spot whom he'd heard of through other criminals. Spot was impressed by Hill's letter and told him to contact him when he got out. On his release, Hill – desperate for cash – teamed up with a character called 'John the Tilter' and they pretended they were detectives to relieve a couple of crooks of their haul of stolen parachutes, which they then sold for £500. Spot was immediately impressed when he heard about the stunt from Billy Hill. Here was a man after his own heart. Spot recalled: 'He was a man I understood and a man whose talents I could appreciate. During the months and years that followed, Billy Hill and me were great friends and saw a great deal of each other.'

Billy Hill reckoned the late forties were a war of liberation against the race gangs: 'The generations of repression, extortion, and blackmail were remembered vividly by the sons of men who had spent years in gaol because of the race gangs,' he later recalled. Hill wanted to make his loot out in the real world, away from the racing game. Billy Hill and Jack Spot had a similar outlook on many other subjects. Spot took Hill under his wing, but Billy Hill was a reluctant sidekick to anyone, let alone Jack Spot.

Then Hill – who'd quickly amassed £10,000 of his own from a rapid turnaround of robberies following his release – surprised the London underworld by announcing he was off to South Africa. He told Spot he wanted to set up a chain of spielers on his own because he didn't want to step on Spot's toes. But, within months of settling in South Africa, Hill was arrested for assaulting one of the country's most powerful criminals after a clash about paying protection money. Hill was thrown out of South Africa and headed back to England. When Spot heard the news he shrugged his shoulders and told one associate: 'Well he'll have to start all over again, won't he?'

At first Hill kept a low profile in the north of England. Then he pulled off a blagging in Manchester with two of Spot's associates, Sammy Josephs and Teddy Machin. A bookies' safe containing £9000 was stolen. But the cozzers were soon on his trail and Hill eventually gave himself up and got a three-year stretch in Wandsworth Prison. Jack Spot reckoned the jail term would teach Hill a lesson.

In prison, Hill decided that once he'd served his time he'd form his own proper mob and then stand shoulder-to-shoulder with Jack Spot. 'He wanted some independence but he also knew Jack was useful,' recalled one old lag. Hill would later dub his gang 'the best mob I ever had'. He reckoned characters such as Slippery Sam, Bullnose Bertie, Billy the Long-Reach and Iron Jemmy Spike would queue up to join him. Hill explained: 'There wouldn't be a safe in the country we couldn't go for and get. Our speciality was going to be post office and bank safes.'

Hill even planned how he'd rent a quiet country house north of London as a hideout for all the loot and then buy an old ambulance because it would be ideal transport for carrying safes. 'The cops would never dream of checking it out,' Hill later boasted.

But first Billy Hill had to serve out his time . . .

♭   ♭   ♭

Spielers were usually tipped off by police for a 'fee' when a raid was on the cards. In the same way that the bookies operated, Spot would then get 'a few mugs' in that day so regular customers escaped arrest; Soho's brothel-keepers were also helped by the police, who offered to 'adjust' certain evidence at a price. The payments covered what an officer might say in evidence relating to a police raid. Hundreds of Soho basement clubs were tolerated thanks to their unofficial contribution to police funds. Uniformed policemen in Soho received up to £60 a week in bribes (the average PC's wage was between £9 and £11 a week by this time). Even in the courts, evidence was frequently 'cooked' by bobbies to benefit the accused. Details of previous convictions were also suppressed on numerous occasions so that defendants were fined rather than imprisoned.

Spot was convinced anyone could be bought. A lot of his ideas came from a veteran New York hood called Sam Clines – onetime member of Murder Incorporated – whom Spot met in Soho just after the war. Clines had just got out of prison after serving a five-year stretch for robbery with violence following his arrival in Britain during the war. Clines told Spot a lot about the way the underworld operated in cities like Chicago and New York. He even taught Spot how to run a crap game, otherwise known as a dice-rolling school. As Spot recalled: 'There was quite a craze for dice at the time and we did very nicely.'

Clines warned Spot to watch his own boys very closely. Spot had long been acutely paranoid about his team. 'I watched them craftily, noticing everything they said and did and stored it away in my memory,' Spot later recalled. Onetime gang member Lennie Garrett had tried to stitch up Spot to the cops following his release from a three-year sentence for laying out a policeman during a robbery. Garrett was angry because Spot had failed to support his family while he was inside. Clines advised Spot to introduce a policy of paying twenty pounds a week to the wife of any member of his team who went to prison in his service. That way he could ensure the loyalty of many, although there would always be the bad eggs prepared to grass him up for a score.

Spot wanted to maintain real power and influence so he began flexing his muscles. He started by adopting an image as a pristine gentleman, often dressed in immaculate handmade suits with a fedora to match and a cigar protruding from his mouth. Clines told him that would give him initial respect from other people.

Then he moved into an enormous office above one of his Soho spielers and started hosting important 'board meetings' with contacts, even including a prominent Tory Member of Parliament. Spot aimed to run the underworld as if he was the head of a legitimate corporation. Clines had told him that was how they did things in America and Spot wanted to emulate the US in every way possible. He explained: 'If ever I had a real spot of bother I could just pick up the phone and ask my MP to sort it out. Sweet as a whistle.' There were rumours that Spot had 'persuaded' his MP to go on his payroll after the politician was caught with two prostitutes in a West End hotel room. Whatever the truth of the matter, Spot was firmly in the driving seat.

Another aspect of his life that Spot discussed with Clines was his relationships with women. The shock of losing his wife to another man meant that Spot had been going through women with reckless abandon. Clines nodded with approval at Spot's confession, because he, too, saw women as nothing more than a useful appendage. Spot then moved into a five-guinea-a-week luxury flat in a redbrick block called Hyde Park Mansions, just off the Edgware Road. That apartment saw dozens of females come and go; a Palladium chorus girl, a BBC sound-effects girl, a 'hello' girl and a dress designer. Spot's problem was that he no longer trusted women so, as soon as they became in any way needy, he ordered them out of his life. The words of his first lover Maggie Klaut back in the East End kept coming back to haunt him. One time he kicked a pretty, young shorthand typist out of his flat, concluding that, 'a daily help was much more satisfactory'. But what he really wanted was more than just a pretty face. His own mother was a strong-willed, independent woman and that appealed to him; but this type rarely came near gangsters with a reputation for slashing anyone who got in their way.

Meantime, the West End was booming. Spot was running numerous protection rackets, taking his cut on gambling and using his power base for one main purpose: the survival of the status quo. He was like a businessman, drawing his profits from a discrete monopoly and only becoming dangerous if he felt his empire was being threatened.

§　　§　　§

In the summer of 1948, Heathrow Airport was being constructed to replace Croydon as London's main airport when Jack Spot masterminded a robbery that looked set to confirm his status as king of the underworld. Sammy Josephs (a.k.a. Sammy Ross), a well-connected Jewish thief told Spot that extremely valuable cargoes were kept at the airport overnight. Josephs had an inside contact who was prepared to let them know when the next big shipment of valuables was en route.

Spot and Ross had worked together on a series of lorry hijacks over the previous few months. Spot believed meticulous preparations were essential so, initially, his boys joined special guided tours of the airport to case the joint. Then bulky parcels were sent from Ireland to test the lorry delivery system. Sammy Ross and another member of the team, Franny Daniels, both licensed truck drivers, found they were allowed into the airport's inner precinct of the customs building to pick up the parcels without an official pass.

Then word came through that a bonded warehouse inside the airport perimeter was taking delivery of £380,000 worth of diamonds and a further £280,000 of cash on the night of 24 July 1948. Spot's team rapidly devised a plan to dope security guards with sedatives in their coffee. Then ten raiders – all wearing nylon stockings over their faces – would follow a single torch light to the customs shed where all the loot was stored.

But someone grassed them up. By 11 p.m. all roads leading to the airport were under surveillance. Thirteen Flying Squad detectives lay in wait in the customs shed and ten more were hiding in a van round the back. As Spot's team crashed in, a bloody battle ensued. Two of Spot's mob, Billy Benstead and Franny Daniels, turned round and scarpered; another gang member, Teddy Machin, escaped by jumping on the back of a moving truck that was on its way out of the airport compound. The rest of the battered robbers were dragged off in waiting black Marias. They were all convicted and received up to twelve years' imprisonment.

Up-and-coming young London tearaway Frankie Fraser knew many of Spot's team. He believes to this day that Spot's London Airport job was doomed to failure because Spot and his team had only carried out a handful of blaggings before. But then there was never any love lost between Fraser and Spot. Fraser later admitted: 'I never liked Spotty. I never liked the way he cut people. But, to give him credit, he had some good people working for him.'

On the underworld grapevine, many were saying that the airport job was grassed up by one of Spot's own henchmen, annoyed that he hadn't been properly paid for a previous robbery.

§   §   §

In the winter of 1948, a pair of young tearaways, aged just fifteen, called the Kray twins, were getting lots of local press coverage in the East End. Reggie Kray won the London Schoolboy Boxing Championships after having been Hackney Schoolboy Champion. The following year he became the South-Eastern Divisional Youth Club Champion and the London ATC Champion. His brother, Ron, won the Hackney Schoolboy and London Junior Championships, and a London ATC title.

Ron and Reg also had their own gang of young hoodlums. They'd been barred from most of the cinemas and dancehalls in the East End. The twins let it be known they kept choppers, machetes, knives, swords and a variety of other weapons beneath the bed they both slept in at their parents' home in Vallance Road, Bethnal Green. It was a tough area where gang fights occurred virtually every night.

By the age of sixteen, the twins had been nicked for GBH on three people during a teenage gang fight involving bike chains and coshes outside a dance hall in Mare Street, Hackney. The Krays were later acquitted of the charges at the Old Bailey. Ronnie Kray even boasted that he'd purchased his first gun before he'd turned seventeen and that he fully expected to shoot someone 'sooner rather than later'. The Kray twins had been brought up on a staple diet of violence. When they slept, they always placed newspapers around the floor so that they'd hear the rustle of the papers if an intruder entered the bedroom of the family home – known as Fort Vallance.

The Krays let it be known on the manor they had a pair of strong right arms and were available to the highest bidder as minders. Ronnie, the more outrageous of the two brothers, liked sharpening his cutlass on oil he spread across the doorstep of Fort Vallance. He'd often swish the blade through the air in an arc, his face contorted with venom and the anticipation of pleasure in combat. One time he turned to his brother and said: 'Can't you see how that would stop them? Half a dozen blokes come at you and then BINGO! the first one gets his head cut clean off his shoulders and it rolls on the floor. Wouldn't that make 'em run!'

Across London, other criminal mobs were flexing their muscles. In a club in Brixton, two gangs had it out with razors and glasses hastily broken on the bar counter. It was a test of strength 'to see who was boss', and afterwards some of them shook hands. But it took four buckets of water to clear the blood from the floor. Incidents like this happened with increasing regularity across the capital. Jack Spot was not the only criminal in London with big ambitions.

§ § §

Spot and his henchmen still frequented Ziggy's Cafe, in Cobb Street, just off Petticoat Lane. Ziggy was a smart-looking, middle-aged man with a stout gut and a fat cigar always hanging out of his mouth. His wife served the teas and lunches in the caff. Ziggy even had a police truncheon on show behind the bar. He'd grown up alongside Jack Spot and even fought alongside him when the Blackshirts marched into the East End back in 1936.

Ziggy's other regulars included characters like Sammy Wilde, a coloured boxer from the Gold Coast of Africa. He had tribal marks cut down the side of each cheekbone and always had a knife in a sheath attached to his waistband. Wilde often wore a small woollen beret with a coloured tassel on top. At night he made appearances on stage as a fire-eater.

Young tearaway Laurie O'Leary and a crew of other teenage hoodlums congregated outside Ziggy's caff by a record stall with dozens of youths from other parts of London. Amongst them were characters called Curly King, Norman Hall, Terry O'Brien and Checker Berry. On one Sunday in 1948 Jack Spot, followed by his henchmen Little Hymie Rosen and Moisha Blueball – all wearing beige Stetson hats – strolled into Ziggy's. Everyone moved aside, giving them plenty of space. There was a respectable hush. O'Leary later recalled that Spot and his boys looked like a bunch of American gangsters straight off a Jimmy Cagney movie.

Also amongst the group of youths outside Ziggy's that day was Ronnie Kray. As Spot and his team disappeared, Ronnie turned round and asked fellow hoodlum O'Leary, 'I wonder what would happen if I shot him, Lol?'

'Shoot Jack Spot, Ron!' O'Leary replied. 'I'd think that if you hit him we'd have to start running, but if you miss, we'd have to run further and faster.' Ronnie Kray's reply was simply that O'Leary was 'too soft'.

As O'Leary later recalled: 'We were kids in comparison to those gangsters. Thankfully, Ron never did carry out his light-hearted threat, but I am certain that that was when he saw the power of Spot and began to want some of it for himself.'

7
THE PICKLED HERRING
TURNS SOUR

In the summer of 1949, Spot's wealthy millionaire backer shut the Buttolph Club down after he heard rumours that Spot had used the Aldgate premises to organise the highly publicised London Airport robbery. Spot later explained: 'I told him [the club owner] that what the boys got up to in their time off was nothing to do with me, but he wasn't having any of it.' By now Spot had a share in at least half a dozen other clubs, plus proceeds from other successful robberies that he'd helped finance, as well as protection money, so he wasn't too bothered.

However, Spot's newly expanding empire needed a trusted right-hand man and he thought that Billy Hill would fit the bill perfectly. Before dawn on a crisp autumn day in 1949, Spot drove to Wandsworth Prison in his flashy white Cadillac Eldorado and waited for Hill to emerge from behind the tall, black steel gates.

Hill was close to middle age, penniless and looked 'as thin as a pickled herring', according to Spot. Naturally, Hill was keen to link up with Spot again. He'd spent many hours in his prison cell planning how he'd organise criminals rather than perpetrate crimes himself. Hill knew that next time he was nicked he'd probably cop a ten-year minimum sentence. Spot offered Hill the chance to oversee his London spielers. Hill knew he needed time to get back on his feet so he was grateful for the 'appointment'.

These clubs had become dens of criminality. Sammy Samuels, who ran small Soho clubs from the thirties to the sixties recalled:

'The gaming clubs and the drinking clubs in and around Soho were meeting places for the fly-boys, the screwsmen and the tea-leafs, the hustlers and the sharpers, and while, on the one hand, the club guv'nor can do without their custom he cannot keep them out of the club. They are part of the set-up. And they often brought with them info about new criminal opportunities.'

Spot believed Billy Hill would ensure that order was kept on his premises. As Hill later explained: 'These places didn't have names and committees and all that stuff. They just started and the word got round that there's a game on. The customers ranged from regular villains to tearaways, to every kind of person from titled aristocrats down to cab drivers and waiters. We never did allow any steamers in. Our game was not to trim mugs who wanted to play for some sort of thrill. There was no need for that.'

Billy Hill came over as a very smooth customer – a cold, hard and silent man with totally expressionless eyes (one villain later said it was like looking into black glass). But, more significantly, Hill was also a skilful gambler, possessing a sixth sense about the draw and fall of a card. Some reckoned Hill could 'set a tone of play and conduct which has never been equalled'.

Despite being of a similar age, Jack Spot and Billy Hill had reached very different stages of their lives. Spot had already run numerous late-night drinking and gambling dens. And, although he still loved the loose women available at the drop of a hat, he'd grown a little weary of the constant round of socialising. Meanwhile, Billy Hill was lapping up the glory – and the cash – like an overenthusiastic kid.

However, Spot and Hill operated together with speed and efficiency when it came to any underworld unrest. When King's Cross leader Harry White – now squeezed off the racecourses and the West End – tried to take over protection of London's greyhound stadiums, he came into conflict with 'Ginger' Rumble and his Shepherd's Bush Boys. Spot and Hill kidnapped both men and forced them to agree a truce, with each man getting a fifty/fifty share of the spoils. Spot and Hill didn't demand a penny from them – just so long as they stuck to their own territories. They didn't even rate the dogs as a lucrative sideline. Their priority was to stop White and Rumble looking for opportunities closer to the West End. Jack Spot later claimed he'd made a big mistake because he'd effectively allowed White's King's Cross mob to start operating again.

Spot's right-hand man Billy Hill seemed on top of things, although his violent habits greatly bothered Spot. One time Hill slashed the face of a pimp who was trying to force Hill's lover back on the game. The first Spot heard about the incident was when Hill phoned him to ask him to check out the hospitals to see what condition his victim was in. Spot personally persuaded the pimp not to grass Hill up to the law. But Spot was furious that Hill's personal life had encroached into 'the business'.

Spot, with his gang of bruisers, and Hill, with his gang of thieves, were by now dominating London's boomtown West End. They ran protection rackets, took their cut of gambling and used their power with one main objective – their own survival. The pair were happy to come to an 'arrangement' with anyone – even the Italians, who'd gradually stepped back in after the war. Meanwhile Spot and Hill drew their profits from a discrete monopoly, carefully preserving good relations with the police, and becoming dangerous only when they felt their empire was under threat.

But all was not so rosy beneath the surface. Billy Hill told one associate Spot was, 'becoming insecure and a bit jealous of me'. Spot later insisted he should have had Hill 'seen to' when he had the chance, because their friendship was far from perfect. But, for the moment, Spot was still the king of the underworld and they continued crushing the smaller gangs with ease. Many traders did not trust the police, or had something to hide, so they turned to Spot and Hill for protection. The two men even recruited a strong army from across the river, at Elephant and Castle, which included such notables as brothers Lennie and Jimmy Garrett plus Bobby Brindle, adding muscle to their number-one heavyweight henchman Johnny Carter.

In the late 1940s, Spot began regularly holding court in the Bear Garden Lounge of the Cumberland Hotel, in Oxford Street, where he offered free drinks to all his boys. The barman, a Scot called Alex, named a cocktail, 'Jack Boss', after Spot. It was a Manhattan made with Scotch whisky and French vermouth (there was a standing joke that anyone ordering a Manhattan had better not expect Italian vermouth when Jack was around). As one of Spot's boys later explained: 'It was the "thing" to be seen having a drink with the boss: it oozed Al Capone and infuriated Billy Hill, who had grand plans for himself.' But Spot had also caught the eye of Fleet Street as well as other villains, and reporters began turning up to see him at the Cumberland. Spot revelled in the attention and fame.

Hill already considered himself on an equal footing to Spot, so he set up similar regular gathering at the Royal Lancaster Hotel, in Bayswater. Hill would sweep through the hotel's double doors with a hefty sidekick in front checking out the place. Then he'd saunter through the lobby, still flanked by bodyguards, two of whom were well-known boxing pros.

When Spot heard about Hill's antics he laughed it off. But some of his most loyal boys told him to keep an eye on Hill. He could be trouble.

§   §   §

Back on the racetracks, business was still booming. Small-time crooks earned a bundle working as bookmakers. Others spent entire weekends at point-to-point races, which were not so well policed. Criminals would go whenever there was a meeting and stand on a couple of boxes beside a post with a bookie's name on it and a board to write the odds on. This was known as a bookmaker's 'joint' but, although it could be put up in seconds, villains still had to pay other spivs for it, plus pay for the chalk and even the water to wipe the board clean between races.

One such classic operation came under the strict control of an independent hard man called 'Italian Albert' Dimes, already known as the 'King of the Points'. Dimes had a fearsome history; in 1941 he'd been involved in the killing of Harry 'Little Hubby' Distleman following a brawl in the Old Cue Club in Frith Street, Soho, which had also left Distleman's friend Eddie Fletcher badly cut up. At the time, Dimes was sidekick to the psychotic Babe Mancini, who'd splattered the ceiling with blood as he slashed away at Distleman with his dagger. Somehow, Dimes had escaped with a caution for unlawful wounding, although he was sent back to the RAF from which he had deserted.

One of Dimes' favourite racecourse ruses was to find a gullible bookmaker and place bets with him just after the end of a race. His right-hand man at the time was a bizarre character called Prince Monolulu, a six-foot-four, broad-shouldered man who wore redskin feathers in his hair. He was also reputed to be one of the racing world's greatest tipsters and sold his tips for a few bob a time.

Albert Dimes also helped organise bare-knuckle boxing bouts at racecourses. Carloads of villains would turn up at places like Epsom with their own favourite fighter to take on an opponent. One Derby Day, Dimes oversaw a fight to the death between one of his boys and a 'pikey' (gypsy) at the Epsom Downs camp close to the track. Straight race goers were barred from the ringside as the two fighters smashed each other to pieces for a £500 prize. More than ten times that amount changed hands in bets.

Dimes also ran other rackets back on the streets of London. One involved a crooked doctor getting people aged eighteen and nineteen exempted from National Service. The parents paid the 'fees' for this service, which depended on their wealth. The cash was split between a tame doctor and the medic in charge of the examinations at a bent medical centre in Mill Hill, North London. As Dimes later explained: 'All parties concerned were happy with the results, especially the young kids who could resume their ambitions without the interference of National Service.'

Dimes had also become expert at getting what were called

dockers' tickets or books, which would then be sold on for a fee. The 'charges' depended on the wealth of the 'client'. The dockers' books enabled anyone to work as a docker at the quayside, loading boats and barges. They were paid vast wages compared with most jobs, even though the working hours were very short. Many dockers helped steal items like jewellery and watches, which were smuggled in from the dock areas without being cleared through customs.

All in all, Albert Dimes was a very smart, supposedly independent operator – just the sort of character who could really cause Jack Spot a few problems. But for the moment, Spot failed to recognise the threat presented by Dimes. He was too wrapped up in his newfound fame as king of the underworld.

ƒ   ƒ   ƒ

At the end of a long day, Jack Spot would return to his flat at Hyde Park Mansions, submerge himself in his favourite armchair, hook his Italian heels on the mantelpiece, and light a big, fat cigar. He felt like an emperor who'd successfully taken over a nation. The troublemakers were off the manor. If Spot fancied a trip to somewhere like Monte Carlo, for a sunshine break, then he could go ahead and do it. No one had a tig on him. He was king of the castle. That's when Spot would blow a huge smoke ring into the air and watch it drift to the ceiling and disperse. Then he'd pause momentarily, wrestling with sudden indecision. Would baccarat or poker best match his mood? He'd soon come up with the answer and head for the door. Poker was a game of wits, baccarat a game of luck. He'd play poker.

Jack Spot also had a tendency to gamble on the loyalty of his childhood pal Moisha Blueball. His attitude by now was: 'I dragged him [Moisha] out of the gutter with me and placed him in a position of trust. He was rolling in dough and working alongside the boss of the underworld.'

Spot reckoned Moisha had never truly understood women and

that he was too soft for his own good. Moisha was already married with a young daughter but he'd never brought his wife out to parties. Spot later recalled: 'I knew how to handle women. With all the dough I was making, I had women crawling to me and licking my boots. I didn't fall for their artfulness. There's only one reason a man wants a woman around: to have himself a good time. But I'm not sure Moisha realised that.'

Spot had moved a blonde, known around Soho as Tiger Lil, into his flat at Hyde Park Mansions. She'd been a stripper in a Paris nightclub before she'd met Spot. He commented: 'She wasn't a bad dame to have around. She gave the apartment that little touch of homeliness that a man needs. She'd flit around in a flimsy nylon nightie, preparing my breakfast before I went to work, and was a hell of a good sport at a party.'

After giving him breakfast in bed, Tiger Lil would sponge Jack Spot down during his morning bath. Then he got dressed and sat down with a copy of the *Financial Times*. Tiger Lil – a genuine blonde, tall and generously proportioned – managed to combine sexual prowess with efficient domesticity. Spot recalled: 'She was glowing and radiant with health and good spirits. And there's nothing that puts a girl on top of the world more than knowing she's putting all the other women around her in the shade.'

Spot and Tiger Lil regularly held parties at Hyde Park Mansions, during which time the drink flowed and the radiogram played at full volume. Spot often picked up the phone and got the apartment manager to send up crates of champagne, plus a tin bath full of ice for the bottles.

But his pal Moisha Blueball was never comfortable at these parties. Spot concluded that he didn't know how to enjoy himself. Moisha saw it a different way. One night he asked Spot: 'Are you really enjoying yourself, Spotty?'

'Enjoying myself? I'm having a whale of a time,' Spot responded.

'I just find it . . . boring,' shrugged Moisha, who told Spot he could never enjoy himself with 'a prostitute'.

'What's wrong with being a tart?' yelled Spot fiercely.

Moisha shook his head slowly. 'I don't understand you, Spotty. Don't you ever feel you want real affection, someone who wants you just because . . . just because you're you?'

Spot's reply summed up his own attitude to women since his wife's betrayal: 'You know where you are with a tart. She tells you outright what she wants and wants it on the nail. The other women, the sentimental types, want a whole lot more. But they don't ask for it outright. Instead they twist you around their little finger to get it.'

Minutes later, with the champagne flowing, Tiger Lil did a striptease for everyone at the party. Spot adored looking at the admiring faces of every man and woman present. As he explained: 'She loved the adulation. I got a kick out of it, a big kick. It was a feather in my cap. Tiger Lil stood out head-and-shoulders above the other women that night, vivacious and beautiful.' Those other women soon discarded their flimsy undergarments, and began, 'splashing in and out of the bathtub like water nymphs'. It was a typical Jack Spot party. Meanwhile shy, awkward Moisha slipped out of Spot's apartment and went home.

A few weeks later, Spot was highly amused to discover that Moisha had walked out on his wife. However, Moisha announced to Spot that his girlfriend 'was not like your tarts' and said he intended to marry her as soon as his divorce came through. Spot told his old pal that she'd lead him up a garden path just like all women. Moisha got so angry that the two friends almost came to blows. Spot eventually met Moisha's girl, who turned out to be extremely quiet and, in his words, 'like a Sunday school teacher'. At one of Spot's parties, the couple sat in the corner hardly uttering a word to anyone. They left when Spot paid an older woman to perform an impromptu striptease for all his guests.

One day Moisha's girlfriend turned up at Spot's club looking for him. Spot showed her into his office and promptly drugged her drink. He wanted to teach Moisha a lesson. Hours later Moisha returned to Spot's office where he found his girlfriend collapsed on a divan. He presumed she'd slept with Spot and blew a fuse.

A fight broke out and Spot flattened his childhood friend with a flurry of punches before telling him to go home.

Spot later claimed that when he walked back into the office after the fight, Moisha's girlfriend was just coming round and that was when he seduced her. The next day he made a point of telling Moisha how the girl had accepted £500 in cash from him. Moisha was so appalled he immediately dropped the girl and went back to his wife. It left a bad feeling between the two childhood friends, even though Spot pointed out that he'd done his old pal a favour.

ƒ   ƒ   ƒ

At the time, Spot spent a lot of his time at the Galahad Club in Soho. Entrance was via a flap in the door, which opened after a password was uttered. The punch-drunk minder on the door had problems remembering his own name, let alone the so-called 'secret' password: 'Whatever you said through the flap would get you in,' Spot later recalled.

Spot and his mob made a point of striding into the entrance of the Galahad in a menacing fashion with their hands dug deep in their pockets and scowling like something out of a gangster movie. As Spot entered, the club's resident three-piece band would stop playing. The club manager plus a couple of waiters would come scurrying over while everyone stared in admiration at the king of the underworld.

Spot recalled: 'Then slowly, with piercing eyes, I'd look search-ing around the club, staring intently into every tensed face. Then having finally assured myself that nobody was waiting to knock me off, I'd give a quick jerk of my head and lead the mob over to the table reserved for us.'

Spot saw it as a bit of harmless play-acting. He and his mob even went into a close huddle once they'd sat at their table. He'd give furtive glances over his shoulder while the customers con-tinued watching with baited breath. One time, the legend was fuelled by a bookie with a grudge against Spot who wormed his way into the Galahad with a razor. One of Spot's henchmen, Johnny Scott, saw the bookie first and got a cut forearm trying to grab the weapon. The bookie was immediately bundled out of the club so the police weren't involved. Word soon got out that there'd been an attempt on Spot's life.

Other regular clientele at the Galahad had a definite touch of the bizarre about them: there were men with thick beards and flashing eyes, accompanied by cigar-smoking women, dressed in men's suits and with boys' haircuts. There were youths in plum-coloured corduroy trousers, yellow shirts and silk neck-scarves. There were also Edwardian clothes, jeans and jerseys, girls with long blonde hair hanging over their buttocks and others wearing a fixed Florence Nightingale expression. Upper-class twits mingled with the tarts, pansies, prudes, cranks, loonies and fanatics, which helped make up much of Soho's turbulent society.

One night in the Galahad, Spot met a tall, blonde girl, called Trudy, dressed in a perfectly fitted dove-grey frock. She was standing at the bar with a whisky glass in her hand pretending to listen to a small, dapper man while she focused her attention directly on Spot. He looked into her eyes for two full minutes. Then she winked. Spot beckoned a waiter who went over and asked her and her companion to join his table.

Trudy said she was a model who'd just auditioned for a BBC TV play. A few minutes later Spot was on the dance floor with Trudy. Within an hour, Spot had given her a bracelet he'd just bought for Tiger Lil. Three days later he'd told Tiger Lil to leave his flat and offered her a 'few hundred nicker' to tide her over while she sorted out a new place to live. Tiger Lil was distraught and rang Spot four times at work that day, pleading to be allowed to stay. As he later explained: 'She wanted to build it into an emotional crisis. And an emotional crisis is one thing I couldn't stand at any price.'

That same evening at around 7 p.m., Moisha Blueball called Spot from the Galahad to say Tiger Lil had shown up and was 'acting strange'. Spot ordered Moisha to get rid of her. But at 8.30

Moisha rang back to say Tiger Lil had stabbed a customer with a piece of glass after the man had refused to buy her a drink. He'd been so badly injured that he might lose an eye. But Spot still refused to come to the club. Spot was in his office discussing an armed robbery he was financing with his latest team. Nothing took priority over a job. Eventually, Moisha turned up and Spot had to clear the room of his team of blaggers. Moisha accused Spot of being callous about Tiger Lil.

'She loved you, Spotty.'

'Bollocks.'

'She might even top herself.'

Spot laughed. 'No dame ever kills herself while she's got a trunk full of new clothes, a jewel case and money in the bank.'

Moisha then revealed he'd paid Tiger's victim £500 to cover up what had happened.

'Now we're even Spotty,' said Moisha.

'What?' asked Spot.

'Remember that £500 you paid out?'

Spot nodded. 'Sure,' he said, recalling the incident over Moisha's girl.

Spot later recalled: 'From that moment on, I wasn't so sure about Moisha's loyalty. He'd obviously never forgiven me for having his girl.'

Later that evening Spot returned to his flat to find Tiger Lil still in residence. He called the apartment-block manager and two porters packed all Tiger Lil's clothes and belongings. In the living room, she sobbed and pleaded with Spot to let her stay. He completely ignored her. Five minutes later she left. He never saw her again.

A few days after, Spot and Moisha had another run-in at Moisha's home in Aldgate. Spot was furious because someone had grassed up his robbery team to the police and he'd had to cancel the job. He thought it might have been Moisha. After a brief discussion turned into a screaming match, Spot laid into Moisha using his fists like battering rams. Then the two men fell onto the floor where they continued hammering each other. Eventually Moisha lost consciousness. His face was battered and unrecognisable, his shirt ripped off his back and stained crimson. Spot got up, walked through into Moisha's kitchen and washed the blood off his knuckles. When he returned to the living room, Moisha was still out cold. Much of the furniture and a glass cabinet were smashed.

The following day, Spot visited the badly injured Moisha in hospital, where Moisha told Spot he understood why he'd given him the beating. Spot was touched by Moisha's loyalty and felt guilty for ever having suspected him of being a grass. Billy Hill smirked when he heard about their bust-up. He knew that such incidents could only be good news for him because they diverted Spot away from the day-to-day running of his criminal empire.

Meanwhile, Spot's latest female acquisition, Trudy, was proving a disaster. 'She lay around most of the day, a lazy good-for-nothing, looking sour every time I told her to do something and pestering the life out of me for bits of jewellery and clothes. She was cold too. I don't mean that she didn't make love. But she didn't seem to have her heart in it,' he recalled. Spot soon found himself remembering Tiger Lil and the tender way she'd stroke his forehead with the tips of her fingers and look deep into his eyes. This time, Spot promised himself he'd had it with two-time girls and hussies. The next one would be the real McCoy.

8

RITA, RITA

In the summer of 1949, Spot travelled north to see how his old mates were getting on in the club world and to keep an eye on the tracks. At Haydock Park racecourse, he met an Irish girl called Margaret Malloy, known to everyone as Rita. She knew nothing about Spot's reputation.

Rita Malloy had been brought up on a gritty tenement housing estate in Dublin. Her parents were extremely poor. Her father had died when she was seven and her mother had struggled to bring up five children. At the age of thirteen, Rita had got a job in a factory, wrapping soap. She'd earned just 11s. 6d. a week. A job as an usherette in a cinema soon followed. By the age of sixteen, she was strikingly pretty and men were lining up to flatter her. Then, aged eighteen, she was involved in a car crash and received a £200 insurance pay out. She used the money to go across the Irish Sea to Liverpool with a vague plan 'to see the world'.

And that's how nineteen-year-old Rita Malloy happened to be at the Haydock Park races. She'd just decided to put a bet on a horse for the first time in her life when she saw broad-shouldered, expensively dressed Jack Spot stood alongside one of his bookies. Rita went across and asked for a ten bob each-way bet.

'I won't give you a ticket,' said Spot, 'but I'll remember your face.'

He later recalled: 'Rita didn't even know I had money! I might have been any other common, working man. Yet she was as sweet and charming as though she didn't care whether I was poor and without influence. I didn't tell her who I was. I was too shy to tell her the real truth. Some women have funny ideas and I sensed she was the sort of girl who'd be upset to think I was associated with the underworld.'

Rita's horse came third, but Spot was so smitten he asked her for a date that evening. Spot stayed up north for another five days. 'I bought her a lorry load of diamond bracelets and dangled them in front of her but it didn't impress her,' he recalled.

Rita Malloy told Jack Spot – eighteen years her senior – that her priority was marriage and kids. Jack Spot insisted that was what he wanted. She concluded that maybe he could be tamed with the right approach. Spot was so bewitched he could see himself settling down with his new girlfriend who was, in his own words, 'a real gem'.

Spot was soon spending so much time with Rita he was starting to neglect his empire. For the first time in his life, Jack Spot was discovering that a woman could want him without any strings attached. She said she didn't care about the money or the lifestyle and her loyalty to Spot quickly became unswerving. She even took him over to Dublin to meet her mother and he made a real effort to forge a relationship with her. Rita later claimed that her mother was initially charmed by Jack Spot: 'He even managed to make the age difference seem unimportant,' she recalled. Spot's Jewish roots were not mentioned at this early stage in the relationship as Rita had warned Spot her mother might not be too impressed. Rita was considered a headstrong girl with a mind of her own and her mother proudly told friends and family in Dublin that she had no doubt Rita would make her fame and fortune in London.

*   *   *

In the summer of 1951, Jack Spot persuaded Billy Hill and Hill's lover, Gypsy Riley, to join him and Rita on holiday in the South of France. Rita was very careful not to tell her strictly Catholic mother back in Dublin in case it upset her. Rita and Gypsy instantly detested each other, which then caused friction between Spot and Hill, who'd left his wife Aggie to run off with Gypsy. 'Rita thought Gypsy was a loose woman who'd bed Spot the moment her back was turned,' one old East End villain explained. 'But actually Gypsy had a heart of gold.'

Despite the tensions, Billy Hill adored the good life on the French Riviera. The sun softened his chiv scars and helped him forget the awful stench of Wandsworth Prison. He knew that his relationship with Spot was far from easy but he tried to laugh it all off as 'a touch of woman trouble'. Both men spent much of the holiday discussing how they'd finance more and more teams of robbers. It was lucrative, low-risk work since neither of them would be directly involved in the crimes. Spot and Hill agreed on one thing; it seemed a natural expansion of their empire.

Shortly after returning from the Med, Rita told Spot she was pregnant. Spot was delighted and immediately promised to marry her. He admitted to one close pal he was really looking forward to settling down with his beloved Rita. All Rita really wanted was a happy, safe life for them and their soon-to-be-born child. She told her sister Carmel that she was determined to tame Jack Spot.

Back in Dublin, Rita's church-going mother was not told about her impending pregnancy. Despite their mother being taken with Spot, Rita and Carmel believed she wouldn't be keen on Rita marrying a Jew. Rita knew this was a sensitive subject for Spot, who hated any form of anti-Semitism.

Spot promised Rita that he might start 'easing off' the day-to-day running of his empire, although he wanted to ensure that no one, especially Billy Hill, thought he was abdicating. Just before the wedding, Spot even leaked a story to the *Sunday People* columnist Arthur Helliwell in which he implied he was 'going legit'. He was trying to keep Rita off his back. Spot had no intention of walking away from his life of crime and emphasised this to Billy Hill. But it seemed to Hill that Spot was trying to have the best of both worlds. Hill didn't yet have the firepower to mount an aggressive take-over but he saw Spot's behaviour as a sign of weakness.

Meanwhile, the two men continued to work in tandem; Spot concentrated on the racetracks while Hill worked the spielers and clubs in the West End. But Government moves were underway to try and clean up racecourse gambling, which meant 'undesirable elements' like Spot would soon be severely restricted by police and racecourse officials. Spot's rake-off from the bookies who set up their pitches at every race meeting was diminishing. Some of Spot's henchmen noticed a change in his attitude. As one of them later explained: 'The day Spotty fell for Rita was the day it all started to go wrong.'

Billy Hill remained in his element in London's clubland. He continued meeting and greeting new contacts and was always on the lookout for 'new investments' to put his money into. He was financing and organising robberies more successfully than Jack Spot had ever managed. But then Spot had his mind on other things.

In the middle of October 1951, Spot and Rita slipped off north, to a registry office in Leeds. Spot didn't want any of his gangster friends at the ceremony and Rita was equally determined to avoid her family. Moisha and Sonny were left behind in London to keep an eye on Billy Hill, who didn't even find out that Spot had got married until after his return.

✠   ✠   ✠

Driver 'Snakes' Clarke eased Jack Spot's white Cadillac from the kerb outside Euston Station and drove the mobster home with the smooth efficiency of a man who could weave a car through traffic with the skill of a twisting cobra. On arrival at Spot's gaff at Hyde Park Mansions, Moisha Blueball was the first to alight. He stood by the rear door, one hand deep in his pocket, watching the street. Sonny the Yank uncoiled himself from the front passenger seat and leaned on the other side of the rear door at the kerb. Hymie, whose face had been permanently disfigured into an evil smile as the result of a nasty chivving by the late Billy Peters, stood by the offside rear door. Snakes remained at the wheel, with the V-8 purring.

Long-legged brunette Rita emerged from the plush recesses of the motor. She was dressed in an emerald green off-the-shoulder number, a white mink stole, green high heels, a diamond necklace and emerald earrings. The previous owner of those jewels had been a Hollywood starlet, but she would never have recognised them in their new settings. Jack Spot only employed the best cutters of stolen stones in the capital. Young Rita might not have approved of her new husband's career, but once he started lavishing expensive gifts on her, she stopped nagging him so much to quit crime.

Spot's big face, beige fedora and stony blue eyes contrasted startlingly with his pallid complexion. His blue, chalk-striped suit had cost him eighty guineas in Savile Row, although the slightly exaggerated cut had almost broken his tailor's heart. Many villains were convinced he'd modelled himself on the American mafioso Frank Costello. His black shoes were handmade in Italy. His socks and tie were silk and exclusive. He smoked a Cuban cigar that was at least five inches long. There were rings on his fingers. He looked like an Italian, except for the eyes.

His beautiful young bride waited on the pavement until Spot joined her. Women had previously been expendable to Jack Spot, but this one was different. Moisha and Hymie closed in either side of the glamorous couple. Snakes switched off the engine, slid from the driver's seat and ran up the steps to the front door to the mansion block, unlocked it, and threw it wide open. Spot and his bride strolled in together arm-in-arm with a look of total indifference. Snakes closed the door on them, returned to the car, and drove off. Jack Spot and his brand new young bride were home.

Within the safety of the spacious Victorian apartment block was a flat furnished in the height of bad taste. Spot's sidekicks poured themselves drinks from the purple, velvet bar in the corner of the lounge before draping themselves untidily around the room. Rita walked straight past them into Spot's bedroom. He paused at the doorway, jerked a hand at Moisha, and followed her a few moments later, a large brandy swilling round in the huge goblet cupped in his hand.

Rita stretched languidly, tightening the gown around her breasts, belly and thighs. Spot placed the glass on the bedside table and began to unloosen his tie. Rita tugged at the zipper on her green dress and it slipped to the floor. She stepped casually from the folds, wearing a black brassiere and black panties and picked up the dress and hung it on a chair. Then she kicked off her heels and began unfastening her bra.

Spot took off his tie and hung it carefully on the tie rack in his wardrobe. Then he removed his coat, shook it out, and draped it on a hanger, where he examined it minutely for stains and sign of wear. He began removing his gold, monogrammed cufflinks from his shirtsleeves. Rita stifled a wide yawn.

Spot intended to show Rita how wonderful life in London could be, especially if you happened to be wife of the king of the under-world. Spot recalled: 'She married me for better or for worse. She tried to make me give up whatever I was doing without even guessing more than a tenth of what it involved. If she'd known the extent to which I was committed, she'd never have slept at nights.'

But life at that moment in time seemed a bed of roses to Jack Spot. Maybe one day he really would ease himself out of the day-to-day running of his empire. But for now he had a beautiful young wife who seemed to genuinely love him. What more could a man want?

ℐ   ℐ   ℐ

Spot's domestic commitments doubled with the birth of his daughter Rachel in April 1952. Rita became much more demanding, but Spot – terrified of making the same mistakes he had with Mollie – tried to do everything Rita wanted. He even began getting home early some evenings, to eat supper with Rita and take his turn feeding Rachel.

Juggling the life of a crime baron with being a new, supposedly enthusiastic father took an enormous toll. Spot was increasingly relying on Moisha and Sonny. He knew this was dangerous because Billy Hill was constantly circling his empire, looking to take full advantage of his frequent absences. Jack Spot was living a Jekyll-and-Hyde existence: a scheming, criminal mastermind yet also a happy, quiet, contented father and husband. And both his friends and foes were predicting it would all end in disaster.

9

287,000 SMACKEROOS

Twelve men arrived separately at a flat in the West End at midnight on 21 May 1952. They knew they were part of a blagging team, but knew nothing more until Billy Hill entered the apartment and told them the assignment. Two hours later, at 2 a.m., a man dressed as a postman walked through the gates of the main London post office, in Eastcastle Street, just a stone's throw from the Old Bailey, on the edge of the City of London. He nodded at the men at the gate and headed towards a group of vans near the sorting office.

He picked out one of the vans, lifted the bonnet and broke a wire that disconnected the alarm, which could be started by the driver if he was in trouble. Then the same man walked calmly out of the complex and got into a car and drove away. He went to a phone box where he called the others at the flat to report his part of the operation was complete. He also had no idea what else was being planned.

Soon after 3 a.m., two stolen private cars with false number-plates were handed over to the gang. The two cars were driven to Eastcastle Street with four men in each vehicle. They pulled up in a mews on one side of the street and waited.

Then another member of the gang went to Paddington Station and watched the post-office van with the disconnected alarm leave the station soon after 3.30 a.m. He phoned the flat. At a bomb-damaged garage in St Augustus Street, Camden Town, another gangster parked up a van filled with empty apple boxes covered in tarpaulins. There was a large square gap in the centre of the apple boxes.

At 4.17 a.m. the driver of the mail van slammed on his brakes after a black Riley swerved in front of him. A green Vanguard then pulled up behind the van just as a man jumped out of the Riley and leaped towards the van driver's door, yanking it open. Two more men followed and hauled all three guards out of the van, attacking them with fists and coshes.

The guards were thrown to the ground. The three robbers climbed into the van and slammed it into gear while another villain got back in the Riley. The rest of the team jumped into the Vanguard and headed off with the other vehicles into Covent Garden, where they took a left into Floral Street. Another car was waiting around the corner in Rose Street. They got in and drove off behind the post-office van at high speed.

At 4.32 a.m., the van pulled up outside the yard compound in Augustus Street. One man jumped over the gates and unlocked them. The other robber followed the van into the yard while a lookout waited in the street. The mailbags were ripped open. Within half an hour they'd counted £287,000 in cash.

Then a brown van was driven out of the compound into Camden Town Road and south through the back of the City, down to Spitalfields Market. Just after midday that morning, the van turned into a country lane and the £287,000 – worth approximately £20 million today – was shared between about fifteen of the top criminals in the London underworld, including Billy Hill.

Later that same day, Jack Spot went to see Billy Hill, who'd taken a suite in the Dorchester Hotel to celebrate the job. Spot recalled: 'There he was dressed like fuckin' Noel Coward, ironing bank notes with his moll, Gypsy, standing alongside him. Across the room was a clothes line with more notes drying out attached with clothes pegs.'

Spot pointed out that it was *their* organisation that helped finance the robbery. Hill responded by handing Spot £13,000 out of the proceeds. Spot didn't even bother saying thanks and left the room moments later. Hill later described that decision as, 'The worst thing I ever did'; Spot should have recognised it as a mark of Hill's under-world ascendancy, but instead he considered it the petulant behaviour of an upstart. He accepted the money believing that Hill was simply rubbing in the fact that he'd pulled off a brilliant crime.

ƒ   ƒ   ƒ

Clubs, dives, spielers, pubs, hotels and private homes were all kept under constant surveillance by detectives investigating the 'Big Job', as it quickly became known. Naturally, Billy Hill and Jack Spot were hauled in by the police for questioning, but they both had good alibis. A £10,000 reward was offered by insurers who later increased it to £14,500 – it was chickenfeed compared with what Hill's team had scooped.

Billy Hill later bragged about the robbery. He said: 'If you went through the most confidential files at Scotland Yard to find out who planned the greatest robbery in British criminal history, you would come to the conclusion that only Billy Hill could have done it. That's what the Yard thinks. It's what the underworld thinks. It's what the insurance people think and the banks and the post-office chiefs.'

But then Hill knew he'd never be fingered for the Big Job. Not even his so-called boss, Jack Spot, would squeal on him to the cozzers. It just wasn't the way it was in those days. Two villains were eventually charged with receiving in connection with the blagging, but Hill nobbled the jury and they were both found not guilty. No one was ever successfully prosecuted for the Eastcastle post-office robbery.

ƒ   ƒ   ƒ

In Soho, many coppers and villains wondered why Spot and Hill carefully avoided involvement in the lucrative vice trade. Scotland Yard detective Bert Wickstead believed they deliberately steered clear of it. 'They just weren't qualified to run that kind of business,'

Wickstead said later. 'Vice is a very specialised form of crime. You need men who can acquire property in the right places and at the right prices. They have to recruit and organise the girls. You need rent collectors and a small army of frighteners to make sure that the girls and the collectors stay honest.'

From the mid-1940s, the notorious Messina brothers ruled the West End vice trade. The two eldest brothers, Salvatore and Alfredo, were born in Valetta, Malta. Then their father, Guiseppe, moved to Alexandria in Egypt and set up a chain of brothels. The remaining boys, Carmelo, Attilio and Eugenio, were all born in Alexandria but, when Guiseppe was expelled from Egypt, he moved the entire family to London, having attained British nationality due to his Maltese citizenship, as Malta was part of the Empire.

Eugenio Messina founded the family's London vice empire by recruiting vice girls from the continent and, as the operation grew, he was joined by his other brothers. By 1946, the family's weekly earnings from prostitution were at least £1000. When four other Maltese ponces tried to muscle into the business by demanding protection money from the Messina's girls, they were cut and maimed by Eugenio and his boys. When Eugenio was arrested for his part in the attack, he even offered £25,000 to anyone who could smuggle him out of London before he was due to be sentenced. The Messina court case publicly exposed the family for the first time.

Then two new premier vice merchants emerged in Soho: Bernie Silver and Frank Mifsud. They'd earlier operated prostitutes, brothels and even gaming clubs in the East End, particularly in the Brick Lane area of Stepney. Silver and Mifsud gained a toehold in Soho through a strip club they ran in Brewer Street. Four prostitutes operated above the premises and, when the notorious Messinas departed in the early fifties, Silver and Mifsud bought up Soho properties through nominees.

Mifsud, a former traffic policeman from Malta who weighed eighteen stone, was known as 'Big Frank'. He was suspected of arranging numerous beatings for rival pimps and prostitutes. 'When you heard Big Frank wanted to see you, it struck terror into the hearts of even the hardest men,' explained Detective Wickstead.

By this time, Soho's favoured tools of the trade were razors, knives, broken bottles, revolvers, hammers, hatchets, coshes and knuckledusters. Charing Cross Hospital employed a special staff of medical stitchers to deal with the gaping wounds made by these weapons. Victims seldom complained but harboured an urge to 'get even' with their attackers. Bert Wickstead recalled: 'One well known tearaway who was "chivvied" had a beautiful "curvature" of the face that stretched from one ear right round his chin to the other ear. He had to have ninety-nine stitches inserted to draw this gaping wound together.'

Scotland Yard supremo Detective Superintendent Ted Greeno had Jack Spot and Billy Hill under close surveillance throughout this period. Greeno was well respected by villains, many of whom he'd known for years. Spot and Hill were in his top three of criminal 'targets'. Greeno had been catching criminals for thirty-eight years and backing horses for thirty-nine. He said: 'If I'd not backed so many winners I couldn't have caught so many criminals, because at both sports you need information, which costs money. A man rarely turns informant just for the money, but he certainly does not remain one without it. And usually it was my own money.'

Greeno had a photographic memory that card-indexed 10,000 criminals in his mind, or so he claimed. That included every villain in the East End. As a young bobby he'd spent hours in an Aldgate teashop overlooking a nearby tram terminus, studying faces in the crowd. One of Greeno's earliest claims to fame was the arrest of two gangs of dippers who'd worked the West End in eight- and ten-handed day shifts for months. They were run by Jack Spot's old school mate Little Hymie. Greeno was highly critical of what he called 'poshing up'. 'It's taken a lot of fun out of the job. The way to catch criminals is to know them, and the best way to get to know them is to introduce them to a police station on a charge.'

Greeno personally handled twelve murder investigations and solved them all including the apprehension of cold-blooded child killers Gordon Cummins and Arthur Heys. Greeno said: 'That hundred per cent record is even better than my record with Derby winners.' Greeno was commended eighty-eight times by judges, magistrates and the commissioners at Scotland Yard; and in 1949 he was awarded the MBE.

Greeno's philosophy was simple: 'When police officers say, "We know who did this, but we just cannot pin it on him," my answer is "Nuts". Either they know or they don't, and if they do then their job is to prove it. I was never rough for the sake of it, but when I saw trouble coming, I forestalled it. I have given some villains awful hidings. I think if more policemen showed more villains that it is not only the lawbreaker who has strong arms, we would be nearer the end of this age of violent nonsense.'

Part of Greeno's campaign against Jack Spot involved pulling him in for relatively minor offences, 'just to let him know' the police were closely monitoring him. On 23 September 1953, Spot was arrested in a West London telephone kiosk with a knuckle-duster in his pocket. He was fined £20 for possession of an offensive weapon. Spot admitted to magistrates he'd bought the knuckle-duster a fortnight earlier. The arresting officer later told reporters: 'To be pulled in, searched and then booked like some petty thief was an intolerable blow to Spot's high opinion of himself.'

When Billy Hill heard about the Spot arrest he tried to turn it to his own advantage. Hill suggested to other villains that Spot was getting 'too close' to certain senior Scotland Yard officers. Hill claimed he'd heard Spot's name thrown into a conversation in a West End club by another Yard legend, Detective Jack Fabian. Later that night Fabian was threatened by three roughs in the same nightclub and he again mentioned Jack Spot's name. Others on the premises raised their eyebrows and took note.

*   *   *

In Soho, Jack Spot still commanded a lot of respect. He continued looking after the families of mob members banged up on behalf of his firm; and when they came out of prison they usually went straight back into his team as a reward for his loyalty. Spot also set them up with cash and clothes as well as a job. Spot pioneered the need for an inner circle of criminal associates, drawing a weekly wage from his organisation. Generous 'salaries' were supplemented by 'nips' from the clubs, pubs, spielers and car dealers that, willingly, or unwillingly, enjoyed the firm's 'protection'. A nip could be free drinks or gratuitous gifts of a wide range of merchandise. When Spot's boys grew too old for active work on the streets, they were found suitably quiet, stationary jobs: some were installed in their own pub, others managed spielers.

And Jack Spot continued to be one of the biggest spenders in town. Waiters stared goggle-eyed as he left enormous tips at clubs and restaurants. In nightclubs he'd order drinks all round and pay bills with crisp, new £5 notes. He delighted patrons by lighting cigars with £5 notes. He splashed out £100 a time for the finest made-to-measure suits as well as silk shirts specially monogrammed at £5 a piece. His tailor-made shoes cost £30 a pair, and even his ties were handmade and cost £3 each – the average wage at that time was around £8 per week. Spot thought nothing of blowing £20 on a dress for Rita or twice that amount for a piece of fancy jewellery. But with such high outgoings, Spot needed to plan new blaggings and increase the protection money at clubs and spielers: takings from racecourses were still dipping alarmingly.

That's when Billy Hill began fuelling rumours that he was now the underworld's *numero uno*. He continued openly boasting about being the mastermind behind the Big Job. And he didn't scotch the stories that Spot had 'gone soft' since his marriage to feisty Rita. Rumblings of tension between Spot and Hill soon caught the ear of new Flying Squad supremo, Chief Superintendent Robert Lee. His officers were in the habit of swooping anywhere in the Metropolitan Police district if Lee requested 'a chat' with a villain back at the Yard. Lee was credited with turning the Flying Squad into the most efficient fighting force of policemen in the world. But probing blaggings like the Eastcastle post-office van robbery had proved a difficult task. Sending out Wolseleys, Bentleys, Morrises, Rileys, Railtons and secret squad cars to hundreds of locations across the capital brought no results. So, with Ted Greeno's backing, Lee decided to turn up the pressure.

Lee knew Spot and Hill had problems and that, if he was patient, they'd start creating trouble for themselves which might give him just the opening he needed. Jack Spot's throne was by no means secure. And there were other younger, far more deadly rivals than Billy Hill, on the horizon.

§   §   §

Just after the Kray twins turned twenty, in the autumn of 1953, they met Jack Spot and members of his firm in the Vienna Rooms, just off the Edgware Road. It was a second-floor restaurant that catered for businessmen, criminals and prostitutes and also happened to be directly opposite Edgware Road police station. Flamboyant Ronnie Kray used a small entourage of good-looking young men to form a spy network in Soho so he knew who all the main men were. The twins were introduced to Spot by Moisha Blueball, who shared their keen interest in wrestling. By this time, Moisha was a smart dresser, but what had impressed the Kray twins were his rarely shown skills as a crooked card player.

That evening, Spot and Moisha Blueball were sitting at a table at the Vienna Rooms alongside the twins when they were introduced to a well-spoken man called Jeff Allen. Moisha took Allen for a couple of grand in a bent card game later that night. Allen told Moisha and the Krays to meet him in a local pub an hour later when he'd pay up his debt.

Allen failed to show up, so Moisha got him on the phone. Allen told him: 'I knew all along I was being conned, and if you come near my home, you'll find me waiting with a shotgun.' Moisha was lost for words and made no attempt at collection. But the twins never forgot Jeff Allen and he later became one of their closest friends.

Other regulars at the Vienna Rooms at that time included Spitzel Goodman, a dapper little character with thick, black wavy hair who'd at one time been manager of Primo Carnera, the Italian heavyweight champion of the world. Then there was a West Indian called Bar who had most of his right ear missing. He'd served seven years for shooting and wounding a club owner who owed him money. No one gave Bar any aggro. He even owned a famous dog called Bar's Choice which won the Greyhound Derby that year.

But it was Spot's old pal Jack Pokla, a respected money fiddler, whom the Kray twins were particularly keen to meet. Pokla bought stolen property from just about anyone and went on to teach the twins how a good fence operated. Another member of Spot's gang who impressed the Krays was Teddy Machin, born in Upton Park in the East End close to the West Ham football ground. He had jet-black hair and the looks of a film star. He'd had a run-in with another Spot gang member, Jacky Reynolds, at the Queen's pub in Upton Park and had smashed a broken glass into Reynolds' face, disfiguring him. Reynolds claimed that dozens of villains called him up to offer to help get revenge on Machin. But Reynolds refused, insisting he was still friends with Machin and that it had just been a drunken brawl which went one step too far. The Krays were impressed with such loyalty.

But it was Jack Spot and Billy Hill who made the biggest impression on the twins. 'They were the centre of attraction wherever they went. They controlled London as bosses of the underworld,' Reg later explained. 'Spot dressed like a screen gangster. Ron remembered him as one of the smartest men we ever met, with lovely overcoats, shirts and ties.'

However Spot didn't realise the Krays had already secretly been in contact with Billy Hill. As Reg admiringly recalled: 'He [Hill] had a good brain, and this appealed to me. I learned a lot by observing the way he put his thoughts into action.'

Hill was flattered by the twins and even put them to a bizarre test. One day Ron and Reg, their brother Charlie and friend Willy

Malone, were at the Kray family home – Fort Vallance – when the phone rang. Ron picked up the receiver and it was Billy Hill on the line. He said: 'Will you come over to my flat quick as poss?'

'OK, Billy,' responded Ron. He then told the others: 'I think he's got some kind of trouble. Let's get over there.'

The twins picked up a shooter each and departed for Hill's flat in Bayswater with Charlie driving. As he walked in, Ron said to Hill: 'What's the trouble? We've bought some shooters.'

Hill laughed, left them in the lounge and went into his bedroom. When he returned, he tossed £500 in brand-new notes on to the table and told the Krays: 'Take that few quid for your trouble and cut it up between you. I was only testing. I wanted to find out if you would get here fast or if you would blank the emergency.'

It was a turning point in the Krays' relationship with Hill. They wanted him at the top while they learned the tricks of the trade. Shortly afterwards, the Kray twins beat up a doorman at one of the many clubs under the protection of Billy Hill. Instead of being furious, Hill commended the twins, chucked a few more bob at them and announced that he owed them because now the owner of the club would never dare to stop paying his protection money.

Reg Kray later recalled: 'To me, Bill was the ultimate professional criminal. I like to think that in some ways I have come close to emulating him, but in many other ways he stands alone. There will never be another Billy Hill.'

And back at their favourite haunt, the Vienna Rooms, the Krays continued making a mark for themselves. Regulars at the club included dozens of prostitutes mingling with customers, led by a big blonde called Kate, whose Maltese pimp so upset the Krays one night they robbed his flat 'because we don't like pimps'. The Kray twins were already proving to be a deadly duo.

10

TAKING LIBERTIES

The evening light was fading as Jack Spot strolled through Soho towards the Golden Ring. The neon signs weren't yet burning brilliantly across the narrow streets, so the twilight mist laid a melancholy black-and-white patina over the area. In the background, the ringing of a black Wolsey police car shrilled along Shaftesbury Avenue. At Piccadilly Circus and Leicester Square, theatre crowds were bustling and noisy. Soho looked drab, forlorn and rather sinister, like a hag who'd removed her day's make-up while there was still light to reveal the ravages of time.

Spot turned in under a sign, went down some steps and entered a bar. His mate Sammy was nowhere in sight. Spot was served by a white-coated queen with ginger hair who then minced off to have a chat with his boyfriend in the corner. Spot sipped his scotch and water before glancing around the virtually empty bar.

Spot put his glass down, still half full, and headed for a door marked 'Here They Are'. He emerged into a damp, small yard with two lavatory doors. He turned right, pushed open a third door and entered an office where Sammy was waiting. A bottle of scotch, a jug of water and one glass stood on the table. The two men nodded. Spot sat down. Sammy said: 'Help yourself, Guv.'

Sammy Passport – mastermind of forgery – gave his nationality as Maltese. In fact he was a Sicilian, from Taormina, but like many before him he knew he was better off being Maltese because of the island's British sovereignty. Sammy was part pimp, part mobster and part thief. He also handled stolen goods and prided himself on his ability to procure a woman to perform any sexual act, however sick and twisted. Spot helped himself to another scotch. Sammy waited for him to speak, but Spot was too wise to commit anything. He was after just one thing.

'There's your dosh,' Sammy said as he pushed an envelope across the desk. Spot drained his glass, ripped open the envelope and stood up. Then he looked down at the still-seated Sammy.

'It's not enough,' he said flatly. 'Tell your mate that from now on protection charges have doubled. I know what he's up to and there's certain penalties he'll have to pay. You also tell him that I'll have him cut if he doesn't cough up pronto.'

But Sammy had some news for Spot that day: 'I been told you're not the man to pay no more.'

'What?' Spot snapped.

'There's another fella who provides much better guarantees,' replied Sammy, before coolly disappearing back towards the bar without uttering another word. Spot clicked his knuckles and marched out of the premises the same way he'd come in. At the end of the street he slipped into a phone box and barked at Snakes Clarke to bring the car over to pick him up. Things were not going so well in Soho and now it looked for certain that Billy Hill was muscling in on his territory.

ƒ   ƒ   ƒ

Apart from clubs and spielers, boxing was the biggest pull for villains. The fight game traditionally attracted a mixed crowd, including movie stars, lords and ladies, MPs, bookmakers, pickpockets, confidence tricksters, former champs, jockeys, football stars, card sharpers, nightclub kings and cheque bouncers.

In the Vienna Rooms, Jack Spot loved chatting to boxers and then persuading them to throw fights. He later claimed he'd once arranged for a world-champion boxer to take a dive in the first round of a title fight. Spot got another fighter to go in the first round with British Heavyweight Champion Jack Gardner. Gardner didn't have a clue his opponent was going to take a tumble.

Billy Hill and Jack Spot turned up in separate limos at the Haringey Arena to see British Heavyweight Champion Don Cockell fight Toni Renato, the Italian champion. They didn't cross paths until the bar during the interval. Spot hadn't confronted Hill about his suspicions yet because he wanted to have all the evidence at his fingertips.

Intrepid *Sunday People* crime reporter Duncan Webb was also at the fight. Webb boasted that both Spot and Hill 'respected' him, explaining: 'We did not get in each other's way. I wanted nothing from them, and they asked no favours from me.' Of course, nothing could have been further from the truth. Webb planned to ask Spot and Hill if they'd been involved in a recent series of lucrative post-office robberies up and down the country. Days earlier, £10,500 had been stolen in cash from a Brighton to London train. Webb intended approaching the two kings of Soho after the fight but, at the end, Spot and Hill bolted for the exit, hats in hand.

Webb just managed to catch up with Hill. 'Well,' he asked, 'What's all the hurry. Something on?'

'See you tomorrow,' said Hill. 'Be at the end of a phone. I might have something to tell you.'

Webb thought nothing more of the encounter and headed out of Haringey to visit several underworld contacts in the West End. He didn't get home until the early hours of the following morning. It was a typical day for the workaholic journalist. He'd started as a cub reporter on the *South London Press* in the thirties, where he had shown a great aptitude for crime stories. After war broke out, Webb served in West Africa before being injured in 1944. He then worked at the *Daily Express* before moving to the *London Evening Standard*, where his obsession with crime hadn't proved popular. He recalled: 'My superiors claimed it wasn't the business of a newspaper to go prying into the affairs of corpses with no arms; Lady so-and-so, the wife of the proprietor, would not like it, I was told. They pooh-poohed the idea: "We are a respectable news-paper," they said, "After all, murders are so vulgar".'

Webb then joined the *Sunday People*, edited by Sam Campbell a keen follower of daring, headline-hitting investigations. By this time Webb was so obsessed with crime that he even assembled dossiers on crimes he hadn't covered and offered them to the police. Webb's involvement with crime even encroached on his love life. He romanced nightclub hostess and murderer's wife Cynthia Hume after convincing her that her husband Donald was guilty of a killing he had always denied. Webb also publicly exposed the Messinas as the main pimps of London in a hard-hitting investigation for the *Sunday People*. Before it appeared, the Messinas sent some of their pals round to Webb's home for 'a chat', but the hack refused to be intimidated. Webb even claimed the Messinas offered him £10,000 to stop writing about them.

Webb's Messina exposé had relied on ingenuity and dogged persistence, and it attracted the interest of Billy Hill, who was happy to see Webb expose the Maltese family because he, 'didn't like ponces or foreigners'. A few weeks later, on the day another of Webb's articles on the Messinas was published, Webb was enjoying a quiet pint at his local with Billy Hill. Then the Messina boys appeared, took one look at Hill's team, turned round and left the pub. Webb soon began writing frequent and highly sympathetic articles about Billy Hill.

Webb's attitude towards law and order was profoundly ambivalent. On the one hand, he nurtured relationships with numerous senior Scotland Yard officers, yet he also helped promote the almost mythical status of the heavy mob and leaders like Billy Hill. Webb described Hill as, 'a crook, a villain, a thief, a thug', but he then added that Hill was, 'a genuine and a kind and tolerant man'. Webb didn't care if Hill manipulated him, just so long as he got a headline-hitting story to blast across the *Sunday People*'s front page. And Webb had heard the whispers about Jack Spot starting to lose control of his empire.

Small incidents had begun happening to Spot: a planned robbery was delayed at the last minute because one of the team never turned up; numerous similar crimes were then cancelled or postponed; his income began to plummet. Some of Spot's more 'unreliable' men now accepted their punishments and then walked straight out on him for a job with another organisation. He couldn't be sure who was running it, but all roads seemed to lead to Billy Hill. Spot began monitoring the newspapers more closely and noticed that other gangs were still successfully committing many robberies. Then the *Sunday People* came out with a series of articles by Billy Hill describing himself as 'the boss of the underworld'. Now Spot knew for sure Hill was after his crown.

Jack Spot later admitted he should have closed up shop and got out the moment he saw the first *Sunday People* article. But he wasn't in a rational mood. Rita pleaded with him to quit while he was ahead. She was under pressure from her mother back in Dublin, who was hurt at her exclusion from Rita's wedding and was now reeling from the news that Rita had given birth to a child, conceived out of wedlock, to a Jewish gangster. Spot continued to assure his young family that he was different from the rest because he was determined not to die in a shootout; he also had no intention of falling out with the authorities. Since the birth of his child, Spot had concluded he needed something more out of life, and his new priority was to be with the young family he cherished and adored.

Rita sensed her husband was walking into a trap. But Spot was spitting fire. No one could talk any sense into him. He'd fallen for the first piece of bait floated in front of him. To prove he was still king of the underworld, Spot tried yet again to organise a job. This time he attempted to assemble a safe-breaking team for a major bank heist. But, once more, the villains pulled out at the last moment before completely walking out on him. At Spot's Soho office, fights were now regularly breaking out between his henchmen. Within hours of each punch-up, they'd quit too.

On the racetracks, Spot suspected one of his most trusted henchmen of betraying him to Billy Hill. Each week, the man's returns from bookies were dropping and he was making all sorts of excuses about problems collecting protection money on behalf of Spot.

Dozens of bookies had fallen behind with their 'dues' to his organisation. When Spot suggested to his sidekick that he was 'losing it'
the man snapped back: 'You can't treat people like dogs. Not these
days you can't. You can't threaten. You have to compromise.'

Spot then began hearing the gossip doing the rounds of Soho.
Other villains were laughing behind his back and saying he'd been
stitched up like a kipper by Billy Hill. Spot decided he had to hit
'em hard, just like he'd sorted out Mosley's Blackshirts all those
years earlier. One afternoon, he ordered Moisha Blueball to join
him in the back of his newly acquired Jaguar and they travelled
across town, driven by henchman Snakes. Spot wanted to mount
a counterattack that would show everyone what he was capable
of. Moisha tried to warn Spot that, if he took on Hill, it would
end in a bloodbath. With henchmen Sam and Mugsy behind them
in a Ford, the two vehicles headed north-west, towards the London
suburb of Hendon.

Arriving at a neat, semi-detached house, Moisha recognised it
as the home of a bookie who had refused to pay Spot protection
money. Sam and Mugsy went to the front door, which was
answered by a woman. They barged past her and, moments later,
Moisha and Spot – still in the back of the Jag – heard a high-pitched
scream. Spot turned to Moisha and then declared: 'There's only
one way to make a man toe the line. Let him feel the keen edge
of a razor.' As Spot's boys emerged from the house, the woman
came out screaming after them: 'They've killed him! Murderers!'

Spot grinned and tapped driver Snakes on the shoulder and
they departed. Moisha, hunched in the seat next to him, was
stunned. 'You'll find everythin' will be different now, Moisha, me
old mate,' Spot said, almost light-heartedly: 'All that bastard
needed was a little incentive to pay up.' That 'incentive' turned
out to be a couple of stripes across his backside with a chiv. That
bookie would remember his encounter with Jack Spot every time
he tried to sit down. Back in Soho, Billy Hill shrugged his shoulders
when he heard the news because he knew what Spot was up to
and he wasn't bothered.

Meanwhile, Moisha Blueball kept reminding Spot that he ought to 'put something by for a rainy day'. He told Spot: 'All the time it's spend, spend, spend. You never think of tomorrow.' Spot was irritated by Moisha. He started to get a niggling feeling about him again. Was he still up to the job? Maybe Moisha was preparing to break away and stab him in the back just like all the others? By this time, Moisha ran all Spot's accounts, which showed exactly who owed what on the racetracks. Spot was powerless without those books. And all Moisha could do was keep reminding Spot to save some money to ensure a long and peaceful retirement.

Spot's paranoia was growing by the hour. He confronted one of his most trusted fences, an old fellow called Chester, when he refused to handle anything from Spot's mob. Spot barged into Chester's West End office with Sonny the Yank, grabbed the old man by the arm and scraped his own diamond ring along the top of his £1500 antique mahogany desk. Spot and Sonny the Yank then marched out of the premises. In the car back to Spot's office Sonny told Spot: 'You worry me, Spotty. You go out of your way to rub people up the wrong way.'

Sonny warned Spot he was asking for trouble. Next day Sonny went back to Chester's office to collect some money and was confronted by two Flying Squad detectives. Spot's once loyal fence had complained to the police. Sonny went back to Spot that day and pointed out to him: 'Things are different now. Face up to it: we're not the only mob. And the other one's rocketing up while we're coming down.'

Spot suspected Sonny's words were part of yet another conspiracy against him. He began watching Sonny and his other main henchmen even more closely. Not long afterwards, he discovered that one of them had been swindling him out of money on a weekly basis. Spot confronted the man in his office.

'I didn't want to hear more of his lies. I went in at him. I drove my left hard into his belly to double him up and get him hugging himself,' Spot recalled. Doubled up in pain, the man held his hands over his face. Spot tried to pull his left hand away and struck out once again. Then he added a flurry of punches. Spot then marked him with a blade. The man fell to his knees, breathing hard. His hands were clasped to his cheeks and blood spilt across the back of his hands. Spot stood triumphantly over his henchman and yelled at him: 'You betrayed me, Judas.' Even his speech now had a tinge of the deranged about it. Then Spot stormed out of his office and headed into Soho.

Although Spot believed he'd been right to cut the man, he didn't like doing it to a once-trusted associate. He walked and walked for hours around his beloved West End. He didn't know what to do next, but he knew that it had to be something really big; something that would make the entire underworld sit up and take notice, especially Billy Hill. Spot returned to his club after darkness fell and walked into his office to begin clearing up the mess caused by the earlier fight.

Then something on the floor caught his eye. It was a post-office savings book. Spot stared at it for quite a while before opening it and seeing that it was made out in his name. He flicked through it and noticed that entries had been made for twenty-seven weeks. Every week the same amount had been deposited. It was a measure of the true depth of Moisha's loyalty. Spot shut his eyes and once again began hearing Moisha's pleading: 'You've got to put something by, Spotty. We won't always have good times.' Spot stood there in the silence of his office, holding the savings book in his hand and looked at the bloodstains on the cover. Then he felt the salt in his mouth. His cheeks were damp and he'd begun sobbing.

*   *   *

In many ways, Jack Spot was courageous. But that didn't mean he lacked fear. On the contrary, his days and nights were now haunted by what – or who – lay in wait around the corner, as he was always convinced some gang or other was out to 'do him up'. He struggled to appreciate that ruthlessness was not necessarily the path to happiness. No doubt sociologists and forensic psychiatrists would say his life was one scarred by the poverty of his childhood, attitudes towards his Jewish blood, his hatred of Fascism and the hard lessons he learned on the streets of London's East End. He undoubtedly suffered from an inferiority complex that compelled him to act in a superior fashion, and it may have been the motivating force behind his criminal activities.

But there was more to Spot than everyday criminality; he certainly didn't lack intelligence and risked many foolish things. Before Spot appeared on the scene, most villains worked haphazardly and spent much of their time behind bars. Then Spot and contemporaries like Billy Hill turned crime into an industry that survives to this day. Every aspect of Spot's criminal enterprises was considered, anticipated and calculated. Just like America's legendary Dillinger and Capone, Spot organised criminals and lawbreaking with such efficiency that crime became almost completely profitable and negligibly risky. He recognised opportunities and took advantage of any openings with great skill.

But now, Spot needed to concede that a new generation was on the horizon, which planned crimes with far more ruthlessness and a lot more violence than Spot could ever muster. His inordinate pride, a touch of paranoia and his unwillingness to concede he might now only be second best were threatening the entire fabric of his life. He didn't want to end up as a burned-out gangster with nothing more to offer anyone, but Jack Spot needed to realise that he'd end up the dead duck of the London underworld if he wasn't careful.

11

A WORD IN YOUR EAR

In the summer of 1954, Billy Hill bought himself a villa in Tangier, Morocco, and acquired a luxury yacht with which he intended to run the occasional load of contraband – cigarettes, not drugs – over to Gibraltar and Spain. Jack Spot presumed Hill was running away, but Hill had no intention of moving out of Soho and saw Tangier as nothing more than a sunshine retreat combined with a lucrative sideline.

Within weeks of Hill's first trip to Morocco, his luxury yacht, the *Flamingo*, sank in 'mysterious' circumstances in the Med as it crossed to Spain from the North African coast with its first load of illicit goods. Hill hadn't been on board at the time, but was seething because he suspected Spot had organised the sinking to teach him a lesson. Back in London, Hill told his boys he wanted to further build his team so as to start taking sole control of the West End.

Spot was infuriated by Hill's reappearance and failed to appreciate Hill's new manoeuvres. Hill put feelers out around various London gangs and a number of meetings were arranged in West End pubs. Elephant Gang member Brian McDonald recalled: 'We all waited our turn. Mine came in late 1954. Hill bought the drinks in the Bath House in Soho's Dean Street, where he'd laid on a tasty buffet.'

McDonald's gang – from south of the river – had earlier formed a tentative alliance with Spot. The Elephant Gang first established its reputation through a series of battles with other gangs in the 1920s and, by the 1950s, had such a fearsome reputation that many gangs in other districts paid to hire the services of the Elephant Gang. Most of the members weren't actually from Elephant and Castle, but from Walworth Road, Old Kent Road, Kennington, Lambeth, Waterloo, Blackfriars, Peckham, Camberwell and the Borough.

One of the few hard men who was totally unimpressed by Hill's grandiose plans was Spot's old sidekick, Johnny Carter. He didn't believe the gangs could work together. They'd have to bury too many hatchets. When Carter attended a meeting with Hill and heard that certain tearaways had joined Hill's team, he was so furious he tried to start a fight with a couple of rival mobsters. Then he turned on *Sunday People* crime reporter Duncan Webb, who'd been personally invited by Hill. McDonald recalled: 'Carter gave Webb a nasty tongue-lashing and we all watched as the others tried to steer him away from Webb's table.'

Carter told other villains he didn't want the 'ponces' (his word for safe crackers, pickpockets and con men) that Hill associated with calling the shots. He could see Hill in the background raking in the money while the soldiers did all the work and then ended up in the nick. Carter still thought Spot had the right idea: 'chiv any bastard that didn't play ball.' The meeting ended with Carter storming out.

A few days later, Billy Hill tried to join forces with the Italian mob, still based in Clerkenwell, but not the force they had been before the war. But, when word got out, Johnny Carter cut Billy Blyth, Hill's emissary to the Italians, and the deal went up in smoke.

Then the increasingly short-tempered Jack Spot gave one of Hill's new, young tearaways a good kicking when he had the temerity to warn Spot not to show his face at one West End club. The man worked alongside fearsome freelance gangster 'Italian Albert' Dimes, whom Billy Hill had recruited as one of his top henchmen. Hill had arrogantly presumed Spot wouldn't work out the connection. But Spot, according to one witness, 'went fuckin' bananas' when he found out.

Within days, Spot and Johnny Carter started mouthing off around Soho that top of their brand-new hit list was Billy Hill. Hill heard the rumours and then publicly recruited Scotch Jack Buggy, a nasty American-born chiv merchant based in Kentish Town, to go after Jack Spot. The cycle of violence and threats was picking up speed.

Elephant Gang member Brian McDonald stumbled on Buggy lurking outside the Galahad Club in Soho. He'd heard rumours about Spot being targeted by Hill. 'I walked right past him. Buggy pulled a revolver from his overcoat pocket and pointed it at my face. I remember the metallic click as it failed to go off. He fled, but he couldn't outpace me. I brought him down by grabbing the belt at the back of his overcoat.'

McDonald alerted Spot and two henchmen to the scene and one of them ran a knife down Buggy's face and thighs, the only parts not covered by his heavy overcoat. McDonald recalled: 'The road was busy, so we left him there. In time he limped back to Kentish Town.' Buggy returned some years later, still making a nuisance of himself. His body was later found bobbing around in the Channel, off Seaford in Sussex, after he was shot – some say on the orders of Albert Dimes.

ƀ   ƀ   ƀ

Billy Hill's reputation as top dog was further enhanced when he masterminded a robbery at the Holborn offices of the KLM airline on 21 September 1954. The robbers got away with two boxes containing £45,500 in gold bullion when a company lorry was hijacked during rush hour. Hill was the prime suspect but, at the time of the robbery, he was in the offices of Duncan Webb at the *Sunday People*, telling his favourite reporter yet another version of his life story as boss of the underworld, to be published the following Sunday.

Hill even tried to imply in the article he was close to abdicating Soho: 'I'm not afraid any more. I know now that the law always wins in the end. So I'll talk. I suppose the least I can do before quitting is to tell those young mobsters who want to be like me a few home truths.'

But it was all a game to Billy Hill. A couple of weeks later, Hill encouraged Webb to publish details of the KLM raid. He wanted the world to know all about this supposedly 'brilliant' criminal enterprise.

On the racetracks, Spot's power and influence took another body blow when a group of Italian bookies led by hard man Albert Dimes took even more of Spot's pitches. Spot knew Dimes was connected to Hill. But he still chose not to confront Hill with the facts. A furious Spot then demanded a meeting with reporter Duncan Webb. It was time to sort out a few important issues.

§   §   §

In early November 1954, Spot met Duncan Webb in a Soho caff and informed Webb he wanted him to write 'a story about the underworld' in retaliation to Hill's articles. Webb tactlessly told him he wasn't interested and suggested that Spot go and see the *Sunday Chronicle*. His dismissive attitude infuriated Spot who then told Webb: 'If you do anything to interfere with this I will break your jaw.' Spot then complained bitterly to Webb about a Fleet Street reporter called Hannen Swaffer whom he claimed had made up a story about him in the *World Press News*. Webb later recalled that Spot was, 'incoherent and terribly excited' at the meeting.

A few days later, Webb was interviewing a contact in the Surrey town of Kingston upon Thames when he got a message to call a 'Mr Nadel'. Nadel said he was calling on behalf of 'Billy'. The message said: 'Phone Holborn 9107.' When Webb did so, a voice said: 'Billy's in trouble.' A meeting was arranged outside a cinema in Tottenham Court Road. The voice was in fact that of Jack Spot, who'd just used the public telephone in the bar of a pub called the King's Arms, in Soho.

Spot walked straight up to Webb when he reached the cinema at 10.30 p.m. and said: 'Come on, it's bad.' As he walked down the street with Spot, one henchman moved alongside them and another behind. When Webb asked Spot what it was all about, Spot ignored him.

As they got towards Bainbridge Street, Spot turned and punched Webb between the eyes, saying: 'Take that, you fucker; I'm runnin' this show.' Spot then grabbed Webb by the lapels of his coat and began shouting: 'I'll give you Billy Hill. I'll give you fuckin' Billy Hill.'

Webb warded off another blow to the lower part of his body. He 'travelled it' in boxing parlance. Webb then saw what he thought was a knuckleduster glinting in the neon light. As Webb tried to get away, Spot struck him in the stomach before missing with another blow.

The following morning Duncan Webb went to Charing Cross Hospital where an X-ray revealed a fractured arm that would be in plaster for months. Webb then reported the incident to the police. When officers called at Spot's flat at Hyde Park Mansions later that day, he told them: 'What's it about – that rat Duncan Webb? He's a dirty rat to the police and the public after what he has put in those articles.'

Spot was arrested and taken to West End Central police station. He was remanded in custody for a week following an initial court appearance the following morning. Three days later an appeal to a High Court Judge in Chambers granted him bail on his own recognisance of £500 with two sureties each for a similar amount.

ß   ß   ß

In January, 1955, Spot's domestic commitments doubled when Rita gave birth to their second daughter, Marion. Rita demanded that her husband spend more time at home with his family. As one associate later pointed out: 'What were the boys to think when the phone rang for Jack and he'd tell us, "Sorry boys, must go home, the baby's crying"?'

Rita's mother died in Dublin just weeks after the birth of Marion. Rita immediately took in her twelve-year-old brother to live with them in London because her sister Sadie couldn't cope with him back in Ireland. As the flat in Hyde Park Mansions became increasingly overcrowded, so did Spot's chaotic life. Luckily, he'd settled his differences with Moisha by now, so he felt he could leave much of the day-to-day running of his fast-fading empire to his old friend.

Just after Marion's birth, Jack Spot appeared in court and admitted causing Duncan Webb grievous bodily harm. The magistrate told him: 'I dislike intensely this idea of taking the law into your own hands. It must be obvious to anyone that this was a premeditated and unprovoked assault which was engineered with considerable forethought.' Spot was described in court as 'the manager of a drinking club just off Old Compton Street'.

Spot pleaded guilty to the attack and was fined £50 plus 20 guineas costs or three months in prison. A further charge of having a knuckleduster in his possession without lawful excuse was dismissed after Spot pleaded not guilty to the charge. Spot contested an application by Duncan Webb for damages, which included £140 for a shorthand typist to type his articles while he was incapacitated, £42 for taxis and also medical fees. Damages totalled £732 against Spot.

Duncan Webb was so shaken up by what had happened to him at the hands of Jack Spot that, when he wrote a subsequent book about his journalistic adventures, he avoided all mention of the incident or subsequent court case.

Back in Soho, Spot's few remaining henchmen were bickering like kids. Two of his toughest boys, Johnny Carter and Bobby Brindle, had a serious falling-out after Brindle's brother, Jimmy, was beaten up by Carter's brother, Nicky. Johnny Carter gave Bobby

Brindle a stripe down his cheek. 'Give that to yer brother,' said Johnny. Brindle left and joined Billy Hill's gang soon afterwards.

ƒ   ƒ   ƒ

Shortly after the Webb court case, Spot attended the Turpin versus Cerdan fight at Earl's Court and sat at the ringside next to Hollywood star Tyrone Power and his wife, Linda Christian. Just before the big fight, Spot was called over to help a boxing promoter who was being insulted by a bunch of Covent Garden porters on a drunken night out.

Spot made his excuses to his celebrity guests and went over to the group of toughies with sidekick Little Hymie and henchman Teddy Machin. They slapped down the group in front of the crowd. When Spot looked over his shoulder, he noticed Tyrone Power and his wife bolting for the exit. Spot shrugged his shoulders. At least the incident might help spread the word round London that Jack Spot wasn't going to give up his crown that easily.

Shortly afterwards, Spot was involved in another ringside punch-up – this time at Seymour Hall, in the West End. The official fight was between highly rated local boys Billy Thompson and Dave Finn. Spot explained: 'The betting boys were dodging around the ringside, kicking up hell of a row and some of the customers at the back didn't like it.' One man jumped down from the gallery and landed at the ringside just in front of where Spot was sitting. Spot later recalled: 'Just because I happened to be the nearest bloke he took a poke at me and that was a mistake. Two of my pals jumped in and beat him up properly. Then the police arrived and wanted to arrest me while they were carrying the other guy out on a stretcher.'

Spot was cleared by local boxing promoter Victor Berliner who told police the other man was a known trouble maker and had asked for it. Yet again, Spot hoped news of his involvement would get back to Billy Hill. The propaganda war was vitally important to both men. Meanwhile, most people in the outside world presumed the West End was still under the control of Jack Spot and Billy Hill.

In early 1955, Jack Spot met the Kray twins again. Spot just wanted a 'friendly chat' with the twins because he knew they were on the rise. He still had no idea they'd kept in close touch with Billy Hill. Attention from Jack Spot fed the now twenty-one-year-old Krays' vanity. They were particularly amused because they'd already decided Spot was not their favourite villain. Ronnie's head was filled with dreams of gang lordship. He wanted the war between Spot and Hill to worsen so that he and Reggie could surge through, to rescue the underworld. They'd fuelled much of the tension, thanks to words in the right ears. One villain from that era explained: 'Ron and Reg were up to no good. They wanted to destabilise Billy and Spotty. There's no doubt about it.' After Spot left his meeting with the Krays, he told Moisha: 'Those two are real trouble. We'd better keep an eye on them.'

In February 1955, Spot got further proof of the ever-widening gap between himself and Billy Hill when a bank strongroom in London was torn open by a gang of highly professional villains. The basement walls were of twenty-two-inch-thick concrete and the massive steel door of the safe was blown off. £20,300, in easy-to-pass fives, ones and ten-shilling notes, was stolen.

Ted Greeno, now one of the top commanders at Scotland Yard, took personal charge of the robbery investigation. He threw himself back into the groundwork he so adored and headed off to round up the usual suspects. Spot and Hill were both top of the list. Spot was happy for the outside world to believe he was involved in the job. But he was really seething because he knew Hill was the organiser and it was another feather in his cap.

Shortly afterwards, the *Sunday Chronicle* published a series of articles by Spot. They were ghosted by Spot's new Fleet Street pal, reporter Vic Sims. Spot informed *Sunday Chronicle* readers he was still the guv'nor of guv'nors, with a duty to make sure that trouble didn't flare up in Soho. Spot boasted how he'd even turned one of his clubs into an 'innocent little place' with a bar and a danceband, which celebrities like Abbott and Costello and boxer Jersey Joe Walcott frequented. Billy Hill read the articles with amusement. Duncan Webb had already told him they were harmless and they certainly didn't refer to anything Hill didn't already know about.

Then the Kray twins got themselves nicked for demanding money with menaces. As they were charged at City Road police station, Ronnie Kray made a reference to Jack Spot, which sent a shiver up detective's spines because they weren't even aware of a connection between the Krays and Spot, let alone Billy Hill. Ronnie Kray insisted to police that he and his brother had been grassed up by people they'd been 'blacking' – blackmailing or demanding money from. Ronnie was also charged with possessing an offensive weapon, a sheath knife. Many years later, the Krays concluded that Spot or Hill might have been behind their arrest. They believed that one of the two men grassed them up because they wanted to teach the twins a lesson. And their money was on Jack Spot.

ℬ   ℬ   ℬ

In March 1955, Spot turned up at the Puckeridge Hunt, a point-to-point in Bishop's Stortford, held on the same day as the Grand National. He refused to let any bookie except his old enemy Harry White take bets on the Liverpool race. That way he knew he was in for a percentage of anything White took. Spot boasted to all and sundry there about how he'd 'smashed up' a bookie at a racetrack up north. It didn't do much for his reputation when it turned out that the man was sixty-five years old when Spot had 'bravely' kicked him with his pointed shoes into the racecourse dirt. Some were now saying that Jack Spot had already lost the plot.

Billy Hill, as a result, recruited more toughies such as Pasquali Papa and Tommy Falco, who'd been working the main race-courses alongside 'Italian Albert' Dimes, already Hill's number-one minder. Spot told anyone who would listen that Dimes 'couldn't bodyguard a flea'. Many at the races warned Spot that Dimes was making great inroads into his business.

Billy Hill seemed to always be one step ahead. In April 1955, he announced that he and his lover, Gypsy, had booked themselves on the luxury liner the *Southern Cross* bound for Australia. The moment Hill departed, Spot tried to rally his depleted troops to reclaim his territory. But Hill had very good cover, and his new right-hand man, Dimes, was ready and willing to take on anyone.

Five weeks after Hill's departure, police boarded the *Southern Cross* as it sailed off the coast of New Zealand, with a message from Australian immigration refusing him permission to visit their country. One of Hill's oldest pals back in Soho had sold the information about his trip to a newspaper who'd passed it on to the authorities.

Billy Hill was soon back in Soho once more. Jack Spot hadn't had time to seize back control of the underworld, and the prints of the manipulative Krays were now clearly all over Hill's throne; they'd been 'keeping an eye on things' while Hill was absent, making sure no one got ahead of them. Meanwhile the new police guv'nor of the West End – Superintendent Herbert Sparks – was trying to make a name for himself by cleaning up Soho. Sparks even used the new Prevention of Crime Act of 1953 to regularly pull in gangsters whom he thought were overstepping the mark. They were seldom charged with anything, but at least the police could fire a few warning shots across their bows.

In Soho, Billy Hill's premier hard man, 'Italian Albert' Dimes, was also creating his own special brand of havoc. At one drinks party, hosted by a well-known West End face, the tall, gaunt-looking Dimes insulted Rita as she walked past him to talk to someone else. Dimes muttered: 'I'd love to get my hands round that.' Rita turned and glared at Dimes and made a point of telling Spot about the encounter later that same evening. Spot was furious and tried to call Billy Hill to complain about Dimes' language but Hill never returned the call.

Another time, at Ascot Racecourse, Spot caught Dimes sneering in his direction. 'That geezer's got dead eyes. He's a right fuckin' nutter,' he told one racecourse pal. 'Someone needs to take a pop at him. Teach him a lesson.' Hill's henchman, 'Mad' Frankie Fraser, insists to this day that Dimes was never an aggressive man: 'But he was six foot, two inches, and very powerful,' says Fraser. 'You'd really have to provoke him before he'd lay a finger on you.'

The feud between Spot and Hill was now an open secret. Elephant Gang member Brian McDonald explained: 'Perhaps it was only possible to have one boss. Those of us hanging around the drinking clubs and spielers could see a rift developing: both were showing signs of jealousy, though I have to say that I thought it was more down to Billy Hill, who was being carried away by his belief in the image which the newspapers were building around him.'

Billy Hill recruited new troops from west, north and east London. And Albert Dimes brought on board two more notorious tearaways, Battles Rossi and Johnny Rice, who'd once been in the Sabini Gang where he'd been known as 'Johnny Ricco'.

Meanwhile, many in the underworld noted that Jack Spot was growing increasingly attached to his home life. Most evenings he'd leave Soho early and slip back to Hyde Park Mansions to spend time with Rita, daughter Rachel and baby Marion. Spot began not bothering to answer his home telephone. Rita encouraged him to 'go off duty' and she continued urging him to think about a career outside crime.

ᛒ   ᛒ   ᛒ

Jack Spot – not fully aware of the Krays' closeness to Billy Hill – invited them to join him at the flat racing at Epsom in the spring of 1955. Spot offered the Krays race pitches and promised them introductions to bookmakers who'd work for them along with the clerks they'd hired. The Krays would keep a 'dollar' (five shillings) in the pound profit. Spot told them they wouldn't lose a penny.

Traditionally, the Epsom races were an annual outing for London villains, who all expected to make big bucks. Whichever gang controlled the leading bookies' pitches was guaranteed a percentage of the take from every bookie on the course. Epsom represented the form sheet for just about every London villain worth his salt. Just a smile or a simple brush-off showed the others who was on the up and up; a handshake made it clear that an old grudge had been long forgotten. Little went unnoticed.

Word had spread that Spot and Hill were at each other's throats so everyone turned up. Jack Spot had swallowed his pride by inviting the Kray twins to help out. He still didn't know they hated his guts. The twins were far from impressed, and had accepted Spot's offer for the hell of it: it might be interesting. 'Interesting' had become a favourite word of Ronnie's. 'We never had liked Spotty. Never thought much of him,' admitted Ron, many years later.

At Epsom, Spot found the twins a good bookmaker to 'mind'; all they had to do was turn up and stand by the pitch, keeping an eye on the percentage. The Krays parked their cars behind the pitches. As Reg later explained: 'Ron and I and a friend of ours, Shaun Venables, had two or three revolvers in a briefcase hidden away in the car, just in case of any gang warfare.' They also kept an eye on Billy Hill who had the number one pitch up by the winning post, and was surrounded by minders. One of them was the notorious 'Mad' Frankie Fraser. Next to him was Billy Blythe, a wild man with a conviction for cutting a Flying Squad officer in the face. And there were many, many more.

Young as the Krays were, they were already up there challenging the big boys. They took a long, hard look at their so-called rivals and concluded they could take them all on any time they felt like it. One Italian gang member sidled up to Ronnie Kray and told him: 'This lot mean business. You two must be stark staring mad to show up here with Spotty. If you want to kill yourselves, there are less painful ways of doing it.' The twins laughed and offered the man a drink. When he'd gone, Ronnie turned to his brother and said, 'The way these old men worry, Reg. Fair makes you sick.'

The twins relaxed, supped a pint or two, chatted and larked around with their mates and roared with laughter at the drop of a hat. The racing and betting took second place. Eventually Ronnie found himself a quiet little corner, yawned and rolled over to sleep. At the end of the day they collected what was owed to them and drove off into the sunset without even a word of thanks to 'Spotty'.

As Ronnie Kray later admitted: 'We just turned out with him to show everyone we didn't give a fuck for anyone. Old Spotty understood. Whatever else he may have been, he wasn't stupid. He knew quite well that, though we were there in theory as his friends, we meant to end up taking over from him.' But was Spot really aware of their plans? He took the Krays racing again to Leeds but he knew he couldn't keep them happy for long. They were constantly lurking right behind him, guns at the ready.

When more of Spot's henchmen quit his mob, Spot took to the bottle. Many noticed he had become increasingly detached from the day-to-day running of his fading empire. Few of his old pals or cronies even bothered to drop in for a chat at his regular sessions at the Bear Garden bar of the Cumberland Hotel. Spot lost himself in a sea of alcohol and didn't even register the ominous signs gathering like storm clouds on the horizon.

♪   ♪   ♪

In June 1955, Rita fell ill with pneumonia and pleurisy and was rushed to St Mary's Hospital in Paddington, West London. Spot was beside himself with worry as he rushed to her bedside. Rita was found to have fluid on her lung. The doctors told Spot that they'd only just caught the illness in time and that Rita would need round-the-clock care and attention. She didn't leave hospital until almost a month later. Rita then went to convalesce in Broadstairs, Kent, but after five days had to return home because her sister, Sadie, was rushed to hospital with a life-threatening illness, and couldn't look after the children. Non-stop phone calls to and from Rita and rushed trips home became the norm for Jack Spot. He was spending less and less time focused on the remnants of his criminal empire.

Back from her sickbed, Rita – still upset by her mother's death – went to her local Catholic church every morning to light candles for her dearly departed mum. At home, she became increasingly upset by her husband's dark moods and short temper, as well as his constant boozing. Rita kept reminding him the only thing that mattered was his family. But Spot was tortured by his lack of both funds and respect. Trying to run a criminal empire and be a good father and husband at the same time was taking an enormous toll. Rita pleaded yet again for him to give up crime. 'Let's go away somewhere, open a small caff and forget all these worries,' she told her husband one day.

But Spot couldn't be sure he'd survive in the real world. Now even his wife was starting to lose faith in him. Spot believed Rita's place was in the home and he didn't like her fretting over his 'business affairs'. He later explained: 'Looking back I suppose I knew then that I was on the way out. But my pride and vanity wouldn't let me admit it.'

Each day Spot dutifully went to his office, drank, brooded and planned. But he was getting nowhere fast. He still dreamed of pulling off a huge job that would save his skin. He had one specific target, a bank, carefully cased. Then he went looking for the right team to carry out the job. But everyone turned Spot down. Even second-division villains didn't want to know. The word was out: Spot was out of the loop.

Then an old mate of Spot, a fence called Nukey told Spot: 'Everybody's been warned off you.' Nukey reckoned Spot's pals had stitched him up. 'They worked you out, Spotty. They've broken you. You're out and the other bloke's in. He's sitting there on your throne and wearing your crown.' Nukey warned Spot to forget trying to put together another mob and advised him to tread carefully. Nukey then upset Spot by suggesting he go and find himself a 'proper' job.

Hill's favourite hard man Albert Dimes phoned Spot that same morning. 'I don't want you to go away racing no more,' he told Spot.

'What the fuck you on about?'

'You've had enough. You been goin' away all these years. It's about time someone else had your pitches.'

Spot was seething, so he headed over to a favourite Soho club for a drink. He later recalled: 'But as soon as I walked in, there was dead silence. Everyone looked at me and then looked away.' As he walked across the dance floor to talk to one familiar face he heard others mentioning his name and then laughing behind his back. Spot was about to front up one of the offenders when he realised there was nothing he could do about it. Spot explained: 'In that moment my brain became suddenly crystal clear. It was as though my mind was split in two parts. One part was goading me on to unleash the rage boiling inside me. But the other was holding me back, reminding me of my two kiddies and Rita and how much I loved them.'

Spot stumbled out of the club in a daze. He began walking across Soho, not even noticing the traffic whizzing by and the familiar faces on the street corners. A name was ticking over and over in his head: DIMES.

Then he bumped straight into Nukey again, who told him that Dimes wanted to see him. Spot was furious. Nukey made it sound like he, the great Jack Spot, was some kind of servant who had to go running when Dimes snapped his fingers. Spot told Nukey where Dimes could go, and then headed west. That night Spot didn't mention a word to Rita about what had happened. But he slept so badly that the next morning Rita asked what was wrong. She thought he was sick and told him to stay at home. Spot ignored her.

At Spot's office later that morning, grease-ball Nukey turned up once again sowing the seeds of doubt and told Spot: 'You've got to go and see Dimes.'

'I told you yesterday. I ain't got no time to waste on him,' responded Spot.

Nukey repeated his advice in an even more serious tone.

'What are you getting at?' asked Spot.

'If you don't go and see him, he's gonna do you up.'

Spot was outraged. 'Albert Dimes has the impudence, the bare-faced, diabolical impudence to threaten he'd do me up,' Spot thought to himself. He was swelling up with a blind rage. As he later recalled: 'I didn't know what I was doin'. The name "Dimes" was still ringin' again and again in my brain.'

A few minutes later, on the morning of 11 August 1955, Spot found himself striding through the West End with a worried grimace on his face. Elephant Gang member Brian McDonald was on his way to a drinking club in Rathbone Place, when Spot came out of Charlotte Street, just north of Oxford Street. Spot clapped a huge arm round McDonald's shoulders, squeezed his arm with his big fist, which had fingers the size of a bunch of Fyffe bananas, and steered him back down Rathbone Place. Spot offered to buy McDonald a salt-beef sandwich. McDonald agreed, none too enthusiastically. The two men then walked out of Rathbone Place, across Oxford Street and into Soho Square. Spot nodded to familiar faces as they strolled.

As the two men turned into Frith Street, morning shoppers crowded the pavements, bustling in and out of the stores. Barrow boys were selling their fruit, bookmakers kept an eye open for the police and women were out doing some shopping. Then Spot saw him.

12

THREE MINUTES OF MADNESS

Jack Spot blinked twice. He couldn't quite believe that the object of his complete and utter hatred was standing there just a few yards ahead of him. Albert Dimes, aged thirty-six, sometimes known as 'Dimeo' and a brother of the notorious Victor Dimes, known throughout Soho. Spot marched straight up to him.

'I want you, Dimes,' panted Spot.

Dimes looked Spot straight in the eye.

'You been talkin' big,' snarled Spot. 'You been spreadin' the word around I'm to come and see you. You been talkin' like a strong-armed guy.'

'Take it easy, Spotty,' reacted Dimes. 'Don't blow your top, mate.'

Elephant Gang member Brian McDonald couldn't believe his ears as he stood nearby.

'You been talkin' too big,' repeated Spot.

'Let's go somewhere quiet and talk it over.'

'Don't treat me like a nobody. I've had my troubles. But I'm still a big man. I'm bigger than you'll ever be.'

Then Dimes said quietly: 'Face up to it, Spotty. You're finished!'

'We'll soon see if I'm finished,' screamed Spot.

Then Dimes repeated his message: 'You're finished Spotty. What's more, it's about time you were finished. You've had your day. And this is a final warning. Get the fuck out of here.'

As he spoke, Dimes gave Spot a big shove, enough to make the red mist descend. Brian McDonald later recalled: 'He put one right on Dimes's chin. Italian Albert went down like a sack of spuds.' As Spot went to give Dimes a few more kicks, another man, Johnny Rocca, grabbed Spot around the waist and tried to pull him off. McDonald then got involved. He explained: 'If I didn't all my respect would have gone with everyone. I jumped on Rocca and we pranced around like a couple of old-time dancers, not really wanting to mix it. He kept screaming at me, "Are you in this? Are you in this?"'

As Spot was hitting out at Dimes, his hand dropped automatically into his pocket, but he didn't have a blade on him that day. Precious seconds of indecision allowed Dimes time to recover. He came at Spot punching out viciously and soon a full-scale battle had erupted.

A woman screamed nearby. That was when, Spot later alleged, he felt a sudden sharpness slice through his arm. The two men fell over some vegetable boxes outside the Continental Fruit Store, on the corner of Frith and Old Compton Street. Spot twisted his opponent's right hand away from him, but as he did so, Dimes yanked back and sliced through the side of Spot's body. The two broke away from each other only to start grappling and, locked together, they tumbled into the greengrocer's shop. Male and female voices shouted. But all Spot could hear was Dimes' heavy breathing and the pain as something plunged in and out of him, over and over again.

Dimes, half stumbling, half shoved, fell through the doorway into the grocery shop. Across the street, Rocca and McDonald swapped a few more blows before Rocca tried to halt proceedings.

'Hold up, what's all this about?'

'I only came here for a salt-beef sandwich,' McDonald replied.

But, inside the shop, the battle was still in full swing. Proprietor's wife Sophie Hyams grabbed the scales, made out of heavy cast iron, and hit Spot over the head, splitting his scalp open. A knife then appeared from somewhere and both Spot and Dimes were soon leaking blood. At least a hundred people had gathered outside the Continental Fruit Store. Then forty-five-year-old Mrs Hyams shouted: 'Stop it, you silly boys.' But they took no notice and the Hyams were soon splashed with the blood of both men.

Spot later claimed that in the shop he wrestled the knife from

Dimes as he realised his opponent was trying to finish him off. Others claim Spot grabbed a potato knife and stabbed Dimes a couple of times. Whatever the truth, the two men fought with the desperation of two wild animals. As they grappled, the strength was ebbing away from both of them. Then Dimes pulled away from his opponent and leaned exhaustedly against the doorjamb before stumbling out onto the pavement. Spot felt a searing pain in his leg and the warmness of blood filling his shoes as he also staggered out of the shop. Brian McDonald watched as Dimes made his way to a taxi, where he was helped in and driven away.

Spot slithered slowly and painfully down a lamppost and then sat expressionless on the pavement. People looked the other way as they hurried past. His neck, ears and head were bleeding and there were chunks torn out of his one-hundred-guinea suit. Spot eventually struggled to his feet and staggered a few yards before slumping into a nearby Italian barber's shop. 'Fix me up!' he told the attendant in front of startled customers looking up at him from their swivel chairs. Spot grabbed a towel and dabbed roughly at his wounds. Then he collapsed unconscious on the floor.

Across the street, McDonald and Rocca took one last look at the scene and legged it. Spot was taken away by ambulance to Charing Cross Hospital. Police cars raced up Frith Street and reinforcements were soon on their way. Within an hour word had got round all the usual underworld haunts that Spot and Dimes had been involved in a fight. And as the names spread across the West End, people who'd earlier been talking openly about what had happened suddenly lost their memories.

*   *   *

At two hospitals, five miles apart, Jack Spot and Albert Dimes lay severely wounded. Both men were vulnerable to any gangland attempt to knock them off. Spot lay in a bed in the Charing Cross Hospital protected from view by a yellow curtain. Two Scotland Yard officers remained close by at all times. A lot of 'family' including nine 'brothers and cousins' plus three attractive women turned up in the hours following the attack, but were told they couldn't see Spot who was by now wearing blue-striped flannelette pyjamas. His head above his hairline was covered in plaster and bandages. He had a black eye and his throat between his Adam's apple and the chin was also bandaged. He was weak and on the critical list. The only words he could muster for police were: 'Can't remember what happened.'

At the Middlesex Hospital, Albert Dimes was being just as tight-lipped. His left forehead cleft was cut open down to the bone. The wound required twenty stitches. He had minor lacerations of the chin and left thumb, a wound on the left thigh and one in the stomach, which just failed to penetrate the abdominal cavity.

One of the few witnesses prepared to speak out said that suddenly one of the two men had brought a stiletto from his inside pocket and lunged at the other. Another claimed he saw the attacked man seize the stiletto from the other. Then there was the mystery of the so-called 'third and fourth men' who detectives believed were present throughout the incident.

Detective Inspector Eric Shepherd of West End Central police station took charge of inquiries into the Frith Street fight. Flying Squad men, and others with long experience of the West End gang scene swooped on houses, clubs and pubs across the capital in the hunt for witnesses.

In south London, another man was linked to the incident after he was found lying, beaten up on a pavement in Elephant and Castle, the night before the Frith Street fight. The man had been heard making threats against West End gang members and police believed that the attack on him might have sparked some kind of turf war between gangsters. The victim refused to give his name and address and told police to call him 'Mister X'. He insisted the injuries were the result of 'an accident'.

Jack Spot suffered a total of nine stab wounds, including a punctured lung just a quarter of an inch from his heart. He'd lost pints of blood as his stomach had been turned into a sieve. So much air had seeped into his belly that he'd swollen up like a half-inflated balloon. Spot had also been stabbed over the left eye, in the left cheek, in the ear and neck, and four times in the left arm.

In hospital, Spot fell in and out of consciousness and hovered close to the point of death while doctors worked furiously to stem the vast loss of blood. As Spot himself later recalled: 'I hovered in a grey, twilight world, punctuated by sharpness, the smell of anaesthetic and constant nausea.'

Rita remained in hospital accompanied by henchman Sonny the Yank while Moisha Blueball made arrangements for Spot's legal defence. 'Dear, sweet, lovely Rita would sit there and pat my hand for hours and tell me not to worry,' recalled Spot. Meanwhile, the police continued to patiently await his recovery. As soon as he was pronounced well enough to talk, Spot told detectives once again that he didn't remember whom he'd fought with. It was more than his life was worth to reveal what had happened.

For the first time in Jack Spot's life, he felt genuine remorse for what he was putting Rita through. As he later explained: 'She was a good, decent girl and I'd married her and dragged her into the shadow of my own bad luck.' Spot warned Rita the newspapers would rip them apart. 'Go away somewhere – and quickly. Leave right away, forget about all my troubles and don't come near me until it's all over.' Rita insisted she and the kids would survive, even though Spot knew he'd blown virtually every penny of the fortune he'd amassed over the previous ten years. Rita immediately hired a good lawyer to defend Spot – and paid his fees by selling one of her diamond rings and dipping into some savings she'd been keeping for just such an emergency.

In the middle of all this, a swastika with a message from the Blackshirt movement – 'Remember 1936' – was delivered to the hospital with a bunch of black carnations. It seemed as if Billy Hill wasn't the only one enjoying Jack Spot's pain.

ß   ß   ß

Mr Hyman Hyams, owner of the shop where the battle took place described the fight as thus to police: 'Albert ran in the shop with his chin bleeding. Mr Comer chased in, after him. Comer said: "So you want to be a fuckin' tearaway; see how you like this." Then he started cutting him about with a knife.'

At the Middlesex Hospital, Albert Dimes was told that he'd also be charged with GBH. He got so angry he told police: 'It was Jackie Spot – I'm not prossing [prosecuting]. Spotty does me up and I get pinched. That can't be fair.' But later in an official statement to the police he would only refer to being attacked by 'a tall man ... I don't know his name. I don't want to kid you, but in the struggle between us I must have cut him up with my knife. If I did use it, it was struggling for my life.'

When Spot heard he would also face GBH charges, he told police: 'Why only me? Albert did me and I get knocked off.' Jack Spot had just given the police an opportunity to tear him and his mob to pieces. As Spot admitted years later: 'For years, like a Chicago gangster I'd strutted insolently around Soho, spending money like water, flamboyantly displaying my wealth and shouting aloud to the whole wide world that I was the mastermind directing successful criminal activity. It was madness. But I didn't realise it then. I'd been so vain, so proud, and so cocky.' He added: 'In three mad, enraged minutes, I'd thrown away a lifetime of carefully planned precautions.' Spot knew that if the police made a GBH charge stand up in court, then that would spell the end of his criminal regime because he'd be sure to cop a prison sentence.

Reporter Duncan Webb gleefully celebrated the downfall of 'Jack Spot – the Tin-pot Tyrant' in the *Sunday People* the following Sunday. He even wrote that, at last, 'the mob had discovered what I had known for years – that Spot is a poseur who had got away with it.' Webb was out for revenge following his earlier encounters with Spot. And Billy Hill enjoyed every word of it.

Frith Street fight witness Brian McDonald was pulled in by the law as an important element of the Spot/Dimes showdown in Soho. 'Words like "conspiracy" were floating about. Conspiracy is a lock-up-and-throw-away-the-key job,' said McDonald. But no one fingered McDonald and Russo, so they got nothing more than a caution.

While Spot and Dimes lay in hospital, Billy Hill and his henchmen were taking over Jack Spot's pitch concessions at race meetings. Scotland Yard feared an outbreak of gang warfare and Soho was flooded with extra police. Traders were better protected than they had been for years. But nothing materialised. Spot and Dimes were both seen sitting up in hospital, receiving their friends and cronies and telling reporters to mind their own business, or words to that effect. Spot's old pal Vic Sims on the *Sunday Chronicle* described him as 'the country's nearest thing to an American gangster chief'. Spot liked that but he had some bigger problems on his plate such as the genuine fear that one of Dimes' boys might try and finish him off. And detectives still hadn't found the knife used in the attack.

Across the Thames, other gang problems were flaring up. Pitched battles took place between gangs from the Elephant and Castle and Deptford. Detectives believed much of the trouble had been caused by thriving street betting. Another south-London gang invaded their neighbour's territory and told bookmakers' runners that, in future, all bets must be placed with bookmakers sponsored by them. A few nights later, the visitors, thirty to forty men strong, arrived prepared to do battle. But a squad of twenty specially selected, uniformed policemen were waiting for them and the battle was thwarted. As one Scotland Yard officer explained: 'The problem is there is only one law out there – the swift and merciless rule of the knife.'

On Saturday 20 August, Detective Inspector Eric Shepherd visited Jack Spot in hospital and ordered him to get dressed and accompany him to West End Central police station. Spot refused, so Shepherd arrested him for causing grievous bodily harm and possessing an offensive weapon, namely a knife. Dimes faced identical charges. Spot was escorted in handcuffs to a waiting squad car.

At West End Central police station, Spot was officially charged and he asked for his brief. As he later explained: 'Me and Dimes weren't being treated like schoolboys who'd scrapped in the street. It was assumed that we'd tried to kill each other. And authority was tryin' to prove both of us guilty. Not just Dimes. But me too!'

Spot faced the prospect of seven, or maybe even eight, years in prison if found guilty of roughhousing with Dimes. He spent that weekend in a cell at West End Central. Being under lock and key marked a new low in Spot's life. For the first time he was frightened, a shell of his former self; he even later admitted he came close to tears every time he thought about his wife and kids. It wasn't the other gangsters who scared him. He just didn't want to be parted from his beautiful young wife and family.

The fight with Dimes made Jack Spot's grand claims to be the great peacemaker of Soho's underworld sound hollow. The police were clearly no longer going to tolerate an uneasy peace with Spot or Hill, or whoever was in command. The publicity surrounding the Frith Street fight had exposed to the British public that Soho was virtually a lawless society. Ordinary, decent citizens were up in arms.

In Soho, Billy Hill's outspoken, estranged wife, Aggie, who ran one of Hill's clubs in an alleyway off Frith Street, told reporters as she waved £2000 worth of diamonds at them: 'You won't find anyone here who knows Jack Spot or Italian Albert. I can only say they are two lovely guys. That's all.'

On Monday 22 August 1955, Spot and Dimes appeared at Marlborough Street Magistrates Court to face the charges. They stood together in the dock with three policemen sitting between them. At one stage Spot looked directly at Dimes who didn't even glance back at him.

Both men were remanded in custody for a week after Divisional Superintendent Herbert Sparks opposed bail. He told the court Spot and Dimes were capable of absconding and that he had reliable information that they both might try and interfere with witnesses. The following day, in custody in Brixton Prison, Spot managed to upset his fellow inmates by insisting that they vacate the interview grilles on either side of him while he received visitors. 'Who the hell does he think he is?' one old lag spat. Spot didn't realise his conversations were monitored by listening posts at either end of the visiting room. During one conversation, Spot was heard discussing the possibility of paying a former Scotland Yard detective £1000 to appear as a witness for him at his trial.

♪   ♪   ♪

On Monday 29 August, Spot and Dimes again appeared before Marlborough Street Magistrates. The public gallery was so over-crowded many had to be turned away. The prosecutor asked the magistrate if witnesses could be allowed to write their names and addresses down rather than say them in open court for their own safety. This implied both men might have witnesses intimidated. One witness was asked in court if he was frightened when the police came knocking. He replied: 'I definitely was.' Another witness was asked if he was scared he replied: 'I definitely was of Comer. He is a notorious cut-throat who runs round the West End. That is what I have heard.'

One witness described the fight and insisted he'd seen Spot first attack Dimes. At the end of the hearing both men were committed for trial at the Old Bailey. Jack Spot was remanded in custody while Albert Dimes was granted bail in his own recognisance of £250 plus two sureties of £250 each. Dimes' Irish QC, Patrick Marrinan, told the court that his client had been attacked by: 'This other murderous, treacherous rascal.' Marrinan raised no objection to the writing down of witness names. He insisted his client had acted completely in self-defence.

Shortly after Spot and Dimes' well-publicised court appearance, Polish pilot Christopher Glinski – whose exploits during the war had won him the Polish Military Cross and the French Croix de Guerre, presented himself at his local police station, West End Central. He claimed he'd been in Frith Street and had seen Spot push the other man. 'Then the other man charged him. The other man took a knife out of his pocket. I saw the knife cut into his arm. Then I saw another blow cut his face. They got hold of one another and, together, staggered into the shop.' The police were somewhat bemused by Glinski's account, but took a statement and warned him that he may well be asked to appear as a witness in the forthcoming trial. What they didn't realise was that Glinski had just visited Spot's flat at Hyde Park Mansions for 'a chat' with some of Spot's associates, including Moisha Blueball and Sonny the Yank. He'd then agreed to go to the police.

Over in West London, another oddball called Pete MacDonough, a.k.a. 'Tall Pat', owed his favourite bookmaker £134. Also in debt to the same bookie was eighty-eight-year-old Reverend Basil Andrews. Both men were under pressure to pay off their heavy gambling debts.

Tall Pat lived in Upper Berkeley Street, in the West End, where his wife sublet small flatlets. She serviced the apartments and he helped, although he had been in bad health for five years. He first met Reverend Basil Andrews when the elderly parson took a short lease on a flat, which he rented for seven guineas a week. Andrews was accompanied by a woman and her teenage daughter and introduced them to the MacDonoughs as his nieces. They even called him 'Father Andrews'.

Tall Pat noticed that Andrews took a lot of phone calls at his flat. The telephone was on the top of a landing, which led down to MacDonough's basement apartment. He later explained: 'Andrews was rather deaf, and we could not but help overhearing, although it was unintentional, a lot of arguments and appointments were carried out by him on the phone. On several occasions I heard names I had known – household names, well-known names.' Some of those names were titled gentry. MacDonough continued: 'He was making excuses on the telephone to some people regarding paying back some money, but it was no concern of mine.'

For despite his distinguished title, Reverend Basil Andrews was far from an ordinary, law-abiding pastor. To the people of

Watlington, Oxfordshire, Andrews was 'the parson with the silver voice'. Before the outbreak of the First World War, he'd been their tall, dark, wavy-haired curate, whose passionate preaching had filled the village church. He'd even had a pretty young wife and a young son. Womenfolk were particularly taken by Reverend Andrews, who would warmly shake their hands after every service. There were rumours that he'd been seen sharing scones and a pot of tea with some of his prettier parishioners in a number of local teashops. Then, one day, Andrews had disappeared from his flock, along with his wife and child. He never even bothered to say goodbye. Local gossips insisted he'd departed suddenly because 'women parishioners were paying too much attention to him'. Nobody to this day seems to know where Andrews moved to. But, somewhere along the way, he parted company with his wife and son and resurfaced alone at the end of World War Two, when he became resident minister at the church attached to a cemetery in Kensal Rise, north-west London. Andrews soon became a regular at a number of local pubs in the area. One of his parishioners later explained: 'He would go in, drink five pints of beer and have a set lunch. It was not unusual for him to leave a half a crown tip. He was a real gent.' Others in Kensal Rise noticed that Andrews always bought a midday racing paper and then telephoned bets for much of the afternoon. 'Sometimes his language was most unclerical,' recalled another of his flock.

ƒ   ƒ   ƒ

On 15 September, Tall Pat MacDonough met up with the elderly Reverend Andrews at the Cumberland Hotel. Also present was Spot's old pal Sonny the Yank. Andrews insisted that he'd seen the Spot/Dimes fight in Soho. Sonny the Yank then informed the reverend father he could earn himself 'a decent wedge' by saying a few words: 'I saw Dimes with the knife.' Sonny also persuaded the cleric to move into a cheap Bayswater hotel rather than continue living in the same building as Tall Pat MacDonough because

The redbrick tenement block of Fieldgate Mansions, in Myrdle Street, Whitechapel, still stands to this day as a testament to the old East End where Jack Spot was born and bred.

Spot *(second from right, top row)* had a tough time in the army after he was enlisted in 1940 and ended up manning anti-aircraft barracks in Somerset.

Jack Spot, still dapper aged seventy-six, and in his favourite suit
and hat, poses at the Frank Bruno versus Tim Witherspoon
fight at Wembley Arena in 1988.

he knew that, if the police discovered the connection, his statement would be thrown out.

A few days later, Reverend Andrews visited Jack Spot's apartment at Hyde Park Mansions. He even managed to avoid being spotted by the hoards of reporters stalking Rita's every move. All callers to flat 12F were met by either Sonny the Yank or Moisha Blueball. In the apartment, Andrews watched with curiousity as Spot's eldest daughter Rachel, then four, opened a drawer and scattered photographs around the room. He noticed the pictures showed Rita's mother's grave and was a tad puzzled, but decided on reflection to say nothing. When Rita politely asked Andrews about his background, he proudly told her he could trace his ancestors back to the Bishop of London. Rita then replied that she had three great-aunts who were nuns in Texas.

Just then Moisha Blueball joined in the conversation and got down to business, as Reverend Andrews recalled: 'He said "You say this," and "You say that." They seemed very delighted about it all. In fact, they told me they had a bottle of champagne to celebrate with after it was all over.' As they relaxed, Rita asked Andrews how he managed to look so well dressed despite his financial difficulties. She later recalled: 'He said he had some very good friends. He even mentioned knowing the French singer Maurice Chevalier.'

Over the following days, Moisha Blueball gave Reverend Andrews a total of £63 (it should have been £65 but Moisha couldn't resist cheating the churchman out of a couple of quid). Moisha also promised the elderly cleric he 'would never want' and 'would always be provided for' if Jack Spot got off.

Shortly before Spot and Dimes' trial started at the Old Bailey, Rita visited her husband at Brixton Prison where he pleaded with her to leave London. 'Go right away with the kids. You can't do anything for me now,' Spot told Rita. 'They've got me where they want me after years of waiting for this moment. I've played right into their hands.'

Spot told his wife to keep some money back from his lawyer as he believed she'd need the cash to survive if he was jailed. But Rita was in no mood to compromise with their future and told Spot she'd done everything in her power to make sure he'd be acquitted. After an emotional, tear-filled visit, Rita left the prison with her head still held up high.

§   §   §

That same day, Billy Hill visited a Brighton bookie called Sammy Belson, the guv'nor of Brighton racetrack and a supposedly close friend of Jack Spot's. Hill and sidekick Mad Frankie Fraser were collecting money for Albert Dimes' defence. They wanted Spot, awaiting trial in Brixton Jail, to realise how popular Dimes was. Bellson, said to be worth at least £80,000, made a generous contribution of £500 because, as he later explained: 'I knew what would happen if I told 'em to fuck off.' Ironically, Fraser was arrested by Scotland Yard detectives later that same day after police heard rumours that he was about to shoot another of Spot's supporters, who was also at the Brighton races that afternoon.

Hill also had no trouble persuading many of Spot's henchmen to contribute to Albert Dimes' defence. Names like Teddy Machin and Jackie Reynolds were happy to drop Spot like a brick. Hill even encouraged them to see Spot in prison and tell him to his face why they were joining Hill's mob.

While Billy Hill's West End headquarters were still at the top of a filthy stairway, above a shabby spieler he ran just off Shaftesbury Avenue, he had two impressive London residences. As well as a flat in Barnes, close to the Thames in West London, he had an apartment in Bayswater, nearer to the centre of town. In the same block in Barnes lived Hill's favourite QC, Patrick Marrinan. There were rumours that Hill paid towards Marrinan's rent. Hill had three full-sized poodles in the flat that he and Mad Frankie Fraser often took for walks out onto the nearby common. Hill was a man of many contradictions . . .

13

FACE TO FACE

On 19 September 1955, Jack Spot, now aged forty-three, and
Albert Dimes, aged forty, appeared at the Old Bailey to face charges
arising from the Frith Street battle. Spot's expression gave little
away as he sat in the dock alongside Dimes. Both men carefully
avoided eye contact and were separated by a prison guard. Spot
was described in court as a 'turf accountant' of Hyde Park Mansions, Marylebone and Dimes was said to be a 'commission agent'
of River Street, Finsbury Park, north London.

The court heard that, during the fight, Dimes got hold of Spot's
knife despite serious injury. Then he was alleged to have done to
Spot what Spot had done to him 'namely, to stab him several times'.
The key was whether the jury felt that Dimes was in lawful possession of the knife, having wrestled it from his alleged assailant.

The Old Bailey hearing was adjourned by the judge at the end
of the first day after the jury decided the two men should face the
charges separately. Spot returned to prison that evening while
Dimes was once again granted bail. Spot's trial was arranged
to take place two days later. One London evening newspaper
splashed the headline: JACK SPOT TRIAL IS FIXED across their
front page. Did they know more than the jury?

On 22 September, Spot returned to the Old Bailey alone. One of
the first witnesses called – Hyman Hyams, owner of the Continental
Fruit Store – said he saw Spot chasing Dimes into the store with a
knife in his hand. He said Spot grappled with Dimes who had nothing

in his hand. His wife Sophie backed her husband up when it was her turn in the witness box. Both told the court they were afraid of Spot.

Then Spot's counsel, a feisty lady called Miss Rose Heilbron took the floor. She had a fearsome reputation in the legal profession – unrivalled for a female QC. She was called to the Bar in 1939 and became the first woman to lead for the defence at an English murder trial when she took on the case for George Kelly, known as the Liverpool Cameo cinema killer, in 1950. She also defended Louis Bloom, a solicitor who was found not guilty of the murder of his secretary. He got three years for manslaughter.

Rose Heilbron began her defence of Spot by questioning fight witness Mrs Sophie Hyams. Within minutes, the Old Bailey judge was urging Mrs Hyams to take a break and have a glass of water as she seemed close to tears. Then Rose Heilbron chipped in: 'Mrs Hyams,' she said softly 'you are a frightened woman aren't you?'

Mrs Hyams did not instantly respond. The Judge then asked her: 'Perhaps you are frightened of Miss Heilbron?' Mrs Hyams responded sharply: 'No I am not.' Rose Heilbron joined in the laughter that echoed through the Old Bailey's Number One Court. Rose Heilbron then asked Mrs Hyams' husband whether Dimes was the aggressor and if Spot was holding onto his wrist, trying to make him drop the knife.

'No ma'am,' replied Hyams. 'I was there. I saw enough, ma'am.'

Rose Heilbron then questioned Pasquail Papa, also known as Bert Marsh the bookmaker, who confirmed to the court that Spot and Dimes were his friends. Miss Heilbron then suggested that Marsh had approached various witnesses for the prosecution and told them that they had better support Dimes. Marsh denied her allegation and her description of being 'feared in the neighbourhood'.

Then Jack Spot told the court he'd gone to Soho to meet Dimes to discuss a warning issued by Dimes for Spot to keep away from racecourses. Spot's counsel, Heilbron, rolled her eyes as Spot tried to convince the court that Dimes had inflicted the knife wounds on himself in order to escape prosecution. Spot then backed his claims by grasping his own wrists and swinging his body about in the witness box. Spot then ducked below the level of the box. 'I had his wrist down there, and it must have gone into him as we came up,' he called from the bottom of the box. 'All of a sudden, he pulls a knife out and makes stabs at me. I put my arm up, and it goes through my arm. I fight my way back to the door of the greengrocer's shop. He goes at me again and gets me in the face. I push him round. We fall over some boxes. I manage to get hold of his arm. He twists away from me and I feel a sharp pain in the side. I cannot get my breath.'

Following Spot's performance in the witness box, it was the turn of Polish war hero Christopher Glinski. His address was Kendall Street, Paddington, and he described himself as an interpreter. Glinski told the court he'd read reports of the case in the newspapers and realised that the details did not tally with what he'd seen. Glinski said: 'I saw the two men arguing on the corner of the street. They pushed and shouted. I saw Comer push the other man. Then the other man charged him. The other man took a knife out of his pocket. The man in the dock lifted his arms to defend himself. I saw the knife cut into his arm. Then I saw another blow cut his face. They got hold of one another and, together, staggered into the fruit shop.' Glinski insisted he had no connections to Jack Spot apart from having seen Spot's photo in the newspapers. He also told the court he did not know Albert Dimes.

Outside in the corridor, clergyman Basil Andrews was also waiting to give evidence. Moisha Blueball had suggested he wait in the precincts of the court until he was called, in case he was intimidated by Albert Dimes' associates. Andrews had spent that morning at Spot's solicitor Bernard Perkoff's office sitting alongside Glinski until he knew he'd definitely be required in court that afternoon.

The Reverend Basil Claude Hudson Andrews, of Inverness Terrace, Bayswater, seemed a friendly, harmless enough old boy as he declared to the court that he'd also read a newspaper report about the case and decided to contact Jack Spot's brief. A man of the cloth would surely tell nothing but the absolute truth under God's oath. The defence even tried to insist that Reverend

Andrews' name not be published so as to protect him. Spot and his team knew full well that someone was sure to recognise the parson's name and his 'unusual' background.

Andrews told the court he was convinced the wrong man had been labelled the aggressor. 'It astonished me,' he said with appropriate gestures and a quiet, almost apologetic tone of voice. 'I thought, 'Dear me! This is entirely wrong! The darker man was the aggressor. He attacked the fairer man.' Andrews identified Dimes as the darker man.

As the old vicar continued giving evidence, cupping his hand to his ear better to hear the questions he was asked, Detective Superintendent Herbert Sparks whispered to his colleague Bert Wickstead: 'Bert, I bet that old parson's bent!'

Then Sparks scribbled something down on a scrap of paper: 'Reverend Basil Claude Hudson Andrews'. That scrap of paper was handed to a detective sergeant who hurried out of the courtroom and phoned Scotland Yard. No one had heard of Andrews, but inquiries were immediately started to find out more about the elderly cleric.

Scotland Yard detective Bert Wickstead later concluded: 'Reverend Andrews' dog collar and clerical garb certainly changed the scales of justice. Those perfect expressions of his as he gave his evidence were so exactly the thoughts of an elderly gentleman who had witnessed a street fight and later read about it in his newspaper.'

Unknown to the police, two London bookies had sent representatives to the Old Bailey to collect some unpaid debts from Reverend Basil Andrews. But they turned up just after Andrews had completed his evidence and left empty-handed. The bookies knew him as the 'knocking parson' and they'd discovered he regularly changed addresses to keep one step ahead of his creditors.

Back at the Old Bailey, Rose Heilbron summed up for the defence by telling the court Spot had suffered much worse injuries than his opponent and she pointed out that Dimes seemed to know a great deal about the knife used in the attack, which had disappeared after the duel.

Judge Sir Gerald Dodson even called Dimes a 'strong-arm man' during his summing up. 'The inference is raised. Why, on going to interview a strong-arm man, did he [Jack Spot] not arm himself?' Judge Dodson even conceded: 'He is entitled to defend himself, and if a knife is being used, he is entitled to turn it on the assailant.' As Spot listened intently from the dock, he now felt more hopeful of an acquittal.

Then the jury retired to consider their verdicts. Two burly warders escorted Spot downstairs to the cells to await their return. Just sixty-five minutes later they emerged. Moments later the judge asked the jury: 'Members of the jury, what is your verdict?'

The foreman climbed to his feet, licked his lips and glanced across the court at Spot and then back again at the judge. Then he said slowly and clearly: 'Not guilty!'

As Spot himself later admitted: 'I wanted to kiss Miss Rose Heilbron, slap each of the jury members heartily on the shoulder, wring the parson's hand and give the judge my deepest thanks. Despite everything, justice had prevailed.'

Jack Spot's acquittal sparked scenes more suited to the end of a world heavyweight championship boxing bout. Spot danced up and down in the dock with hands clasped over his head. He pranced, smiled, bowed, until the judge snapped, 'Behave yourself, Comer!'

Spot then strolled down to the cells to collect his shaving kit and other personal items before being virtually carried out of court by his waiting friends and associates. Spot told reporters: 'If you want to write a story, write one about Rose, Miss Rose Heilbron, the greatest criminal lawyer in history.'

Back at his flat at Hyde Park Mansions a few hours later, with champagne flowing, Spot telephoned Rose Heilbron and told her: 'You are the greatest lawyer ever!' Top of the guest list at Spot's bash that evening were Moisha Blueball and Sonny the Yank. Spot proudly described them as: 'They're the best friends I've got. They've stood by me all the way through.'

Four storeys below, on the street outside Hyde Park Mansions, a black taxi drew up containing Reverend Basil Andrews. He told the driver to wait and walked hesitantly up the eight steps to the intercom and pressed the button marked flat 12F. When he announced who he was, a voice at the other end told him to 'fuck off'. Andrews sloped off into the night, mightily upset. He'd been expecting to be paid a 'bonus' for his efforts on behalf of Spot's successful defence. Andrews later insisted he'd only been looking for Spot's solicitor Mr Bernard Perkoff that night, but few doubted Andrews was after a final payoff for his false evidence.

The following day telegrams, letters and cables of congratulations flooded into Spot's flat. Spot announced to the press that job offers had been flooding in since his acquittal, including 'one from the Kabaka of Buganda, who wants to hire me as a bodyguard'.

Spot insisted his next move would be into the textile trade with friends. He said he was easing himself out of the underworld and Soho. He also pledged to write a book 'about the racing game'. He explained: 'There's still lots of people who would be amazed at the full inside story.' But Spot's first aim was to take a holiday. 'Possibly I'll go to the south of France with the wife and kids,' he added.

Meanwhile, a few of Reverend Basil Andrews's 'friends' began phoning Scotland Yard and Fleet Street, telling them all about the colourful private life of the not-so-saintly Reverend Andrews. Some of the callers were bookmakers who said the Reverend had reneged on bets. Others came from anonymous people who pointed out that Dimes was the innocent party. Further inquiries by Scotland Yard established that at least six London hotels and two book-makers were currently looking for the elderly parson to collect unpaid bills. If the police had known about him earlier they'd have tried to discredit him in the witness box.

Jack Spot's first morning of freedom after his acquittal consisted of breakfast in bed with a copy of the *Racing Post*, even though he'd promised Rita he would change his ways.

Spot invited Fleet Street journalist John Ralph into his apartment for an exclusive interview and pictures in exchange for a fee. There, he made a very public display of hugging and kissing Rita and the children in front of the reporter. When Ralph asked why his defence had been entrusted to Miss Heilbron, a thirty-nine-year-old wife and mother from Liverpool, Moisha chipped in, 'A Jewish lady she is. It's an education just to listen to her speak.' Spot added: 'And to think, when one of the boys suggested Rosie should defend me I had my doubts. 'A woman defend me,' I said, 'You're crazy. But my solicitor thought it was a wonderful idea – if we could get her. Best lawyer there is for a man who wants a real deal.'

On the expensive sideboard of Jack Spot's apartment in Hyde Park Mansions a large picture in a gilded frame took pride of place. 'Rose Heilbron,' Spot told the reporters, 'I call her my pin-up girl.' Just then, Sonny and Moisha chipped in, 'Pin-up girl. Rosie in good times and bad.'

Spot then returned to the subject he most enjoyed talking about: himself. 'I've been through hell,' he told John Ralph. 'Hospitals, prison cell, no bail, nothing, treated like a criminal. I was a worried and sick man.'

Then Ralph asked Spot about his 'star' witness, Reverend Basil Andrews. Spot turned the question around skilfully. 'Miss Heilbron was gentle with him, drawing out the facts. I listened with astonishment.' Spot insisted there were no connections between his mob and the good Reverend Andrews. He said the vicar's evidence only came to light after an approach was made to one of his wife's friends, who'd read about the case in the newspapers.

But Fleet Street soon uncovered a gambling cleric desperate to make a few bob to help pay off his appalling debts to bookies. The *Empire News* claimed to be the first newspaper to get on the trail of Reverend Basil Andrews. *Empire News* reporters had earlier spotted Andrews getting out of the taxi at Spot's home at Hyde Park Mansions on the night after the end of the trial.

Reporters uncovered that Andrews' favourite trick was to say he had a niece called Barbara, who was in fact the daughter of a friend of his, a Mrs Owen. Barbara was just sixteen years old and Andrews frequently claimed she was due to inherit £100,000 at the age of twenty-one. Then he'd try and borrow hundreds of pounds off innocent punters.

The following Monday, on 26 September 1955, it was Albert Dimes's turn to appear at the Old Bailey to answer the same charges as Spot. Dimes's counsel, Mr Alan Roberts, QC, insisted there was no evidence to go before the jury. 'I submit that when a man runs in the street, runs in the shop, runs until he cannot get any further, then it is a grave misuse of language to call that a fight.'

Mr Roberts also told the court nobody could describe as fighting the reactions of a man who was struggling for his life against an aggresor with a knife. The prosecution insisted that the green-grocer shop could be considered, in law, a public place but Judge Justice Glyn-Jones disagreed. He responded: 'I doubt whether I can allow what took place in that shop to be treated as evidence on a charge of having made an affray in Frith Street.' Mr Roberts argued that it was 'grotesque in its absurdity' to charge Dimes with being in unlawful possession of an offensive weapon when, with his remaining strength, he had wrested the knife from his assailant. He then submitted that there was no evidence against Dimes of wounding with intent to cause grievous bodily harm to Jack Spot.

The prosecution then took the Judge Glyn-Jones' advice and unanimously voted to withdrew the charges against Dimes. The judge told the court: 'From the moment the [Spot] verdict was announced on Friday night, it would be quite improper for a jury to be asked to find him guilty on this charge, especially as all the other witnesses in the other case said the other man was the assailant. It is not for Dimes to prove that he was acting in self-defence. It is for the prosecution to prove that he was not.' The judge then said: 'I think in all the circumstances, all I can do is to discharge the jury.' Albert Dimes walked out of the Old Bailey laughing.

14

'A TOUCH OF THE SECONDS'

A team of Scotland Yard detectives had watched the jury members closely throughout the two Old Bailey trials to guard against possible interference and became convinced some of the jury had been nobbled. Police spotted Soho gang members circulating close to jury members in lunch breaks and during adjournments. But they were unable to prove anything concrete.

The media naturally chose to put their own unique spin on the 'fight that never was'. Respected author Alan Tietjen wrote: 'Remember, it was not the police, judge or counsel for the defence who acquitted them. It was twelve ordinary members of the public who were responsible, and who had taken the oath ending with the words and true verdict given, according to evidence. That evidence was perjured. So what could the jury do? There was a doubt – a doubt about who initiated the attack and whether or not Jack Spot was defending himself from a murderous attack by Dimes, or vice versa. I was present throughout the trial at the Old Bailey, and I must confess that in my humble opinion the verdict of the jury was surprising.'

Two days later, Tall Pat MacDonough met Reverend Basil Andrews in a West End restaurant. Andrews was accompanied by his friend Mrs Owens and her sixteen-year-old daughter. Tall Pat and Andrews went outside for a quiet chat, and Tall Pat immediately asked him if he was all right and if he had seen what the newspapers were saying about him. 'I don't read the papers. Of course I'm all right,' Andrews snapped back.

They left the restaurant in a taxi together. During the journey MacDonough gave Andrews £25 in £5 notes. The following day Andrews met MacDonough again and was given a second installment of £25 in £5 notes.

ʃ   ʃ   ʃ

The world was expected to believe neither man had attacked the other, even though they both had been seriously wounded. Home Secretary Major Lloyd George opened an inquiry into the acquittals. He explained to the press: 'There is a need for an inquiry as to whether or not some witnesses were tampered with.'

The authorities had been made to look pretty stupid by the not-guilty verdicts against two protagonists who so obviously had a vicious fight. For years, the good citizens of Soho had been told that the police would guarantee their safety from such hooligan elements and now two such characters had been allowed to walk free. Newspapers ran cartoons and blasted leader articles across their pages referring to the 'Mirage in Soho'.

Then intrepid *Sunday People* reporter Duncan Webb got a tip from Albert Dimes about even more interesting details about Reverend Andrews's 'background'. The following Sunday he had his latest scoop plastered across the front page of the *Sunday People*. The headline read: PARSON'S DUD BETS START HUNT BY BOOKIES.

One bookie told Webb that Andrews owed him £35, yet a few days later the old parson had laid a bet with another West End bookie and lost £15.10s. Then Andrews went missing. At a West End hotel, he borrowed £1 from the manager soon after his arrival. He repaid it, but when his bill was presented later he announced he could not pay it. The manager then impounded his luggage and, once again, Andrews disappeared.

The publicity surrounding the 'fight that never was' showed the great British public that a thriving criminal underworld still existed on their very doorstep. How could a bunch of Soho gangsters 'bend' vicars to give false testimony? Witnesses were known to have been paid to have second thoughts, or what was known in the underworld as 'a touch of the seconds'. It was the 'gentlemen of the chin', as chiv-merchants were called, who'd become the feudal lords of the manor of Soho, with their own version of the Ten Commandments beginning 'Thou shalt steal' and ending with 'Thou shalt bear false witness aginst thy neighbour'.

Then Reverend Andrews received a postcard at the hotel in Inverness Terrace, Bayswater, where he was staying in room twenty-three. The unsigned card read: 'You dirty beast. Why should you poke your nose in where it is not wanted? Let me tell you if this case comes up again, you will not live for long.' The card had been posted at 3.45 p.m. the previous Wednesday in the E6 London postal district.

Obviously disturbed by the threat to his life, Andrews then began singing like the proverbial canary. He visited the offices of his favourite, extremely friendly and generous newspaper, the *Daily Sketch*, where he dictated the following letter:

'I am fully aware that cowardly people who dare not come forward into the light of day are suggesting that I am a fraudulent witness and that I hoodwinked Mr Comer's legal advisors. I would recall to you that when I gave my evidence last week I gave it on my solemn oath, and I need not remind you that I am a Clerk in Holy Orders also.

'I therefore wish to affirm in the most solemn terms that what I said in the witness box was the whole truth and nothing but the truth. I wish to deny that I have committed perjury. I wish to deny that I have any hopes of material gain from having come forward as a witness. I did so only in the interests of truth, and I am willing to tell the police that if they come to me.

'Any financial difficulties due to my change of address and my harmless flutters in the sporting world are only temporary, due to my age and inexperience. Those who are dunning me will soon be repaid if they have patience – some debts have been settled already.

'I am a man of peace, as well, I hope, as one of God's humblest servants and workers. I would like to bring about a reconciliation between the parties in strife, who seem to have forgotten that, by what they have done, they are debasing the sacred Brotherhood of Man.'

What Basil Andrews didn't tell the newspaper was that he'd just been to see the Bishop of Kensington to try and borrow some money. The Bishop had told him to get on his bike. The day after giving his statement of denial, Andrews found himself summoned to Scotland Yard by Commander Ted Greeno, now one of the Yard's legendary 'Big Five'. With Greeno was Commander George Hatherhill, head of the Yard's CID, Superintendent Herbert Sparks and Superintendent William Judge. They talked late into the night with Andrews in a small room overlooking the Thames. At one stage during the interview, Greeno got an anonymous phone call saying Jack Spot was planning to flee London. Greeno immediately got two of his detectives to check out Spot's movements.

As word of the parson's interview spread, crowds gathered outside the Whitehall entrance to the Yard. The iron gates remained firmly closed. Asked why he'd lied at the trial Andrews finally admitted the truth to Greeno: 'It was very wicked of me. I was very hard up and I was tempted and I fell. It is rather humiliating for me to have to tell you I was desperately hungry. I had had what is called Continental breakfasts and nothing in between. I should not have yielded but I did. Thank God I have asked to be forgiven!'

Greeno and his colleagues grilled Andrews for three-and-a-half hours. Eventually, a dark-blue squad car drove out of the Yard with Greeno and Sparks. Sitting between them, half covered by a blanket was Andrews. He was taken to a suburban hotel where he spent the night after being advised by the Yard that he should accept their offer of twenty-four-hour protection as there was a genuine fear he might be the target of a reprisal.

Back at the Yard, dozens of pages of notes were being transcribed by a team of typists to add to the report. When complete, it would be sent off to: the Home Secretary Major Lloyd-George; the Director of Public Prosecutions, Sir Theobald Matthew; and the Commissioner of Police, Sir John Nott-Bower. Another copy was due to be sent to the Attorney-General, Sir Reginald Manningham-Buller.

Over at West End Central police station, a special team of detectives were working around the clock on the Frith Street fight inquiry. Scores of people were interviewed and numerous statements taken. The other 'key' witness, Chris Glinski, discovered that detectives were showing his photograph to staff at West End hotels. The officers asked barmaids and waiters if they'd seen him drinking with a certain woman.

Glinski was so worried he issued a statement through his solicitor: 'I have visited two big hotels recently. I might have been approached in one by a dark-haired woman, but I do not remember the incident.' Then he added, somewhat confusingly: 'I am beginning now to remember things, which had previously slipped my memory. I shall be able to tell the police all about them. It is strange how one's memory fades.'

Then an extraordinary story about Reverend Andrews came to light, concerning an alleged marriage between one of Andrews' women friends (the young girl he described as his niece) and an elderly man he'd borrowed money from. Andrews was said to have conducted a marriage ceremony for the couple in which the princely sum of £365 had changed hands.

Ted Greeno's investigation into the Frith Street acquittal put a lot more pressure on Jack Spot. Spot was in an angry mood when, one day, he returned to Hyde Park Mansions and was asked by reporters what he thought about the inquiry. Spot snarled: 'Leave me alone. I've nothing to say.'

Reporters remained outside Hyde Park Mansions twenty-four hours a day. When Rita got her sister Sadie to take the children to Dublin, they were even followed by reporters to Paddington station. In Dublin, another pack of reporters were waiting for them. After four days, Rita went to Dublin to bring the children back. When she got to Ireland she found her youngest daughter, Marion, was ill and had to take her to hospital for injections. Then older daughter Rachel had an accident and went to hospital with concussion.

On 29 September, the *Daily Sketch* newspaper announced to its readers that it had concluded a 'full investigation into the Jack Spot affair'. The paper continued: 'The investigation has been carried out non-stop, day and night, for seventy-two hours. This newspaper has uncovered a sensational new situation, which is being reported to the authorities today.'

The paper demanded swift and fearless action after it revealed to the world what everyone had known for at least five years: that Spot and his gang were running the race-tracks up and down the country. The *Daily Sketch* claimed their findings would help allay public fears following the acquittal of Spot and Dimes.

Certain Fleet Street newspapers were incensed that people like Jack Spot and Billy Hill had been allowed to thrive and then boast of their crimes in the pages of rival newspapers. Newspapers who'd failed to secure the villains' exclusive stories were trying to turn the case into a moral crusade. There were also demands for more arrests following the internal investigation by Ted Greeno at Scotland Yard.

Meanwhile, self-styled king of Fleet Street, Duncan Webb, continued his obsessive campaign against Spot by writing an article in the *Sunday People* with the headline: TINPOT TYRANT WAS 'TRIED' BY HIS OWN MOB. Webb claimed Spot was on the run from his own mob. He also reported that Spot had been tried in his absence and the other thugs had passed judgement. 'It was decided to tell Spot to get out of London – and stay out.' Then, really sticking the knife in, Webb went on: 'The mob has discovered what I had known for years – that Spot is a poseur who had got away with it by boasting.'

Webb even recalled to his readers how Spot had asked him to

pen his life story just before Spot attacked him in the West End a year earlier. 'But the story I got from Jack Spot was not the facts as I knew them. I refused to write anything about him.'

The fact that Billy Hill had his fingerprints all over the article became crystal clear when Webb added: 'Billy Hill has earned his position as London's Gangster Boss, and by the sheer force of his personality he has kept the peace in the underworld and seen fair play.' Spot was once again furious about an article written by that 'toe rag' Duncan Webb and inspired by Billy Hill.

By the end of September, gossip was rife in Soho that other mobs were planning to take the place of Jack Spot and his boys. Many of the new faces hung out at the Granada coffee bar, in Berwick Street, where they also happened to demand money with menaces from the owners. Old habits died hard.

15

BANG TO RIGHTS

On the last Friday of September 1955, Jack Spot left his flat at Hyde Park Mansions sparking a flurry of ludicrous newspaper headlines, summed up by that afternoon's *Evening Standard*: JACK SPOT MYSTERY DEEPENS. But behind the fun and games lay a serious problem for Spot. He knew that it would only be a matter of days before Scotland Yard came knocking with some conclusive evidence about the background of at least two of the witnesses at his recent trial.

Spot realised he was now considered the grand old man of the underworld. Certainly, he'd mellowed since his early days, although he remained immaculately groomed and well tailored, usually wearing a brown suit, brown fedora hat and his trademark handmade shoes. Meanwhile Billy Hill – although slightly older – was still considered the young upstart. Scotland Yard detective Nipper Read described him as 'short, slim, and with hair greased and pasted back, looking every inch a spiv of the 1950s'.

The day after Spot's departure from his flat, on Saturday 1 October, the *Daily Sketch* Crime Squad produced a story headlined: WHERE IS SPOT? 2AM MYSTERY AT FLAT. The *Daily Sketch* reported: 'Jack Spot left his London flat at 7.40 a.m. yesterday for the first time since Monday. At 2 a.m. today he had not returned. A young man with an Irish accent, who appeared to be the only occupant, said that Jack Spot's wife Rita Comer was not there either.'

The next day, Spot was back in residence at Hyde Park Mansions claiming he'd been at home all the time. He emerged with Moisha and Sonny escorting him as hoards of reporters tried to grab a quote while he walked along Cabbell Street towards the Edgware Road.

That afternoon, Spot stepped on to the tiny balcony of the fifth-floor flat, his broad shoulders hunched under his braces and leaned on the railings while waving to his adoring public waiting on the street below. Spot stood sniffing the air in the bright afternoon sun. Just across the street, at Edgware Road tube station, newspaper bills still screamed out about the mystery of his 'disappearance'; yet, here he was trying to prove to his rivals that he wasn't running.

After a few moments, Rita joined him on the balcony, dressed in a light brown skirt and white blouse. She casually slipped her arm in his and looked down at the reporters, pointing them out to her husband. Spot focused on one friendly Fleet Street face. Rita shook her head violently – she hated most reporters by this stage. Spot ignored her and moments later turned and went back into his flat with his wife behind him.

A few minutes later, that same journalist climbed the seventy-eight red-carpeted stairs to the Spot home. The locked-doors-and-secret-knock routine of just one week earlier had been dropped. Chimes pealed inside the flat as the hack rang the doorbell.

Then Rita's voice came through the frosted glass. 'Who is it and what do you want?'

'I'd like to speak to Mr Comer, please.'

The door opened. Pale-faced Rita, now wearing a black housecoat, asked what the reporter wanted.

'Is your husband here?' he responded.

'Of course he is,' she shouted. 'You've just seen us from the street.'

Then the door slammed shut. A few minutes later, Rita left the apartment block. Fifteen minutes afterwards, noted reporters, she returned. And so their surveillance went on.

At about 4.30 p.m., Rita left the flat again wearing a black coat with a deep fur collar. With her was an older, grey-haired woman. The two women walked towards the Edgware Road and then disappeared amongst a crowd of Sunday-market shoppers.

Over in Dublin, Jack Spot's sisters-in-law, Sadie and Carmel Molloy, denied to reporters that Rita's two young children had arrived to stay with them, even though they were happily playing inside Sadie's home in Townsend Street, in the centre of the city.

Meanwhile, detectives visited Brixton Prison where Spot had been earlier held on remand, and interviewed warders and staff who'd been in contact with Spot. They wanted to find anyone who'd swear they had overheard Spot giving instructions to bribe Reverend Basil Andrews.

By now, Rita was close to buckling under the pressure. Newspapers stalked her every movement and there was a real danger she might now be implicated in persuading Andrews to give evidence. Spot hoped that with the two children in Ireland, things might calm down. 'But the reporters were like bloodhounds,' Spot later explained. 'It was impossible to shake them off. They followed us every inch of the way.'

Spot then persuaded Rita to join the kids in Dublin and she quietly slipped out of Hyde Park Mansions one night in early October. Spot believed he was better off handling the flak in London without his family. But before Rita had even got to Heathrow Airport, Fleet Street was on her tail. On the plane, a reporter snatched a few quotes off her, which she later denied.

Then Jack Spot called up his Fleet Street friend Vic Sims on the *Sunday Chronicle* from a 'secret address somewhere on the Edgware Road'. He told Sims: 'I've been so pestered by people calling at my flat that I have had to leave. I've nothing to hide – I never had. It's all lies that I'm thinking of leaving the country.'

Spot then conceded to Sims that his reign as king of the underworld really was over. 'As soon as I was taken to Brixton prison I knew that I was finished. From messages I received from the outside I learned that men I had called my friends for years were deserting me in scores. I decided then and there to finish with the game. Then when I was in the dock at the Old Bailey I looked up to the public gallery and saw a man sneering at me. A few minutes before he had been my friend. I felt like spitting in his face. Yes, I think you can call me the last gangster. Ruthless men think they are now in a position to dominate London's underworld. Most of them have served long terms in prison. Unless the police act quickly, gang warfare on a large scale will soon break out both in London and the provincial cities. For the past ten years, while I was the acknowledged boss of the racetracks, all was peace and quiet. Now anything is likely to happen.'

In Dublin, Rita's sister Carmel Malloy denied to reporters that Rita was hiding in Ireland, even though she'd been shadowed all the way there by Fleet Street reporters. Carmel also strongly defended Spot: 'He's a good man. Not one of you is fit enough to lick his boots,' she said. Just then, the hacks came under fire from a hail of stones thrown by kids from the balconies of the surrounding blocks of council flats.

♪   ♪   ♪

Elsewhere, old enemies were coming out of the woodwork. Bookie Harry White spat on the floor of a Holborn club, turned to a reporter and said: 'That's how frightened we are of Jack Spot and his men now . . . he hasn't got five men he can rely on to stand at his back.' White and Spot had been sworn enemies ever since their battle in the West End a couple of years earlier. White, who still had a razor scar across the top of his scalp from Spot's blade, also spilled the beans about Spot's protection rackets and his criminal dealings on the racetrack.

Meanwhile, Reverend Basil Andrews' relationship with the *Daily Sketch* had become so close that when Scotland Yard decided to interview him a second time, they had to make a request to the *Daily Sketch* Crime-Squad team for permission. An appointment was fixed at the office of Andrews' newly appointed solicitor.

Fifty minutes beforehand, detectives drove in a red Flying Squad car to the City-square offices of the solicitor and took up positions watching all approaches.

At 4.32 p.m., Detective Superintendent Bert Sparkes and Detective Inspector Eric Shepherd entered the building by a back alley and hurried into the solicitor's office. The brown shutters across the windows were slammed shut and Andrews was grilled. Points he made in his first statement were checked against evidence gathered from underworld sources. Andrews was then shown photographs and positively identified two men and a woman. None of the people mentioned in his statement had yet been interviewed, but detectives were watching the suspects day and night while minor holding charges were being prepared. Three other men were also named by Andrews, but police knew it was highly unlikely they would also be brought to trial because of a lack of evidence.

On 6 October 1955, Jack Spot travelled by the mail boat to Dun Laoghaire, Dublin. Gone was the familiar fedora hat and, in its place, he wore a flat cap. Spot took a taxi to Dublin's Westland Row station where he switched to another cab after meeting Rita. City cabbie Christopher Hogan recalled that the couple did not utter a word of conversation during the trip. The couple eventually decamped at a house in the suburbs where Spot was reunited with his two young daughters.

At 8 a.m. on 7 October 1955, Detective Chief Inspector John Mannings visited the home of Polish war hero Christopher Glinski in Kendal Street, Paddington. Mannings told Glinski he was taking him to West End Central police station, to be put up for identification in connection with the Spot/Dimes trial.

After being cautioned, Glinski asked for his solicitor to be called before leaving his home. Chief Inspector Mannings recalled: 'While Glinski was shaving, I stood quite close to him, and on the mantelpiece I saw a newspaper cutting from the *Daily Telegraph* headed: HOME OFFICE CALL FOR JACK SPOT REPORT.

Glinski spotted Mannings looking at the cutting and said: 'That won't prove I committed perjury, and everyone knows what you're after. Look, the trial is over. I never talked about the evidence of the parson and nobody can prove that I did.' Glinski then let slip that he suspected Spot's pal Hubby Distelmen of grassing him up. 'It must be him because he's the only one who knows about me going to Comer's flat. I will still beat you. I refuse to be put up. Whatever you write down I won't sign it.' At the police station, Glinski was identified by a woman who said she saw him at Hyde Park Mansions before the trial. Glinski had insisted at the original trial that he'd never visited Spot's apartment.

Still in Dublin, Spot heard from sources that the police now had Andrews and Glinski on side and had even offered them immunity from prosecution in exchange for their evidence. Then Albert Dimes decided to tell his side of the story to *Sunday People* crime reporter Duncan Webb. Dimes insisted he was nothing more than a bookmaker 'who unwittingly led the revolt against Spot and his gang who'd been trying to bleed us white. We bookmakers were showing Spot that we were not afraid of him. So in an effort to show his so-called power, he decided to "fix" me – with a stiletto.'

Then in a deliberate attempt to wind up his arch-enemy, Dimes told Webb: 'It was Spot's last fling to try to impress the Underworld with his power – so that he could make a come-back. But Spot chose wrongly. He knew I was no fighting man, so he thought I would take it and not hit back. I didn't take it.'

Dimes insisted: 'The real mobsters of the underworld despised Spot. They said he was no real criminal, but just a cheap slasher.' Dimes said Spot had made it impossible for small bookmakers like Dimes to make a living.

But the most damning accusation came when Dimes claimed Spot was a police informer. 'The Underworld was shocked. The "boys" have a code of their own, and the first rule is that no gangster must inform to the police against another, still less give evidence against him.'

Jack Spot was furious with the article, even though it was obvious Billy Hill had planted it with his old pal Duncan Webb.

Spot told one friend: 'It's all a pack of fuckin' lies. It makes me look like a right prat.'

Spot was powerless to do anything about the Dimes article. 'He couldn't exactly sue for libel, could he?' one old wag said at the time. Accused of being a squealer was the ultimate insult to Jack Spot. That name started ringing over and over again inside Spot's brain:

DIMES

DIMES

DIMES

DIMES

§   §   §

Then Jack Spot heard in Dublin that Scotland Yard wouldn't be making him stand trial again on any count arising out of the Frith Street trial. Although there was enough evidence to support the perjury charges, detectives had to prove the fight with Dimes had actually happened. This would have been tantamount to a rehearing of the original case. So they switched their attentions to Rita and Spot's associates, whom they believed had been involved in a conspiracy to get Spot acquitted through illegal means.

Spot was under pressure to return to London from Dublin for other reasons; he needed to collect money from his few remaining criminal enterprises. He feared he might be lured into a trap but he had no real choice in the matter. On 18 October, Spot and Rita returned to their Hyde Park Mansions flat. Spot was dressed in a blue pinstriped suit with a grey felt hat pulled over his right eye; they were accompanied by another woman. A few minutes after entering the flat, Rita reluctantly opened the door to waiting pressmen: 'We've been here all the time. We never went to Dublin,' her dark green eyes flashed. 'It's absolute nonsense. We haven't been anywhere and we intend staying right here.'

Rita, standing in her stockinged feet, claimed she and her husband had just been to visit her sister Carmel in hospital. But where was Spot? She looked over her shoulder. 'He won't talk to you. He's just gone to bed.' However Rita did admit the children were away 'because there have been so many callers'.

Fleet Street remained camped outside Hyde Park Mansions day and night, and newspapers openly reported that Reverend Andrews had been bribed to give false testimony in court. The net was closing and Spot now realised that Scotland Yard were after his wife and associates. Within twenty-four hours, Rita was sent back to Dublin to see the children again after Spot was tipped off that Scotland Yard were about to swoop.

The following day, investigators obtained three warrants at Bow Street Magistrate's Court before booking flights to Dublin for Scotland Yard's Detective Sergeant Shirley Becke and Detective Inspector Eric Shepherd. The main warrant charged Rita with conspiracy.

At 1.00 a.m. on 21 October 1955, DS Becke was accompanied by DS Frank Carey of Dublin CID to the Townsend Street home of Rita's sister Sadie. They had to knock very hard to get a response. Eventually DS Becke was allowed in and she told Rita to get dressed. When she heard the charges she replied: 'Conspiracy? How many am I supposed to have conspired with?' She kissed her sister goodbye before she left in a squad car handcuffed to DS Becke. Rita was wearing a black coat, a fawn woollen frock, and had a blue scarf over her head. The children remained in the house, still fast asleep.

Within half an hour, Rita was locked in a cell at the Bridewell Detention Prison. The following day she was taken by police to Dublin Airport, where she was escorted onto an Aer Lingus flight under the name of Mrs Brown. On the flight back to England, Rita told DI Eric Shepherd: 'I suppose this means the Old Bailey all over again, with me this time, instead of Jack. Moisha and the others said the old parson would give evidence for a few quid.'

At London Airport, one of the officers held Rita's arm as she was led from the plane as it stood on the tarmac. Chief Inspector Charles Allen of Special Branch was there to meet them. Minutes later, Rita was driven off at high speed in a black squad car and taken to Bow Street police station. Bail for Rita was refused after police put up an objection that she might abscond and return to Ireland. Spot was furious because now she'd be parted from her beloved children.

♪ ♪ ♪

As soon as Superintendent Herbert Sparks got a phone call from his officers, saying Rita was back in the country, he headed over to Moisha Blueball's home in Gore Road, Hackney. As he knocked on the door, a window opened and a voice asked: 'Who is it?' Sparks replied: 'A friend.' Then the door was opened. Sparks told Moisha to stand at the back of the room and not to move while he opened drawers and took out papers and photographs. Sparks took a telephone notebook and papers, before he turned to Moisha and said: 'Get your thinking cap on, son. We've picked up Mrs Comer.' Moisha asked Sparks: 'How many others have you nicked? They say you can't do Jackie again.' When Moisha was told this could not be discussed, he said: 'Don't be silly, Mr Sparks. What about the old fool that shopped us? It was all in the papers.'

An hour after Moisha Blueball's arrest and incarceration at West End Central police station in Savile Row, Tall Pat MacDonough, of Berkeley Street, Marylebone, was also nicked by Sparks. Within minutes, Tall Pat was singing his head off: 'I didn't think I would be involved in a state case. After all, I didn't give evidence. I felt sorry for Mrs Comer. I daren't open up. You understand, Mr Sparks, there are too many people involved. I just daren't. I have not had a penny piece out of this. I regret the day I ever met Father Andrews.'

Later that same day, Sonny the Yank was arrested at his Aldgate home. He told Sparks: 'If I'm picked out, I'm not going to take it lying down. I was only there under the Old Pals Act. I was only looking on, making the tea. I will cream my head off in the witness box.'

The following day the *Daily Mirror* ran a vast banner headline: 'SONNY THE YANK' IS ARRESTED. As one retired copper later noted: 'These fellows were being built up into movie stars. I was astounded by how much publicity they generated.'

The next day all four: Rita, Moisha, Sonny the Yank and Tall Pat MacDonough, appeared in court charged with conspiring to pervert the course of justice. Spot immediately began collecting money in the East End for the cost of Rita's defence, which, it was estimated, would be at least £6000. Spot also claimed he was about to visit Dublin to begin negotiating for a caff in Grafton Street. There were also rumours he was going into the racing game in Ireland once Rita was home safely.

Meanwhile, Fleet Street continued its campaign against organised crime in London. The public's feelings about such matters were at a high pitch of indignation and the authorities felt under immense pressure to prove they were trying to clean up the capital.

Just before the conspiracy trial was due to start on 15 November 1955, Billy Hill poured further salt on Jack Spot's wounded pride by holding a high-profile launch for his autobiography entitled *Boss of Britain's Underworld*, ghost-written by Duncan Webb. Spot hadn't even realised Hill was preparing a book, which was also serialised by Webb in the *Sunday People*. It was very similar to the previous series of articles written by Webb in the *Sunday People* more than a year earlier.

Hill and Webb hosted a lavish launch party at Gennaro's Restaurant in Soho to encourage mass-media coverage for the book. The *Daily Sketch* ran a picture story on page one the following day: SOHO GANG BOSS NO.1 SCANDAL. PARTY COCKS A SNOOK AT THE POLICE. The first sentence read: 'There has been nothing like it since the days of Al Capone. It was the most insolent gesture the underworld has ever made.' The *Daily Mail* reproduced the invitation sent to its reporter and concluded with a comment: 'A sorry day, I feel, when a gangster's book justifies a gilt-edged invitation.'

Spot read with irritation when the *Daily Express*'s William

Hickey gossip column described Hill as courteous and intelligent. Spot had once again lost the publicity battle. He lacked Billy Hill's barefaced cheek and, of course, he didn't have a book to promote. Billy Hill, the famous author, even announced to the press at his book's launch party that it was he rather than Spot who'd broken the power of the Harry White mob. Hill projected himself as an uncompromising and unapologetic criminal and the public seemed to like him for it.

The *Daily Mirror* coverage of the launch was summed up by the headline: EX-GANGSTER THROWS AN AMAZING PARTY. Below was printed a photo of Billy Hill enthusiastically kissing London socialite Lady Docker while her husband Sir Bernard looked on adoringly. In the *Sunday Express*, cartoonist Giles turned the Dockers presence at the Hill party into a Damon Runyon-style cartoon. The ever-so-posh Dockers later claimed they'd attended the party without realising 'criminal' Billy Hill would be present. They insisted they thought the event was being hosted by Hill's ghostwriter, Duncan Webb.

Jack Spot got hold of an advance copy of the book and 'went ballistic' when he read the following excerpt: 'If you stand in any part of Soho at any hour of the day or night you will be spotted by at least six of my men. Walk a mile in any direction and you will pass a dozen. This is the centre of my empire, the district from which I rule the underworld of Britain. Walk up Shaftesbury Avenue and ask the first gangster you see who rules the underworld. If you don't know any, then ask a copper. He'll tell you that Billy Hill is the guv'nor.'

Hill referred to Spot as a character called 'Jack Delight' (he never called Spot by his real name throughout the book, on the legal advice of his publisher). Hill wrote: 'To give him his due he could have a fight, that Jack Delight. I had to carve him to ribbons before he swallowed it. Then he broke all our codes by going to the law. He had to be given a talking to.' Spot feared everyone in Soho would be even more convinced he was a grass, a police informant.

Hill even claimed in his book that he'd stopped one pair of rival gangsters from killing each other by buying them a drink. He also told how champion jockey Sir Gordon Richards's home was robbed and it was Hill who had got all his personal belongings returned. He also wrote of a far-fetched plot of his, to kidnap the disposed Sultan of Morocco from exile in Madagascar and return him to Tangier. The only good news for Spot was Hill's proclamation that he was planning to retire sooner rather than later. 'I'm on the way out. By the time you're approaching the middle forties it's time to think of retiring. Villainry and crime are a young man's game.'

Throughout the book, Hill threw down the gauntlet to Jack Spot: 'I am the gangster boss of London, Britain's Public Enemy No.1, if you like. The undisputed king of the underworld. Yes, I ruled the asphalt jungle of Soho as 'Scarface' Al Capone did years ago in Chicago. My word is law in the jungle. Today there isn't a single crook or hoodlum with the guts to challenge it. Those who did cross my path when I was battling my way to the top, all bear the same ugly trademark a long, livid chiv scar across the face.'

One of the few reporters on Jack Spot's side, besides Vic Sims, was Gerry Byrne of the *Sunday Chronicle*. He'd written judicial comments about Hill being 'a miserable little character' and ran stories about how Hill had allegedly poisoned the pigeons of Trafalgar Square and put green ink in the fountains. Hill had then got his kid brother a job as a Trafalgar Square photographer, after moving in him and five thugs to operate the pitch. Gerry Byrne's black Morris saloon was systematically wrecked by vandals shortly after he wrote the articles.

Scotland Yard detective Bert Wickstead and many of his colleagues were outraged that Spot and Hill could find public platforms with such ease. He summed it up thus: 'They dropped their razors and picked up their pens to be the first to rush into print and proclaim themselves "Gangster King of Soho".' Wickstead recalled: 'These villains write books, give press receptions and, thumping their wheezy chests, give long interviews to the reporters telling how they rose to power. Having achieved their immunity from the law by a series of false alibis, bought witnesses, intimidation and fear. One should not be hoodwinked by the vapourings of these mean bullies who, for forty years, have fashioned their own laws in the belief that they are beyond the pale of the ordinary criminal code.'

What further infuriated officers like Wickstead was that the police knew only too well that Hill and Spot had secretly financed numerous robberies that endangered citizens on the streets of London. These included post-office van hold-ups, bank heists and even a number of raids in the Hatton Garden jewellery district. Yet here they were, brazenly living off the fame of their crimes.

Meanwhile, Spot's few remaining friends urged him to quit the underworld while he still had a chance. But Spot first had to get Rita through her trial. He felt guilty about her involvement and was prepared to do anything to ensure she didn't get a prison sentence.

16
SELF DEFENCE

Rita found herself sharing a cell with a shoplifter in Holloway Prison, North London. Spot tried to ease her hardship by having food and flowers delivered to jail, which was allowed because she was still awaiting her trial and had not been found guilty of any crime. Rita was, however, refused permission to share the gifts with other prisoners, and she later said this was a shame because she made two or three good friends in jail. As usual, she tried to put on a brave face. Rita later recalled: 'But all the time my heart was aching for my two babies. I lost two stone in weight pining for them. But the prison authorities did their best for me.'

Rita arrived for the first day of her Old Bailey trial, on 2 November 1955, immaculately dressed in an expensive designer outfit; she looked like actress Margaret Lockwood in *The Wicked Lady*. She played the loyal, devoted wife to perfection – but then Rita didn't have to act the part. Also in the dock were Tall Pat Mac-Donough, Sonny the Yank and Moisha Blueball. All were accused of conspiring to defeat the course of justice by getting Reverend Basil Andrews to give false evidence at Spot's earlier trial.

Solicitor General Sir Harry Hylton-Foster, QC, described the case as 'a sordid story of an interference with justice in a civilised country'. Hylton-Foster told the court it was imperative for Spot to establish that Dimes was the aggressor. That's why Reverend Andrews had been wheeled out. 'He is very old, and of an age when some of us may hope to be free from the temptations of this world,' Hylton-Foster told the court. 'He was, to the knowledge of MacDonough, very short of money indeed, and was, in his view, "an old villain".'

Earlier statements made by the accused, including Rita, were read out to the court. Each admitted knowledge to police investigators of Reverend Basil Andrews, although Rita later strongly denied ever having made such a statement.

Hylton-Foster told the court: 'One cannot help but feel a certain sympathy for a man of eighty-eight, left to face the world upon an income of fifty-five shillings a week – a man of education and refinement, of, I suppose, a fairly good upbringing. It is not merely the question of committing perjury for money but other things: borrowing money right and left, not only from the rich or the titled, the well-known, or actors or household names, but sometimes going and telling the tale to fellow clergymen who spare some money so that Andrews can live at the Mostyn or Claridge's Hotel and take a flat above his means.'

Solicitor-General Hylton-Foster then outlined how, the week before the Spot trial, on Tuesday 13 September, Andrews had met MacDonough at the Cumberland Hotel, in Marble Arch. He explained how, the next morning, Andrews was picked up by a car at his hotel in Inverness Terrace and driven to Rita's flat, where several people were present. 'In Mr Andrews' words, "people sort of drifted in". There were, in fact, four or five men at one stage, in addition to Mrs Comer. Mr Andrews was asked to say he was passing through Soho and witnessed a fight. The fight was described to him. He was asked to say it was the dark man who had the knife – that would have been Dimes – and struck Comer.'

Then the court heard how Andrews was given a one-pound note, for a taxi home. The next day, by arrangement, he again went to Hyde Park Mansions, where the suggestions of the previous day were confirmed and Andrews was given more cash.

Reverend Andrews might have been eighty-eight years old, but he still refused a chair when it came to giving evidence in the witness box at the Old Bailey. QCs even had to raise their voices because of the parson's deafness. One asked him if he had scrounged from people. Andrews didn't understand the word 'scrounge'. The counsel repeated it again. He shouted it. Finally he spelt it. Andrews then replied: 'I don't know what it means.' Andrews impressed all who saw and heard him at the Old Bailey. But his 'deafness' was the deftest touch. As one barrister explained: 'The subtle tones of cross-examination, the change of inflexion, the hint of sarcasm, of disbelief, are dealt a shattering blow when the man in the witness box, instead of blanching with fear, cocks one hand to his ear and says, "Eh?"'

The elderly cleric confirmed in court that he did know the defendants. Asked how Moisha Blueball and Sonny the Yank had reacted when MacDonough told them about his offer to give evidence, Andrews replied: 'They seemed to be delighted. They expressed their pleasure and relief that somebody was found who would come forward and help them, and they made rather a fuss of me.'

'What form did the fuss take?' asked prosecutor Seaton.

'Oh shaking of hands and saying, "How splendid!" and all that sort of thing . . . I can't tell you the exact words.'

The judge asked Andrews if he thought Rita knew why he visited the Spot apartment at Hyde Park Mansions.

'I think she did,' he replied.

'What did she say?'

'She said she was so pleased to see me, and it would be a good thing if I could help her in any way to have her husband released or freed.'

'What else was said?' asked prosecutor Seaton.

'I cannot really remember. You see, I am an old man. I am eighty-eight. My memory is not so good as it was.'

As Andrews spoke, Rita, pale-faced, raven-haired, stared fixedly at the lights in the ceiling of the court.

Andrews' most repeated answer was a weary, 'I don't remember.' He also showed flashes of anger, too. When defence QC David Weitzman called him a 'self-confessed liar' he straightened up in the box and shouted: 'Your object is to condemn me.' Andrews also raised his voice when it was suggested he'd been seen drinking at a bar with a dark-haired woman; and then that he frequented an inn, often drinking five pints of beer in one session. The churchman countered that charge angrily: 'I never drink beer. It gives me rheumatism.' Andrews' evidence provoked many outbursts of laughter –which he never joined in with.

Facing Weitzmen, Andrews said: 'It is awful having your sins thrown at you after you have repented them. You don't believe in repentance do you? Even the penitent thief on the cross was pardoned. I have no pardon. I have come here . . . to speak the truth, the whole truth and nothing but the truth. In the silence of the night, it was brought to my mind the sin I had committed and the wickedness I had done, and the harm I had caused by acting as I had done.'

When Andrews was asked where he'd stayed the previous night. He replied: 'Do I have to tell? I have been told that if I am seen by any of the gang I shall have my throat cut.' Then it was suggested in court that the *Daily Sketch* was 'paying his hotel bill to induce him to rig the evidence he gave'. Andrews would only concede that, within a day of publication in the *Daily Sketch* of his 'I am not a perjurer' letter, he went to police and told a different story.

Rita's counsel, 'Khaki' Marshall, said: 'I am not suggesting the *Daily Sketch* asked him to do that. He is cunning enough, crafty enough, to realise that position, and it was worth his while to change his story and say that his first story was untrue. It was not a case of £50. It was a case of considerably more. We know that, since then, he has been moved about and his hotel bills have been paid by the *Daily Sketch*.' Prosecutor Hylton-Foster immediately objected, calling it a 'lunatic proposition' that Andrews had made up being paid by Spot's associates purely to sell his story to the *Daily Sketch*.

Andrews claimed he had repented, and condemned his lying on behalf of Spot as 'committing a sin in the eyes of God'. He added: 'I may say, though I don't like uttering a word which could be considered cant or hypocrisy, that I have always asked God to forgive me, though I can never forgive myself.' Then Anthony Marlowe, QC for Sonny the Yank, asked the churchman to fix a date for his repentance.

'How soon after the Comer trial did you repent?'

'You mean when did I come to my senses?' asked Andrews. 'It was in the still watches of the night.'

'Which night?'

'I cannot tell you that. Have you ever heard of a sudden conversion?'

'Indeed I have and I am asking when it took place?'

'I cannot tell you.'

'Was it a week after?'

'It might happen in an instant.'

'Can you tell us roughly? Did this conversion in the still watches of the night come in September or October?'

'I daresay. I don't know.'

'We might take it, then, that after you had this vision you have been telling the truth?'

'Yes, exactly.'

'Then this vision on the still watches of the night came before November 2?'

'I suppose so. I am fogged over dates.'

Amid laughter, Marlowe said quietly: 'So am I and I want to get you unfogged.'

When Mr Marshall, QC for Rita, rose to question Andrews, there was an air of expectancy. He started by saying to Andrews: 'You must be very tired of being asked questions?' Andrews bellowed: 'What did you say?' Then added, 'I must say many people talk indistinctly.' Then Marshall spoke more slowly and loudly: 'I want to ask you, in particular, about some of the better things in your life; that would be a change wouldn't it?' 'It would indeed,' replied Andrews. 'It has been sordid up to now.'

'There was a time when you interested a very wealthy man in a down and out?' asked Marshall.

'I don't know what you are referring to,' responded Andrews.

'Do you remember it was a matter which arose at a funeral and the wealthy man was in the wine and spirit trade?'

'I remember the whole of that. Has it anything to do with this case?'

'The fact was that at one stage of your life you obtained for a down-and-out a job which lasted something like fifteen or twenty years.'

'I was delighted at it because nothing gives me more pleasure than to help a lame dog over a stile. Is there anything wrong in that?'

'You must not get angry with me yet.'

'I am not getting angry with you. But I feel rather strongly that whatever I say has a doubtful interpretation put on it. I suppose you and other people here will think I was asking for myself. I never received anything.'

'You can be sure I am not criticising you for this. You are rather surprised I know something about this?'

'I am, but very glad.'

Marshall then switched tack: 'Let me put another personal matter: You are in the habit of taking one main meal a day?'

'Yes.'

'You like also and, believe me, I am not criticising, to have a bottle of your favourite wine with it?'

'I don't drink wine much.'

'But you like it.'

'I have not got a favourite wine; I don't know what it is.'

Silence swept the courtroom for a few seconds then Marshall asked Andrews if an ancestor had been Bishop Andrews of London.

'I did have, but I don't want to boast about it,' responded Andrews.

Then Marshall got to the point: 'You see, Mr Andrews, all these matters are matters that could only have come in the first place from you. I am under instructions to put to you that in conversation with Mrs Comer the first time you met you told her of these matters.'

Andrews asked bemusedly: 'Did I? I can't imagine I did. But if she said I did I suppose it is true.' The elderly, repenting, gambling clergyman versus the Soho gangsters was a magical recipe for Fleet Street. As they say in newspapers, this one was destined to run and run.

17

ROLL UP, ROLL UP

Jack Spot monitored the court proceedings through newspapers and radio. He was worried about Reverend Basil Andrews' testimony and told one friend: 'Right then, if I could have wrapped my fingers around his scrawny neck, I would have choked him to death coldly and deliberately and with the full knowledge of the penalty I'd have to pay for so doing.'

At the Old Bailey, Andrews finally stepped down after giving seven-and-a-half hours of testimony. Then Superintendent Herbert Sparks appeared in the witness box. He was asked about 'the outcry in the press' following the September trials of Jack Spot and Albert Dimes. Fleet Street had blatantly inferred that witnesses had given false testimony and there had even been suggestions the jury was nobbled. Sparks replied: 'Articles were written to that effect, but the police do not bother about articles in the press.'

Then came defendant Moisha Blueball, who described himself as a bookmaker, married, with an eighteen-year-old daughter. Moisha told the court he visited Hyde Park Mansions once every three or four weeks and had been present when Spot was originally arrested. Moisha denied in court that when he was driven to West End Central police station, following his own arrest, he had told one detective: 'You can't do Jackie again.' He also denied telling police: 'He must have told you who was at the flat. You have only got his word for it . . . Glinski's schtum.'

Moisha told the court that 'schtum' was a Yiddish word for

'quiet'. He then explained: 'Unfortunately, I suffer from a little Jewish persecution complex, and I would not say that word in the car, one Jewish man amongst three Gentiles, especially when I have never spoken to them in my life.' Moisha denied giving Reverend Andrews any money.

Next up was Spot's other lifelong pal, Sonny the Yank. He said he'd also known Spot since boyhood. His job was given as a donkey greaser – a driver or attendant of a ship's 'donkey' boiler, who works the winches. Sonny raised tearful laughter in court by taking his false teeth out while giving evidence, in his trademark Cockney with a Hollywood staccato, about a telephone call made by Rita to her solicitor. Then, with teeth in hand, he turned to Mr Justice Ormerod and said: 'I'm sorry to do this, sir.'

There was more laughter when Sonny was asked by Solicitor General Sir Harry Hylton-Foster, QC, if he was glad about Jack Spot's original acquittal. 'Yes, more than glad,' replied Sonny. 'There was plenty of Scotch about that day.' Again, the ushers had to call for silence in court.

Rita appeared in the witness stand wearing a tight-fitting black suit with silk, embroidered facings. She immediately denied any part in the alleged plot and then clasped her hands together in a prayer-like motion and looked appealingly across at her counsel. She even said she knew nothing of her husband's bookmaking business and had only been to Soho three times in her life.

Rita insisted she had only first heard of Reverend Andrews the night before Jack Spot's trial commenced, when Andrews turned up at Hyde Park Mansions. 'He talked a lot about himself. He said he was not a wealthy man and had only a small pension; he said after he had paid his rent he had only a very little left, sometimes about thirty shillings or three pounds.'

Rita told the court that, as Andrews was leaving the flat, she went into the bedroom and got him some money for a taxi. She said it was a couple of pounds. Testimony from others suggested it was as much as twenty-five pounds. Rita told the court she had been 'overjoyed' when Moisha Blueball called her on the telephone to say that Reverend Andrews was willing to give evidence on Spot's behalf. She insisted she should 'have been a little bit more clever' but she never even considered he might be trying to make some money.

Summing up, Ashe Lincoln, QC for MacDonough, described Reverend Andrews' evidence as: 'Like the curate's egg – good in parts and bad in parts.' He added: 'When an egg is bad in parts, it is safest to reject it all.' David Weitzman, QC for Moisha, told the court in his summing up: 'This is not a fair with a showman with a lucky dip who shouts: "Roll up, roll up, roll up," and you pick out any story you like.'

Anthony Marlowe, QC for Sonny the Yank, told the court: 'We have every reason to suppose now that the law was cheated of its victim. But it would be deplorable if, because that happened, because public opinion as expressed is the press howling for victims, the balance must be redressed by seeing that some of his friends are punished.'

Then it was Rita's counsel, Khaki Marshall's turn. 'This is probably one of the oldest problems that individuals face . . . the problem of conflicting loyalties. She must have been wracked with deep anxiety. She has already greatly suffered and you may well feel that here is a case of someone caught up in a stream of events that was too strong for her . . . a case which may well deserve your mercy and your pity.'

ƒ   ƒ   ƒ

At 7 a.m. on the last day of the trial, Jack Spot hurried out of Hyde Park Mansions to buy a newspaper. At 8 a.m. he drank a cup of coffee at a local caff and told one reporter: 'They're crucifying her. She's already done eight weeks in prison. She's ill.' Spot still insisted that neither he or his wife had any connection with Reverend Andrews: 'He was a pathetic sight in the witness box, and one which would have aroused pity if it were not that in his fumbling, doddering way he was accusing my wife and others of a crime that would bring them imprisonment. His evidence should have had no value whatsoever in a court of law.'

At 9 a.m. a restless and gloomy Jack Spot went to a local barber's shop. A nearby street-corner bookie was laying on odds of 4–1 that his wife would be acquitted. At 10 a.m. Spot went window shopping in the nearby Edgware Road, while pals patted him on the back and told him not to worry.

Back in the Old Bailey, Judge Mr Justice Ormerod was summing up the case. He told the jury that Reverend Basil Andrews was 'an accomplice and an avowed perjurer'. Of Rita the judge said: 'Although it may sound hard-hearted, I am bound to tell you that you must not be swayed by pity, by sympathy for her, much as she may very well need it.'

Then the judge laid into the press. 'Mrs Comer was apparently pestered night and day by representatives of the press. Of course, the press has not had an opportunity to reply to any criticism made. But you may think that if half of what she says is true about the way she was treated by them, they went far beyond the bounds of what anybody would regard as ordinary decency in this matter.'

At 11 a.m., a car took Jack Spot through Soho and past the shop where he and Albert Dimes had fought. At 12 noon, he arrived at a meeting in Aldgate. Two miles away – outside the Old Bailey – one of Spot's associates told waiting newsmen: 'Jack's not a bad boy. They're trying to get at him through his wife.'

At 1 p.m. Spot had a light lunch while his associates continued calling the Old Bailey to see what was happening. Forty minutes later Spot pulled up near the Old Bailey in his two-tone blue and cream Ford Zephyr. They stayed in the car.

At 2.09 p.m., the eleven men and one woman of the jury finally retired to consider their verdict. At 3.04 p.m., the jury returned with a question which was quickly answered. Rita looked on in a state of distress. She and the other accused had been allowed to remain in the court rather than be taken down to the cells below.

At 3.25 p.m., the jury announced they'd reached a unanimous

verdict: All four of the accused were found guilty. Rita's cheeks paled. She bit her lip. The others dipped their heads to the ground. Moisha twisted his fingers into his palms tensely. None of them looked at each other.

Outside a thumbs-down signal from a pal told Spot, waiting in the Zephyr, of the verdict. 'They can't do this to her,' he said. 'I love her.' Spot, the tough guy of Soho, then collapsed in floods of tears and sobbed: 'What can I do? What can I say?'

Spot then cursed British justice. To a bystander, he sobbed: 'You've got a wife to go home to, but now I've got nothing. My wife is going to prison. She's done nothing wrong. It's not justice to take her away from our two babies.'

Rita's suspense over her prison sentence lasted another fifteen minutes while QCs gave their mitigation speeches. Her counsel, Khaki Marshall, said: 'She has already greatly suffered . . . caught up in a stream of events too great for her. I commend her to your lordship's pity.'

Rita looked at the judge with an ashen and impassive expression on her face.

Then the judge announced: 'I realise that as the wife of Jack Comer you were strongly tempted. At the same time I cannot allow this offence to go unpunished. But Mrs Comer, I am not going to send you to prison.' He paused. 'Fined fifty pounds.'

Rita lowered her head and murmured: 'Thank you, my lord.'

But the other defendants were not so lucky. Moisha copped a two-year sentence, while Sonny and Tall Pat got one year each.

After the sentencing, Rita swayed in the dock. Then she walked down towards her counsel blowing her nose in a lace handkerchief. A minute later one of Spot's boys ran down Giltspur Street, arms waving wildly. The pal yelled: 'She's off Jack! It's a fifty quid fine.' Jack Spot tumbled from his car. His face was wet with tears.

Spot hugged a complete stranger who just happened to be walking by. Then his two friends seized him. One kissed his cheek. Spot shouted with joy. Suddenly his curses against 'British justice' had turned to public praise of it. It was 3.52 p.m.

Back in court, Moisha scowled and looked flushed as he left the dock to start his sentence. Moisha's only previous conviction had been after his arrest during the Cable Street riots alongside Spot. Sonny the Yank glared at the jury, tightened his lips, bowed to the judge, and went to the cells with a snicker of a smile. Tall Pat MacDonough, head bowed, followed him.

At 3.54 p.m., Jack Spot bounded up the marble steps to the Old Bailey, in his grey trilby hat. His overcoat hung open and two men marched alongside him. As he reached for the door handle, a policeman put out his arm and refused to let him in. There was an argument. 'This is Jack Spot,' said one of his henchmen. The policeman said he didn't care, the court was closed. An inspector arrived at the scene. 'This is Mr Comer, her husband,' said the second man. 'He wants to go in to meet her.'

Finally, Spot was allowed in and joined his wife's sister Carmel in the hallway. He said: 'Thank heavens the judge had a kind heart.' A minute later, Spot walked into Number One Court where Rita was talking to her counsel. He embraced and kissed her wildly then said: 'Come on, love. Let's go.' Rita insisted she paid her fine immediately so Spot took fifty pounds out of his wallet before sitting down on a nearby wooden bench. He told one reporter: 'Thank goodness this is all over. I'm going to take her straight home to the children. They're dying to see her. Thank God the judge had a soft heart.'

Rita emerged from the cells below, carrying a brown paper parcel under her arm, which contained the personal belongings she'd had with her during her incarceration. She now wore her favourite black swagger coat with a fur trim, and her make-up was fresh. She smiled and waved towards her husband and relatives. More kisses and hugs followed.

Spot then guided his wife out of the courtroom. Reporters rushed around them, but he brushed them aside. She buried her head in his shoulders. There was confusion at the main swing doors. Everyone was pushing. Spot and Rita just managed to squeeze through.

They walked down the main staircase as the wives and children of Moisha, Sonny and MacDonough were descending more slowly. Some were weeping. Spot then turned to Sonny's wife and said: 'I'm so sorry, dear.' Rita lent over and tried to hug Sonny's wife. She pushed her away and spat out just two words, 'Fuck off.'

Traditionally, Moisha and Sonny's families would be looked after by Spot while they were away. But they both knew that Spot was not as wealthy as he used to be and he'd be unlikely to give their families any money this time. They'd just taken the heat for getting him off the original charges and now his wife was walking free while they copped a long stretch inside. Nothing had gone according to plan.

ℐ   ℐ   ℐ

Rita and Spot stood on the pavement outside the Old Bailey, facing a crowd of at least two hundred. Spot told reporters he was quitting the racetracks and abdicating as boss of Soho. He said he was going to open a little caff and sell tea and buns. Police struggled to hold people back, and two men were knocked to the ground. Then the couple climbed into the back of the Zephyr, which headed off up Seacoal Lane. For the first time in living memory there was no Moisha or Sonny to protect them from hacks and hard men. As the couple drove back to Hyde Park Mansions, they talked eagerly about their future together – away from a life of crime. Spot said he'd changed his mind about moving to Dublin because it had so many connections with Billy Hill and other villains. Rita told Spot she was prepared to stay in England if they could find a house somewhere in the Sussex countryside. 'We'll be safer if anyone makes threats to kill us,' she said.

Spot went to bed early that night. Only a few weeks earlier, Moisha and Sonny had chorused: 'Justice had been done,' when they celebrated Spot's acquittal with champagne and chicken in Spot's flat. Back then, Rita had raised her glass of bubbly to Moisha and toasted: 'To the best friend anyone ever had.' Moisha, red-faced with embarrassment, sat in a chair grinning broadly, everyone slapped him on the back. Now he and Sonny were starting lengthy prison sentences connected to the same case.

The only legit callers at Hyde Park Mansions that evening were Tall Pat MacDonough's wife and daughter. They were allowed past a 'guard' of three porters at the flats' entrance only after Rita's sister, Carmel, had checked them out first. They stayed twenty minutes, during which time Spot made a donation to Tall Pat's 'fighting fund'.

Spot reckoned Rita's legal battle had cost him at least seven thousand pounds, and admitted to one journalist that it 'damn near ruined me, too'. But none of that mattered because he had his beloved Rita back home: 'I would do anything for Rita. She's proved herself a wonderful wife over and over.' His friends Sonny and Moisha no longer seemed to matter.

18
HOME SWEET HOME

That night Jack Spot awoke shivering. He thought he heard someone on the roof. He stayed in the freezing bed without moving for
a few seconds. Then another sound came from the sitting room.
As he got out of bed, he felt a draft rush around his legs. Creeping
through to the sitting room, he found the main window wide
open. That's strange, Spot thought to himself, I'm sure it wasn't
like that when I went to bed.

Outside, patches of mist swirled around Hyde Park Mansions
as the wind whistled lightly in the distance. Something stopped
Spot from going to the window and closing it. He felt the presence
of someone in the apartment. He glanced out of another, smaller
window but could only see a few feet because of the fog. Just then,
he heard movement on the roof again. Spot turned and ran back
into the bedroom. He grabbed the phone and dialed 999.

Within minutes, three dark-blue Wolsey squad cars had
screeched to a halt outside Hyde Park Mansions. Five uniformed
policemen and a detective examined the roof area. There was no
one there and they left after five minutes. But the incident confirmed to Spot that 'certain people' were after him. But then others
had paid an even heavier price for their part in the conspiracy
that had helped acquit him.

ß *ß* *ß*

A few days after the end of the trial, Billy Hill commissioned his young henchman Mad Frankie Fraser to hurt one or two of Spot's boys. Fraser was a typical hired hand: prepared to kill or maim anyone for the right fee. Within days, Fraser stabbed a boxer called Bobby Ramsey, who sometimes worked as a minder for Spot, just as Ramsey was entering a club in Crawford Street, Marylebone. Fraser recalled: 'He was with a brass who used to hang out in Gerrard Street. I cut my hand as I was stabbing him.' Moments after slinging the knife away, Fraser was arrested by police.

Fraser arrived at the police station at the same time as his injured victim Ramsey. Fraser insisted he'd been helping Ramsey instead of stabbing him. The prostitute backed his story and Fraser ended up being taken to hospital to have a few stitches in his own injured hand. Fraser later claimed that Billy Hill paid off a detective to ensure that he was never charged in connection with the knifing of Bobby Ramsey.

When Spot found out about the incident he decided to retaliate. 'If he'd done nothing, things would have all died down,' said Fraser. Spot persuaded his new strong-arm man, a young tearaway called Joey Cannon, to recruit three other men who were then given guns by Spot to shoot Billy Hill and Albert Dimes. So much for Spot's 'retirement'.

Every Sunday, Billy Hill had lunch in Kentish town with his ex-wife Aggie and their children. Spot instructed his team to make preparations to hit Hill outside the house. They then began boasting about the scheme in the West End. Hill and Dimes soon heard about it. They grabbed Spot's team and, as Frankie Fraser later recalled, 'gave them a slap, and explained the facts of life to them'. Joey Cannon and the other men bottled out and handed their weapons back to Spot, who knew big trouble now lay ahead.

Hill and Fraser held a meeting at Hill's flat in Barnes and decided to punish Jack Spot for daring to put together a hit team. Hill gave Fraser a shillelagh, a wooden stick traditionally made in Ireland, to use. Fraser recalled: 'Bill and Albert thought that, if I had a knife, I might get carried away and kill him. And I might have done because I think he deserved it, getting hold of those four boys and giving them guns.'

Spot got a tip that things were about to get very personal, so he went round to Paddington police station, pleading for protection, but the police refused to help because Spot didn't have enough evidence. Spot genuinely feared for his own and his family's safety. He'd also convinced himself that others were to blame for his own misfortunes. 'They were all to blame. All my friends. Even Blueball and Sonny! I'd known them since we were kids and all these years I'd looked after them. I dragged them up with me, put them on top when I was on top and gave them every opportunity. Sometimes I even prejudiced my own interests to give them a break. They were friends. I thought I could trust them.'

There were also other more practical problems on the horizon. Money was running out fast. The approaching new year of 1956 looked set to be a disaster. Spot later recalled: 'Those long weeks in prison awaiting trial had aged me. And those long, fretting weeks of waiting while Rita's fate hung in the balance had aged me even more.' Spot owed money everywhere. His one remaining Soho spieler in Dean Street was forced to close down. He tried to collect money owed to him by various people, while at the same time keeping his own creditors at bay. No more handmade suits, champagne and caviar.

But Fleet Street's obsession with Jack Spot continued despite his fall from power. On 9 December 1955, the *Daily Mail* caught Spot with a folded carrier bag under his arm, wearing a neatly pressed blue suit and a grey trilby, popping out to do some shopping near the family flat. The Mail reported that 'if he has abdicated as boss of Soho's underworld he looked like qualifying for the title of Perfect Husband'.

Other papers reported that Albert Dimes now insisted he wasn't after Spot's racing interests, even though he was negotiating with the Jockey Club over new regulations proposed for point-to-point meetings. Dimes claimed he'd been appointed by the bookmakers to represent them, and, in discussions with Colonel Blair, chief of the racecourse personnel, argued that the Jockey Club's plan to charge bookmakers £5 each for pitches was 'a liberty'.

Dimes also made a few bob when he was awarded £666 damages against a firm whose taxi collided in September, 1952, with a car in which he was a passenger. Lawyers even referred to the Frith Street affray, asking: 'At that time you were sufficiently well to stab Comer?' Dimes claimed in court his average earnings were in the region of £10 a week. He had also been fortunate enough not to pay income tax since 1951.

Mad Frankie Fraser later summed up Billy Hill's attitude towards Dimes: 'Bill was a manipulator, he was made that way. He was jealous of Albert although he would never admit it. Bill wasn't natural like Albert Dimes, although he could be a very charming man if it suited him. He was like a very good snooker player, thinking not of the next shot he's going to take, but of four or five shots after that. He would put people in brackets. "That Albert could be very useful to me, although I don't particularly like him and I'm a bit jealous. Nevertheless he's a good man and I'll keep him for a move or two ahead." Bill had a great brain; there's no two ways about it.'

There was further fallout from the Spot/Hill feud when, in early 1956, a small-time villain called Tommy Smithson was shot dead in a brothel in Maida Vale. Smithson's speciality was demanding protection money from strip clubs, Maltese pimps and spielers. He'd even been rash enough to try and muscle in on some of Billy Hill's empire and had twice been severely beaten for his troubles. Many saw his death as a warning sign from Billy Hill to Spot never to put together another heavy mob. Smithson also helped foster the up-and-coming Kray twins, even helping them set up in a nightclub in Hackney. Smithson was assassinated by a gunman whose two accomplices waited in a car outside the brothel; a Maltese pimp was later arrested for the hit. Fleet Street was appalled by the Smithson shooting and started exerting pressure on the Government to rescind plans to abolish the death penalty. Newspapers described the slaying as, 'an almost exact copy of the movies'.

Billy Hill and the Krays brazenly turned up for Tommy Smithson's funeral. Hill used the occasion to ensure the twins continued their unsteady alliance with him. He informed the Krays he would eventually pull out of London altogether to live at his new villa in Marbella, Spain. His estranged wife Aggie was already running his New Cabinet Club in Gerrard Street and Hill wanted certain guarantees that she would not be bothered by the Krays. Hill would retain interests in a couple of other West End clubs, and intended popping back and forth from Spain to keep an eye on his businesses. Hill knew he was better off out of London. He'd tried often enough in the past to head for fresh pastures but this time he believed he'd found a formula that would enable him to have the best of both worlds.

By the summer of 1956 the Krays had set up their headquarters in the Regal billiard hall, in Eric Street, off Mile End Road. The twins were already committing regular acts of extreme violence. They'd taken over most of the East End and were heading west with a vengeance. They called their organisation 'The Firm', Ronnie was 'The Colonel'. But they still lived at Fort Vallance, their mum's home.

Spot hadn't even merited a mention when the Krays met up with Billy Hill at Smithson's funeral, although the twins told another associate at the time they were 'disappointed' Spot hadn't put up more of a fight to retain his throne. They'd have loved to see a real bloodbath. 'It's a shame 'cause we'd have liked to have had a right dig at Spotty,' Reg told his associate. The Krays kept a close eye on Jack Spot just in case he tried to put his few remaining troops back on the streets. They agreed with Billy Hill that, if Spot put a foot wrong, they'd all come down on him like the proverbial ton of bricks.

♪   ♪   ♪

Meanwhile, Hill's henchman Mad Frankie Fraser teamed up with Raymond Rosa and Richard Frett, also known as Dick Dodo, and some other criminals to go after Spot's long-time hard man, south Londoner Johnny Carter. They broke down Carter's front door in Peckham before beating him with hammers, coshes, knives and shillelaghs. The attack on Carter was seen as another warning to Spot to keep out of the underworld. Once again, London's gangland resembled Chicago in the worst days of Prohibition.

Jack Spot let it be known he still expected to be treated with respect. But he remained worried about the safety of his family. He'd broken his promise to Rita to move to the Sussex countryside because he was so short of cash. For the moment he and his family were trapped in Hyde Park Mansions – which, thanks to Fleet Street, was one of the most famous addresses in London.

Scotland Yard detective Nipper Read, the man who would later help bring the Krays to justice, encountered Spot when he visited the Yard demanding protection after receiving yet more phone threats. He told Read that his local police station had refused to help. Read recalled: 'But the evidence was vague, and the police was unable to act unless there was more concrete information.' Spot was again told to stop asking until he had 'some real evidence'.

But the intimidation continued. Spot was stopped in the street by three tearaways warning him that 'Rita and the kids are goin' to get cut.' Spot went back again to see Nipper Read again at Scotland Yard. 'Nipper, they're definitely going to get me,' he told Read.

The detective later recalled: 'I listened and sympathised, but there was really no way I could help him. As a betting man, he must have known it was 6–4 on that he would eventually become a victim, but it was difficult to offer him protection in a situation which he had manufactured for himself.'

Every morning, as a sign of defiance to his enemies, Spot left Hyde Park Mansions, walked across the road to his barber's for a shave and then down to the Cumberland Hotel, where at a corner table in the Bear Garden, he still held court. Despite his problems he looked immaculate and still seemed to be modelling himself on his favourite American gangster heroes.

Spot scraped together £50 a week to pay Joe Cannon to be his personal bodyguard. Spot believed he was now on a hit list and he needed protection, as well as keeping one step ahead of the enemy. He had no idea that Joe Cannon's boasting about the plan to knock off Billy Hill had led to its failure. Spot tried to contact Hill to sort out their problems, but Hill refused to take Spot's calls. For the first time, Spot began questioning the reasons behind his split with Hill. Previously, he'd blindly countered force with more force. But he knew that, unless he got some answers, the battles between them would develop into something more deadly. Why, after all these years of peace, had Billy Hill turned against him? Was it pride, stupidity, suspicion or arrogance? Spot just couldn't come up with the answer.

As Spot started touring Soho, trying to drum up support for his cause, he began to hear more and more about the Kray twins. To this day, many villains in London wonder why the Krays were so obsessed with violence and yet remained such outsiders as a result. Ronnie Kray did not like any threat of competition from other criminals while Reggie was always urging his twin brother to be more cautious. But Ronnie was permanently out for blood and could come up with a thousand reasons to chiv any person he deemed to be an enemy.

The Krays' Firm, even in those early days, was in a permanent state of readiness for battle. Their soldiers could be swiftly mobilised to clamp down on any perceived threat. New arms were always being purchased and caches of guns and ammo were stashed in different parts of London. Every member of the Firm was issued with his own automatic. Ronnie and Reggie purchased their own VIP Browning machine guns for £75 each. Ronnie even tried to splash out on Limpet Mines and Mills Bombs but couldn't find a suitable supplier.

The twins were more than just aspiring to be the most powerful criminals in London. They avoided macho gang fights to show who was boss. Now, everything had to have a purpose. Even their base at the billiard hall was more like a business headquarters than a club for villains. News was travelling around the East End that the young twins were 'genuine guv'nors who looked after their own'. This gave them improved status, which increased their ability to attract recruits.

The Krays installed a sense of real discipline into their firm. Ronnie's dream was to replace all the tearaways there with genuine criminals. By 1956, the twins' power had spread through Hackney and Mile End along to Walthamstow. Every thief, gambling club, many businesses, and most of the pubs were paying protection money to the Krays. Reggie bought himself a flashy convertible Caddillac not dissimilar from the one that Jack Spot had once owned.

Criminals around London began referring to them as 'the most dangerous mob in London, the boys with the real future'. But they still lacked the strength to expand. Ronnie wanted to sweep into the West End, but no other gangs would form an alliance with them because of their deadly dangerous reputations. Ronnie Kray wanted to take them all on. He constantly talked of 'doing' people. He didn't help his unhinged, violent reputation by talking about how he believed he was psychic and could read people's motives from their auras. Reggie disapproved of his brother's spiritual obsessions but felt under the power and influence of Ronnie. The Krays were here to stay.

19
CHIV MERCHANTS

On 2 May 1956, Jack Spot visited a pub called The Little Weston, off Praed Street in Paddington, on behalf of a secretive financial backer who was prepared to buy the property. Spot had agreed to run the tavern if the deal went ahead. At 10.40 p.m. that night, Spot and Rita plus an Irish friend called Paddy Carney were walking back to Hyde Park Mansions from the pub. As they approached the apartment block, three cars screeched to a halt thirty yards further up the street. Rita heard the sound of people running behind them. Moments later, at least half a dozen men – some with handkerchiefs tied loosely around their faces – emerged from the dark and steamed right into Spot. One of those men was Mad Frankie Fraser. Spot hit the deck in seconds as a cosh ripped open a gaping wound in his skull. Then he felt sharp pain tearing at him as blades sliced through his flesh.

Rita let off an ear-piercing scream before flinging herself at the attackers. She kicked and scratched them to try and get them to pull away from her husband. Spot scrambled back onto his feet and started hitting back as a few local residents emerged from nearby homes.

Rita later recalled: 'I was pushed against the railings and fell to the ground. Jack got hold of me and tried to push me up the steps. We got up three steps to a platform and both fell again. I got up, but my husband was still on the ground. Men were galloping all around us. There were lots of them. They were whacking at both of us.' That was when Rita spotted the shillelagh being used on them. It was one she'd brought back from Ireland, which her husband had insisted on giving to Billy Hill as a gift. She also recognised a tearaway called Billy Blythe amongst their assailants.

Spot lay helpless on the ground as they hit him over and over again with the shillelagh before booting him in the face. Another man they knew to be Hill's associate Rossi then came up the steps and attacked them with what looked like a butcher's chopper. Another thug called Dennis joined in with an iron bar. Rita shrieked at him, 'I know you,' but he didn't reply. The couple's friend, Paddy Carney, disappeared into the darkness, never to be seen again. Police sirens sounded in the distance. The men hastily scrambled back towards their cars before driving off.

Rita grabbed her husband's arm and dragged him up the steps. With blood streaming from his face and body, plus one ear flapping, Spot tried to focus on the front door of the mansion block. Then he collapsed as everything went black. He later recalled: 'This wasn't a run-of-the-mill cutting job. They intended to kill me. The razors could only slash me to ribbons. But the chopper, the iron bar and the coshes were intended to finish me.'

Dr Howard Bourne, a scientist, was driving his cream-coloured Morris Minor along Marylebone Road when he heard a woman screaming. He then saw at least three men running off as he stopped his car. Dr Bourne found Spot collapsed on the steps with blood gushing out of a gaping face wound. One of the men he saw running off he would later identify as Mad Frankie Fraser.

Blood already stained the steps on the entrance to Hyde Park Mansions as twelve-year-old neighbour Philip Bergman looked out of the window. He saw a group of men running down the street towards Marylebone Road. One had a handkerchief across his face and another carried what looked like an iron bar. None of them wore hats. The third man had an overcoat. 'That's when my father pulled me away from the window,' Philip later recalled. Mr Maurice Bergman confirmed his son's story: 'I saw the man on the steps outside my flat. It was Mr Comer. I know him well. Beside him was his wife with her hands clasped over her face. As the men ran off I saw one of them carrying a long knife.'

§   §   §

But where was Spot's bodyguard, Joe Cannon, when the thugs struck? He later claimed that Spot had told him he was taking Rita out for a meal and that he should meet him back at the flat at Hyde Park Mansions. Cannon said he took his girlfriend, Ellen, out for the night and forgot all about the time. 'When I looked at my watch it was one o'clock in the morning, long past the time I was due to meet Jack and Rita. Still, there was no use crying over spilt milk, so I spent the rest of the night with Ellen. In a way I was lucky. If I'd been with Jack when he made his way home I would have been dead or, at best, seriously injured.'

Mad Frankie Fraser later insisted there was no intention to murder Spot: 'The thing was to teach Spotty a lesson. He wasn't important enough to kill. The death penalty was about, but you couldn't care less about that because you could easy have killed him by mistake anyway. That's the chance you take. But the purpose was to let him see what a loud-mouthed chump he was.' Usually Fraser was paid cash up front for such an attack but, on this occasion, he'd waived his fee because he knew that once word of the incident spread through the London underworld, his reputation would be second to none. Within hours of the attack, Frankie Fraser had hot-footed it to Brighton on the south coast. From there, Billy Hill had arranged for him to fly to Ireland where Hill had rented a doctor's house on the outskirts of Dublin.

Meanwhile Jack Spot was rushed by ambulance to St Mary's Hospital, Paddington. Semiconscious, and with Rita beside him, he was immediately given blood transfusions and emergency surgery. Rita's injuries were slight and she only required outpatient treatment at the same hospital. When a detective asked Spot if he recognised any of his attackers, he simply shook his head.

Rita, on the other hand, was far less inclined to let the attackers get away with almost murdering her husband. She said one of them had hammered into her husband with that shillelagh Spot had given Hill in the days when they were still friends. Nothing would shake Rita from her conviction that the men should be brought to justice. Why should she play the underworld game of never betraying another villain? That night she provided police with a sworn affidavit that would help them gain arrest warrants for tearaways Mad Frankie Fraser and Bobby Warren. She also 'suggested' some other names, although she admitted she wasn't one hundred per cent certain about their identities.

At 1 a.m. that night, one of the senior registrars at St Mary's Hospital emerged to tell reporters: 'The deep wounds to his face were the most serious. His life is not in danger and his eyes were not affected.' Outside Spot's ward, Rita sat, chain-smoking, and hid behind a screen whenever any visitors appeared. Spot was then transferred to a general ward where Rita and Scotland Yard detectives could talk to him. But he continued to simply shake his head whenever asked about the names of his assailants.

At 2 a.m., police officers left the hospital carrying a bloodstained jacket and a small, roughly tied parcel. An hour later, Rita spoke to newsmen: 'They must think they're very brave for twenty-five of them to set on just one man. He's badly cut . . . they kicked me as well you know . . . I tried to shield his face when he was on the ground. But Jack's going to pull through as he pulled through the last time.' Then she paused before raising her voice: 'I know who did it. We didn't stand a chance. They hit us with everything but their fists. But they're going to pay for it.'

At the crime scene, police scoured the area for the weapons but all they eventually found was a man's heavy gold signet ring. In the early hours of the following morning, police raided a well-known Soho club and interviewed numerous villains with records of violence. They were asked where they were at the time of the attack and their clothing was examined for bloodstains. The only good thing to come out of the attack, as far as Jack

Spot was concerned, was that police now agreed to mount a twenty-four-hour guard on his wife and children.

That morning, Scotland Yard detective Nipper Read visited Billy Hill's flat in Moscow Road, Bayswater, to question him about the attack on Spot. Read later recalled: 'He took his time getting dressed and smartened himself up. Just before we left, he went to a sideboard, opened a cupboard and took out a roll of notes, which would have choked a pig.' 'S'ppose I'd better bring a few quid, just in case,' Hill told Read, as if he didn't have a care in the world.

Over in Clerkenwell, Albert Dimes was equally co-operative with visiting detectives. Both Hill and Dimes were taken to Paddington Green police station for interviews but they had strong alibis and were never charged. Scotland Yard believed that neither of the men were directly involved in the attack. 'It would have been too obvious. These men were astute criminals. Not idiots,' said Nipper Read. But the Yard let it be known that Hill and Dimes had been able to provide detectives with 'valuable information'.

Meanwhile Spot lay in the end bed of the Lewis Lloyd Ward at St Mary's, Paddington. He was hidden from his twenty-three ward mates by a patterned screen. Detectives watched him round the clock and tried to extract some details without any success. Rita, looking tired and pale, returned the next morning at 10 a.m. After more than an hour she returned home to have lunch with her children and ignored the packs of reporters lurking outside Hyde Park Mansions. Two of Spot's henchmen escorted her up the steps.

But in the London underworld, Jack Spot had already been branded a squealer because he couldn't stop his own wife from shooting her mouth off. Jack Spot still didn't know at this stage that Rita had even spoken to police.

§   §   §

The Kray twins had steered well clear of the aftermath to the Frith Street fight 'that never was'. But on this occasion, they made a point of popping in to see Jack Spot in hospital the day after his admission. Rita was far from happy when Ron and Reg strolled in, dressed in black suits and black overcoats. They assured her it was a well-intentioned visit so she allowed them to pull aside the curtain surrounding Spot's bed to have a chat with him.

Both Krays gleefully examined his injuries before Reg got straight to the point: 'Who the hell did this to you, Spotty?' Jack Spot didn't even glance up at the twins. He simply rolled over and looked the other way. They even tried asking him a few more questions about the identity of his attackers. But Spot said nothing as the twins persisted like blood-hungry bulldogs knawing away at a piece of meat. Eventually, Spot closed his eyes and pretended to be asleep. The Krays smiled to each other, did their customary shrug of the shoulders, and headed for the exit.

That evening, the twins held a celebratory drink at their favourite boozer, the Blind Beggar, in Mile End Road. 'They were that happy to see Spot out of circulation,' one former Krays man explained years later. Around midnight, Ronnie Kray paid a visit to the Italian Club in Clerkenwell with his latest toy – a heavy Mauser automatic. He threatened one of Hill's associates. It was all done for show to make Spot believe they weren't involved in his beating and slashing. Back in the West End, police warned that it was highly likely the attack would spark fresh friction between London gangs.

Billy Hill had wanted Jack Spot taken off the streets permanently. Perhaps this time Spot would get the message loud and clear.

At St Mary's Hospital, Paddington, Spot continued suffering appalling pain and discomfort. He later recalled: 'It was sharp, biting pain. There was the white ceiling of the operating theatre, the smell of the anaesthetic and the greyness of the cotton wool that clogged my brain. Choking tubes were inserted down my throat.' And through all the haze came a voice constantly asking Spot: 'Who did it?' 'What are their names?'

Later that day Spot requested an urgent private chat with Rita and asked his police guard to leave them alone for a few minutes.

'Have you talked?' Spot asked Rita cautiously.

At first she didn't reply, but looked down at his injuries with concern.

'Have you talked?' repeated Spot.

Rita began crying. 'I thought they'd killed you, Jack. I thought they'd killed you.'

Jack Spot now had a lot more problems on his plate than just a bunch of life-threatening injuries. He'd refused to co-operate with police. But Rita had grassed on everyone.

Later that same day, Spot posed for a photograph for the *Sunday Express* with Rita at his side. His arm was encased in plaster, his nose and mouth twisted, both eyes blackened. He told the paper: 'I'm the toughest man in the world. I am staying on in London. Nobody will ever drive me out.' Rita added: 'Let 'em all come. We're not scared.' Rita got £300 for the article and neither of them meant one word they were quoted as saying.

Two days after the attack, Spot's so-called bodyguard Joey Cannon got a call requesting that he attend a meet at Billy Hill's office in Warren Street, just off the Tottenham Court Road. Spot still trusted Cannon and he advised him to take a .45 revolver with him just in case there was any trouble. Cannon informed Hill and Albert Dimes that Spot wished to convey a message that he, Jack Spot, would talk Rita out of giving evidence re the attack. The quid pro quo was that Hill should put a lid on the escalating violence between them. Hill was not pleased and told Cannon that Spot was a wrong 'un and that he would do no such thing. Cannon only survived the meeting because Mad Frankie Fraser put in a good word for him.

ƒ   ƒ   ƒ

On 5 May, tearaway Bobbie Warren – one of the men recognised by Rita during that attack outside Hyde Park Mansions – was arrested. Warren knew the Whites of Kings Cross and his own brother had been beaten up by Spot in 1947; what goes around comes around.

Just over a week later, Mad Frankie Fraser was picked up by the police after they got a tip that he was flying back into Heathrow from Billy Hill's rented house in Dublin. As Scotland Yard detective Nipper Read explained: 'We went in three cars to London Airport – two of which broke down on the way – and by the time we arrived the passengers had disembarked. We looked around desperately and I saw him, suitcase in hand, at the bottom of an escalator. His face was livid when it dawned on him that he was about to be nicked.' Fraser later recalled. 'I'd telephoned England to get someone to meet me and the phone had been tapped. I didn't have a clue. I came off the plane and half a minute later I was surrounded.'

On 19 May, Fraser and Warren – described as a twenty-eight-year-old scaffolder of Chatham Avenue, Islington – were remanded in custody at Marylebone Magistrates Court on GBH charges. Police opposed bail because of fears about intimidation of witnesses. Meanwhile Spot still played dumb. 'I don't know who was there,' he told police for the umpteenth time later that same morning.

Billy Hill hired his crooked legal pal Patrick Marrinan, QC, to defend his boys. Marrinan, son of a Royal Irish Constabulary officer had climbed the ladder to become a barrister after studying law at Queen's University. He'd been a well-known face at Belfast clubs and greyhound racetracks for years. Marrinan was also a keen boxer who was heavyweight champion of the Irish Universities. Back in 1942 he'd been convicted of harbouring black-market goods in Liverpool. This had held back his ascendancy to the Bar until 1951. Marrinan was a greedy, unscrupulous character.

Mad Frankie Fraser and others regularly socialised with QC Marrinan at Billy Hill's luxury flat in Barnes. Fraser recalled: 'He was a good drinker; he'd start with Guinness and go on to Irish whiskey. I think Marrinan was a rebel. It was the unfairness and corruptness of the legal profession he fought against. Also he got better money from fighting hard for a case. Billy Hill was intelligent enough to recognise this.' And on the face of it the evidence

against Warren and Fraser was not impressive. Even Rita's identification of them had been contradicted by Jack Spot himself.

On his release from hospital, Jack Spot had so little faith in the
police guard assigned to protect Rita that he went everywhere
with her. He explained: 'And everywhere we went the detectives
followed on our heels, prepared for any attack,' he later recalled.
For once in his life, Spot didn't mind being in the company of
police officers because his number-one priority remained the protection of Rita and the kids.

ƒ   ƒ   ƒ

There was a serious knock-on effect from the adverse publicity
surrounding the string of underworld court cases featuring Spot
and his mob. MPs began asking questions in the House of
Commons about whether 'effective steps were being taken by the
police to prevent the operation of criminal gangs in the London
area'.

Mr Anthony Greenwood, Labour MP for Rossendale, asked
Home Secretary Lloyd-George: 'How long have the public got to
wait before the activities of these squalid, cowardly and small-time
hoodlums like Comer, Dimes and Hill are going to be effectively
curbed?' Lloyd-George replied: 'In the Jack Spot case, within hours
the assailants were apprehended.' He went on to assure the House
that it was his duty to 'put them out of harm's way'. But other
plans were afoot.

ƒ   ƒ   ƒ

Billy Hill's gang never even considered that they would be identified by their victims Spot and Rita. As Mad Frankie Fraser later
recalled: 'Spot should either have been killed, I should have
masked myself up, or no one he knew should have taken part.'
Everyone involved knew it was only a matter of time before other
arrests were made. And the underworld blamed it all on Jack Spot

– the so-called tough guy who couldn't even get his wife to keep schtum.

Meanwhile Spot edged closer and closer to bankruptcy. Much of his legendary bravado had been replaced by downright fear. He slept badly and often lay awake at night, replaying the fights and razor attacks that had dominated his life over the previous thirty years. And his drinking was getting heavier. In the West End, it was said that many were after Jack Spot with a vengeance. Surely it was only a matter of time before they nailed him.

20
DOGS OF WAR

The Warren/Fraser trial commenced before Mr Justice Donovan in Number One court at the Old Bailey on 9 June 1956. Billy Hill rounded up a bunch of his boys who'd been cut by Spot and arranged for them to sit in the public gallery. As Mad Frankie Fraser later explained: 'They were there to let Spotty know. He went white when he saw them.' Court officials even had a special buzzer warning system installed to call police reinforcements to any part of the building in case there was trouble. An emergency switchboard was also erected by the porter's lodge at the main door to the Old Bailey.

As with the previous trials, this one got Fleet Street banner headline coverage. And the stench of corruption reeked inside the Old Bailey itself. Early on in the proceedings, prosecutor Ronnie Seaton, QC, asked Fraser an awkward question which Fraser hadn't 'squared' with one of his tame witnesses.

Fraser then got a message to counsel Patrick Marrinan to make sure that what had been said was conveyed to his witness waiting outside the court. Marrinan stood up, bowed to the judge and indicated that he wished to go to the lavatory. Outside, Marrinan saw the tame witness and told him what Fraser had said. That witness later gave exactly the same evidence as Fraser. Then Fraser did himself no favours by proudly telling the court he was a great friend of Hill and Dimes. 'They said I should have said I just knew them, but I couldn't bring myself to deny they were my friends,' Fraser later explained.

Billy Hill, sporting shades and a snap-brim hat, and his mob made their temporary headquarters at the Rex Cafe, opposite the Old Bailey where they drank tea, smoked cigarettes and monitored proceedings. Many looked as if they'd walked off a Hollywood movie set: broad-shouldered, broken-nosed and razor-slashed characters who swaggered in front of press photographers and muttered threats for the benefit of anyone who cared to listen. They also watched the police who were watching them.

At the end of each day, Billy Hill reported back to the Kray twins at their billiard hall in the East End. The Krays assured Hill there was no way Jack Spot would ever be allowed to make a comeback.

ƒ   ƒ   ƒ

On the second day of the trial, Jack Spot took the stand at the Old Bailey and insisted, naturally, that he hadn't seen any of the men who attacked him. Years later Spot explained why his wife had contradicted him: 'Rita is a decent, honest girl and she married me without knowing my way of life. I was attacked and she saw only her husband being slashed to pieces before her eyes. My wife was not bound by the unwritten law of the underworld. She knew only the bonds that tie a woman to her husband.'

Later that same day, Rita was called to give evidence at the Old Bailey and identified the shillelagh used in the attack after examining it closely. A few minutes later, Rita insisted to Warren's QC Patrick Marrinan that she hated all publicity before he pointed out that she'd just been paid £300 by the *Daily Express*. Mr Justice Donovan interrupted to say the matter was irrelevant, but Marrinan persisted. 'If the witness is prepared to commercialise her husband's injuries for £300 and she says she shuns publicity . . .' The judge then commented that he wished the *Daily Express* would pay him £300 for his photograph! Ignoring the remark, Marrinan asked, 'Is it not the truth that you are most anxious your husband should become the underworld king again?' Rita hit back: 'I would be very happy if they let my husband and me alone. I'd like him to get just a small job . . .'

When it was Mad Frankie Fraser's turn to give evidence in his own defence it was pointed out by prosecutors that he'd told police after his arrest:. 'Look here, you know I was in it, but you have got to prove it, and I'm not saying anything more.'

Fraser claimed to the jury that what he really said was: 'Look here, if you know I was in it, you can prove it, and I am not saying anything more.' He insisted on the night of the attack he was in Brighton, working for a bookmaker. He said he often did that, earning £1 or £2 a night, adding that he didn't have a PAYE card, or an insurance card.

Prosecutor Ronnie Seaton then questioned Fraser about his visit to Ireland immediately after the attack on Spot. Fraser responded: 'I asked for a week's holiday the same night Mr Comer was attacked . . . I thought I might be able to earn a living smuggling. I can't say any more as it might involve other people.'

Then up stepped turf accountant Samuel Belson from Hove, near Brighton. He admitted he'd done six months inside for stealing women's coats, but insisted he'd since built up a good reputation in Brighton and was a friend of leading police officers in the seaside town. Belson backed Fraser's alibi that he was in Brighton at the time Spot was attacked.

The prosecution suggested to the jury that Spot's failure to ID the men in the dock that day was because he intended to deal in his own way with the attack. 'He is saying, in effect, this has nothing to do with the law. It is my affair,' said Ronnie Seaton, QC. Then he added: 'If it were to be said that that is the way we are going to govern this country, we may just as well adopt the law of the jungle. Success would go to the gentlemen with the sharpest knives.'

Defence counsel Patrick Marrinan then rounded on Rita during his summing up by describing her as 'sweet-face little Miss Comer who comes into the court as tearful wife and mother. Yet this is the woman prepared to live with a gangster and have a voluntary association with him . . . the sweetest little person, crying out to God almighty with a trembling voice.'

Marrinan described Spot as: 'That vile cut-throat gangster . . . that corner boy of the lowest look . . . a man who prides himself on being king of the underworld . . . this scum of the earth.' Marrinan added: 'This case has a background that is unpleasant – unpleasant and unnatural. People in it do not lead the sort of lives which ordinary respectable citizens lead. There is a background which shows that people are prepared to go to most tremendous lengths to pay off feuds.'

Judge Mr Justice Donovan summed up, 'this much is clear: one side or another is doing their best to deceive you by hard lies. They are doing their best to see that a wrong verdict is recorded.' Then the judge leaned forward towards the jury: 'The civic value of the man Comer is neither here nor there. We are dealing with a very bad case of violence in the public streets of this day. If this sort of thing is allowed to spread, it would not be safe for any of us to walk the streets.'

The jury then retired to consider a verdict. Outside, a chocolate-suited Billy Hill now sat with henchmen on a Lest We Forget seat in the garden of remembrance in St Sepulchre's Church and sent messengers scurrying back and forward across the street to the Old Bailey.

Two hours later the jury returned. Warren and Fraser were brought back into the dock looking tense and pale. Then the verdicts were announced 'Guilty . . . Guilty . . .'

Rita sat on a side seat and put her hand over her mouth. Spot shook his head. It was only then the court heard both defendants had criminal records. Fraser was a razor slasher skilled in the use of broken glass or a bottle as a weapon. He had fifteen convictions, two of them involving violence. Warren had also been prosecuted for a number of serious crimes. As Mr Justice Donovan gave each man seven years, he told them: 'I have been affected by what I have just been told. Otherwise sentence would have been much longer.'

Hill and his heavy mob went bananas when they heard the verdict. There was shouting and swearing in the courtroom and more than a dozen uniformed cozzers forced Hill's boys to leave the room before any of the legal teams and their witnesses. Many of them were once again swearing revenge on Jack Spot. The Bailey was ringed with more City of London police and Mr Justice Donovan was given a police escort. Police feared reprisals on Spot, so detectives immediately put his flat under even tighter surveillance.

Outside the court Rita and Spot were bundled into a waiting Jaguar amid popping flashbulbs and a teeming crowd of bystanders. Their limo headed south towards the embankment.

Fleet Street was outraged that Billy Hill could so brazenly continue to run the underworld in full view of the authorities. Columnist 'Cassandra' in the *Daily Mirror* complained: 'These hoodlums who have never done a day's work, who were brought up in borstals, who have criminal records that leave the ordinary citizens reeling with horror at their callous brutalities, turn up in vast shiny limousines outside the courts of justice to encourage "their boys" when, all too occasionally, they land in the dock.'

ƒ   ƒ   ƒ

A few days later, a Scottish gangster called Johnny 'Scarface' Russo was out walking along Frith Street, Soho, when a large cream-coloured Buick pulled up alongside him. An electric window slowly slid down and a finger beckoned Russo over. He recognised Billy Hill immediately. Russo had known Hill since 1940 and had even slashed Hill's brother, Archie, on an earlier visit to London when he'd tried to end a love affair between Archie and a pretty blonde club girl called 'Manchester Maisie'. Russo had also borrowed cash off Jack Spot on one or two occasions to help get him out of a fix.

At the wheel of the Buick was Hill's henchman, Johnny Rice. Albert Dimes and another man were also inside the car. As Russo leaned closer, Hill turned to Dimes and said: 'He'll do.' Hill then told Russo, 'We want someone to take a "strike" from Spotty and nick him, so that he gets some bird.' In other words they wanted somebody to allow himself to be slashed and then frame Spot for the job, meaning certain arrest and prison. Russo accepted a ride in the Buick to nearby Warren Street and agreed to meet Hill again at Peter Mario's restaurant, in Soho, scene of the much-publicised launch of Billy Hill's autobiography.

At the restaurant the following Tuesday, Hill told Russo: 'I'll give you a monkey [£500], plus the expenses of a plastic operation if you'll do it.' Russo scratched his chin thoughtfully for a moment then agreed. But he said he had to go to Scotland the following Friday so it would have to be before that. 'That's alright,' said Hill. 'We'll make it for Wednesday. It'll happen comin' out of the Astor club on Wednesday morning. I'll get two straight witnesses.'

Two days later, Russo took an early train to Scotland and called Hill to say: 'Thanks but no thanks. I changed my mind and if you ever come to Glasgow, we'll send your body back in a sack!'

'But we've got it all lined up,' said a furious Hill.

'Then do it your fuckin' self.'

*   *   *

Following the Warren/Fraser trial, Rita received telephone calls and anonymous letters threatening to scar her face with acid and kidnap her fifteen-month-old baby and four-year-old daughter. One letter warned her to keep silent or, 'it isn't your nest that will be feathered but your coffin'. A sketch enclosed in the letter showed a woman with cheeks cut to ribbons and with a dagger in her heart.

Rita told one reporter: 'Sometimes it's threats, sometimes it's somebody trying to find out where Jack will be at certain times. Sometimes they just hang up as soon as I answer. What makes me so wild is that the bell rings right outside the baby's nursery – and a lot of these tough characters ring up in the early hours. It's a war-of-nerves trick. And it wakes my baby.'

Whenever Rita heard the phone ring, her only sign of nervousness was a little nervous tic of squeezing her long, slim hands together. Whenever she heard footsteps coming up the stairs outside the flat she'd pause for breath. But she told reporters: 'I'm not afraid of cowards who threaten women and little children.' Rita took the children to the park every day, did her shopping and even made a point of taking the girls out for tea two or three times a week.

One morning Rita left Hyde Park Mansions with the children, and noticed a man following close behind them. Every time she turned he was there, smiling in a chilling kind of way about fifteen yards behind her. Rita then took a long loop around a nearby park just to be certain. He was still there five minutes later. Then the man walked towards her with his hand in his pocket. Rita grabbed the children and pulled them close to her. Just then the man pulled his hand out of his jacket to shake hers. He was congratulating her on not running away from London. 'Just a stranger, but it might have been a stranger with a knife,' Rita later recalled.

But despite everything, Rita continued to publicly support her husband. 'I love him,' she said to any reporter who asked. But behind the scenes she was far from happy with the situation. 'What future will there be for Rachel and Marion? I wanted them to have the chance in life I never had,' she yelled at Spot one morning shortly after the end of the Fraser/Warren trial. Later Rita told one friend: 'I'm determined to get a business. I'm not afraid of hard work. Because I had it so hard in my early years I thought it'd be wonderful to have money, clothes and other luxuries. But I've certainly found out how wrong I was. Your values change as you get older and wiser. The big time only brings terrible worries. However hungry and poor we were when I was a girl, we were free. We could walk about without looking over our shoulders all the time. That's the way I'd like it to be again – to be able to laugh and joke with my husband and children with no worries on my mind. But no matter what happens, nobody is going to frighten me out of my home.'

Jack Spot told journalists he knew the man behind it all. 'He used to be a friend of mine, and I once helped him out of a difficulty.' Everyone knew he was talking about Billy Hill.

                                          ƒ   *ƒ*   *ƒ*

The pressure was making Spot begin to question his own sanity. He became so stressed that he secretly began consulting a Harley Street psychiatrist. In the mid-1950s, such a thing was very rare, especially for a gangster, but Spot thought it might help, and later described his shrink as 'an intelligent man'. At first, Spot didn't even tell Rita about his visits to the psychiatrist. If news of his treatment ever got out, he'd be the laughing stock of Soho.

Spot carefully absorbed the wise words of his shrink, who assured him that a lot of his problems were a direct result of his impoverished childhood. At the time of Spot's psychiatric sessions, there was also a genuine belief that biological inheritance was a major factor in the making of a criminal. Spot started to believe that he was a victim of circumstance rather than a cold-blooded character who crashed into the world of crime with the greatest of relish.

His psychiatrist knew only too well that the career of a criminal took the form of climax followed by anti-climax – the climax being the crimes up to their arrest and trial, and the anti-climax being everything that followed. Gangsters like Spot, Billy Hill and the Krays began their criminal careers breaking the law in a rush, motivated by rage or vengeance. But, when they evolved into established criminals, lawbreaking got much easier. The villains then became intoxicated by their celebrity and continued to commit crimes to maintain the euphoria. But, like all addicts, they soon got so strung out they inevitably made a mistake. The psychiatrist's words made Spot begin to think about his actions. He even started questioning the wisdom of being a part of the underworld in the first place.

The most important question in the psychiatrist's mind was why had Jack Spot become a criminal mastermind? He had catapulted himself into the history books by developing a unique criminal strategy; he was a criminal of his time. Spot's 'work', as criminologists call it, combined his criminality with the urge to be famous. Spot's nature gave out the impression of someone with great feelings of invincibility, and his psychiatrist later said that he'd rarely come across someone quite like Jack Spot. 'The brazenness, the openness were highly unusual,' the psychiatrist explained. 'There was a lot of arrogance at work here. He was thumbing a nose at everyone.'

The psychiatrist concluded that Spot was a complete chameleon who could switch from happy, loving family man to cold-blooded criminal with the flick of a switch. As another observer later concluded: 'He seemed to adjust his persona to his surroundings. We are talking about a multiple personality here.'

Perhaps Jack Spot was in some way insane. That at least would account for part of his behaviour. Spot had undoubtedly left his own 'calling cards' from the moment he began breaking the law as a schoolboy; he liked the world to know when he had been 'at work', and deliberately left a trail so no one would ever be in any doubt about the perpetrator. But Spot's psychiatrist found Spot genuinely believed he was superior to all authority: 'He thought he was immune or impervious to capture. Spot wasn't that discrete or careful to hide his crimes.'

Spot might be a dream case for a psychiatrist but these sessions weren't going to simply wipe out the past. And there were many problems still on the horizon.

♪   ♪   ♪

Spot knew only too well that Billy Hill and Albert Dimes were still after him. He was worried about Rita and the children although she believed that if the police continued protecting them, then nothing could happen. Spot agreed, but in his heart he knew the police wouldn't be able to save him.

Rita and Spot were prisoners in their own home. Neither of them dared venture out into the West End. And Rita knew from the worried expression on her husband's face that he still expected something bad to happen, sooner rather than later. And the threatening phone calls increased. Sinister, husky voices left messages claiming to be Spot's friends and asking where he could be found that evening. One time Rita told a caller her husband was out shopping. Within ten minutes, three carloads of men were waiting on a street corner within striking distance of Hyde Park Mansions, but out of sight of the two-man police guard parked by the apartment block. As Rita later explained: 'Fortunately Jack was in the flat all the time. But we can't keep living this way.'

In the summer of 1956, Billy Hill and many members of his team disappeared from their usual haunts. They had heard a rumour in the West End that Scotland Yard had 'secret agents' living and working in the London underworld, building up evidence for eventual prosecutions intended to break the rule of the mob. Now was the time to keep a low profile.

Hill and his mob's absence provided a useful opening for the Kray twins, who were busy exploiting the marketplace with cold efficiency. The Krays had been breathing down Billy Hill's neck for ages, although it was still in their interest to let him continue his reign for a while longer. As old-time face, Jimmy McShane, explained: 'Ron and Reg wanted all the pieces of the jigsaw puzzle to be in the right place before they swooped in to take over everything.'

21
A DIABOLICAL LIBERTY

On 20 June 1956, Tommy Falco, an olive-skinned, part Maltese, tic-tac man, was admitted to St George's Hospital on Hyde Park Corner, as the victim of 'a road accident' which required forty-seven stitches. Within an hour, Falco let it be known Jack Spot had given him the wound and detectives were dispatched to interview Falco. The left sleeve of his jacket and shirt was taken away for forensic examination. Falco was found to have a thirteen-inch long cut along his left arm, which varied in depth from an inch to one third of an inch. It was a clean, single cut and looked as though it had been caused by one continuous stroke. The doctor who treated him later concluded it was most unlikely that the wound was self-inflicted.

Once Tommy Falco's wound was carefully stitched and dressed, he was taken by squad car to West End Central police station. Also in the vehicle was 'witness' Johnny Rice, broad-shouldered, six-foot-five inches tall, dressed in an expensive double-breasted blue, serge suit and wearing square-lensed, horn-rimmed spectacles. He was fingering a heavy gold signet ring on the little finger of his right hand.

Falco and Rice provided officers with full statements and a warrant for Spot's arrest was signed by local magistrate Mr Robert H. Blundell. Johnny Rice described himself as a 'steel merchant' in his statement. In fact, he was a getaway-driver for bank robbers, as well as Billy Hill's principal driver. He'd also featured prominently in pictures taken at Hill's book launch in Soho. One newspaper also had snaps of Johnny Rice manning a bookmaker's stand at Brighton races. Rice told police he was about to leave Falco outside the Astor Club at 2.15 a.m. when Spot had attacked his friend with a weapon. He caught Falco as he began falling, and carried him back into the club. He did not follow Spot as he ran away, but he heard a car start up not long afterwards. At just after 5 a.m. that morning the head porter of the nearby Lansdowne Club, John O'Brien, found an open razor on the pavement lying outside the home of a member of the Luxembourg royal family, close to the Astor Club.

At 10.30 a.m., detectives approached Spot as he was leaving St Mary's Hospital, Paddington, after receiving further outpatient treatment for the injuries received in the earlier attack on him and Rita. Spot was taken to West End Central, where he was interviewed by Detective Chief Inspector John Mannings. He was asked for an account of his movements the previous evening. Spot insisted he hadn't left his flat from 10 p.m. Tuesday 19 June until 8.45 a.m. 20 June, when he went to the hospital. 'This is a diabolical liberty,' he told Mannings. 'I'll get ten years for nothin'. You see what they do for me. I should have named the twenty of them.'

At the same time, another Yard team arrived at Hyde Park Mansions looking for evidence of the Falco attack. Detectives noted there was no trace of blood on Spot's clothes. Rita then insisted on being taken to see her husband at the police station. She made a statement backing her husband's alibi that he had never left the flat. But that didn't prevent Spot being charged with causing grievous bodily harm to Thomas Joseph Falco. Spot was kept in a cell overnight to appear at 10 a.m. the following morning at Marylebone Magistrates Court.

Crowds began gathering around West End Central police station as word of Spot's arrest spread. 'Victim' Falco and his wife had to be smuggled out of the back entrance in a police car. Rita swept out of the same building shortly afterwards and went immediately to the offices of the family solicitor. A couple of hours later, Rita arrived back at Hyde Park Mansions with a three-man bodyguard of CID men. Two more officers already stood guard outside the apartment block. As Rita travelled up to the fourth-floor flat, where her two children and sisters Carmel and Sadie were waiting, a police guard was placed at the foot of the stairs.

That afternoon, Scarface Russo – the petty crook asked by Hill to set up Spot – left Ascot racecourse and was heading home on a train to Glasgow when he read that Falco had been slashed. Back in Scotland later that evening, Russo made a drunken phone call to Billy Hill to tell him he was about to go to the police. He said he wanted to give Hill a chance to drop the charges before Spot appeared in court. Hill was not impressed and told Russo to fuck off. Russo then called the police to say he'd been propositioned to let himself be slashed.

Meanwhile, 'victim' Falco was given a twenty-four-hour guard at the home of his father, sixty-seven-year-old Alphonso Falco, of Gray's Inn Road, in Holborn. Police were aware that Tommy Falco had attended the earlier Warren/Fraser trial when he'd been working as a henchman for Billy Hill. Now he had a forty-seven-stitch wound, allegedly caused by Jack Spot.

At the preliminary hearing at Bow Street Magistrates Court the next morning, Falco alleged that after the knifing Spot had said, 'This one's for Albert.' Chief witness Johnny Rice recalled the quote slightly differently: 'This is one for Albert Dimes.' Falco explained to the court that he was employed by Dimes. 'I work for Albert Dimes when we go to the races . . . when he wins I get wages.' He added: 'The whole of my evidence is the truth. I am a Roman Catholic, and I don't give evidence unless it is true.'

A few minutes later Rita burst into tears as Spot was remanded in custody for a week. That evening in Brixton Prison, Spot began reading detective novels at the rate of one a day. He was allowed numerous privileges because he hadn't yet been convicted; he could order meals from a caff behind the jail and drank a daily half-bottle of wine from his local pub, the George IV. He even got free writing paper for as many letters as he liked.

In the prison hospital, Spot also continued to get treatment for wounds from his earlier attack. Rita took in flowers and fruit and regularly met with Spot's defence counsel, Ellis Lincoln, at Hyde Park Mansions to discuss developments. Spot's earlier legal heroine, Rose Heilbron, QC, had sensibly decided against representing her great fan Jack Spot for reasons she never explained. Many believed it might have something to do with the question mark over her client's innocence in the Spot/Dimes fight trial.

Over in Soho, Billy Hill, short, slim, and with his hair greased and pasted back, was once more openly playing the role of king spiv of the underworld. Rumours about undercover police agents had subsided and he had many businesses to attend to. Hill was smart. After that drunken phone call from Russo, threatening to go public about Hill's scheme, Hill (accompanied by his brief, naturally) had visited his local police station and told them Russo was a cheat and a liar and not to believe anything he told them. He'd immediately confronted the cozzers and virtually challenged them to charge him or forever hold their peace. After a thirty-minute interview he was told he was free to go.

On 29 June, Jack Spot was taken from his cell at Brixton Prison back to Bow Street Magistrates Court. His lawyer Ellis Lincoln asked for bail and told the court: 'There is a complete answer to this charge and it will reveal a vile and treacherous conspiracy on the part of certain people to wreak vengeance for some reason on Mr Comer.'

Detective Chief Inspector Mannings succeeded in opposing bail for Spot on the basis he might abscond. Jack Spot later claimed his incarceration gave him even more time to reflect on his past and some of the conclusions reached by his recently acquired psychiatrist. 'I had given up fighting. I didn't even hate my jailers any more. I almost couldn't feel any more. I was just ... the ex-king of the underworld.'

ƒ   ƒ   ƒ

Up in Scotland, Scarface Russo welcomed two Yard investigators into his home. Russo made a full statement to the officers saying he'd been offered £500 to 'take a small stab here, one here and one here'. He pointed at his face, shoulder and middle of his chest. Russo said Hill wanted the attack to happen at the Astor Club because it came within the auspices of the West End Division of the Met, suggesting that Hill had some very powerful 'friends' amongst his local constabulary.

♪   ♪   ♪

On that same day, Fleet Street reported that Hill associates Billy Blythe and Robert Rossi had been named in connection with the attack on Jack Spot and Rita outside Hyde Park Mansions. 'Little Billy Boy' Blythe – just five feet tall – had always fancied himself as a big-time operator. In teenage fights during his East End childhood, Billy always got a thrashing. He'd joined the army before the war, only to desert and then end up serving a long stretch in boot camp. Then he'd got into gambling and encountered Jack Spot at point-to-point meetings. Little Billy then served a real prison sentence – this time for cutting a copper. After that he ran a gambling den in Smithfield until the police closed it down. Finally, he went for broke and joined the team that was after Jack Spot.

The following day, Blythe and Rossi, who had been living at Billy Hill's rented house on the outskirts of Dublin for three weeks, were grabbed in a city pub at gunpoint by five plain-clothes police officers, including one from Scotland Yard.

Billy Hill's favourite brief, Patrick Marrinan, turned up in Dublin to try and prevent the extradition of Rossi and Blythe. In court the following day, a Dublin judge made an order directing that the men could not be taken out of the jurisdiction of the Irish courts until he gave a final decision about their detention.

Two days later, a Dublin judge ordered the release of Rossi and Blythe because the warrants they'd been arrested under were 'inadequate'. But as the pair strolled out into the sunshine laughing and talking, London CID officers swooped once again with new charges. They were seized and hustled back to the cells. Half an hour later, the two men were driven to the Killeen Customs post, near Newry, on the border with Ulster where the car was met by a police patrol, which headed straight to the Belfast police office, a new building nestling against the wall of Belfast Prison. Blythe and Rossi were pushed along a tunnel that ran under the prison wall and into a detention cell.

An hour later, they were bundled into a grey police van with darkened windows containing two Scotland Yard detectives. Then Blythe and Rossi, cuffed and with their heads covered in raincoats, were escorted onto the 6.15 p.m. London flight.

Rossi informed one detective: 'I told Blythe, Hill would put us away when he could see the law was getting nearer to him. I shall have to take my chances. I shall say I was not there.' Just then Blythe chipped in: 'You all go and fuck yourselves. They came at me with guns tonight. I only wish I had one. I would have blown holes in the lot of you. You can't do this to me. This is kidnapping or high-jacking or somethin'.'

Meanwhile, in Brighton, another suspect in the attack on Spot and Rita – car dealer Edward 'Ginger' Dennis was allowed to have tea while police searched the house he was staying in. Detectives then found two letters referring to the attack on Spot and Rita. As police left the house with Dennis in handcuffs, he asked one officer: 'Can't you bang those letters back to the wife? It's worth half a hundred to you.'

Rossi, Blythe and Dennis were all booked into Paddington Green police station at 9.30 p.m. on 2 July. They were charged with maliciously wounding Jack Spot and told they'd be detained overnight. The next morning, a parade of twenty-five men was arranged. After consulting with the men's solicitors, that figure was reduced to sixteen men, but then the three prisoners refused to take part in the parade. Then a detective said to them: 'In that case you will be confronted with the witnesses.'

In the presence of a solicitor and other police officers, Rita was shown Rossi and said hesitantly: 'Yes, I think.' Rossi chipped in: 'You're wrong. I never saw that woman in my life. Why don't you answer instead of "I think, I think, I think"?'

Then Rita was shown Blythe and she said, 'Yes.' Blythe interrupted: 'You identify me? This is ridiculous. I want you to state that I'm innocent.' Two other witnesses were taken to the cells by police, but both said they were unable to positively identify either Blythe or Rossi.

Meanwhile, Ginger Dennis had changed his mind and agreed to take part in an ID parade. Rita then hesitantly fingered Dennis, telling police: 'I think that is the man, but I'm not sure.' Dennis was so upset he grabbed the two men nearest to him in the ID parade and said: 'You heard that.' Then he called his solicitors and said he wanted her indecision to be recorded.

The following day, Billy Hill's QC, Patrick Marrinan, representing Blythe, told Marylebone Magistrates Court: 'There is still such a thing as the presumption of innocence. It seems to be quite a fashionable thing for Mrs Comer to point the finger at anyone and say this is an enemy of hers or of her husband. It is quite apparent she is not a reliable witness.'

In court, Blythe offered to take a lie-detector test to prove his innocence even though he was the one man Rita had recognised instantly. Back in Soho, Scarface Russo was set upon by three men and warned he'd get a much worse beating if he gave evidence. Soon he was under siege from death threats. There were obviously a lot of reputations at stake.

In his Brixton Prison cell, Jack Spot tried to make sense of it all. Something his psychiatrist had said to him about how he believed himself to be invincible rang in his ears. Spot's bragging now sounded rather hollow.

22

COMMONSENSE PREVAILS

On 16 July, Rita was escorted through passages and lifts at the Old Bailey until she got to the cell underneath the court where Jack Spot was locked up awaiting the opening of his trial later that morning. Spot, sipping a cup of tea as he peered through the wire grill, tried to assure Rita he'd be alright, but she could tell from his crumpled demeanour that he was very worried. As she left the cell area, Rita blew him a kiss and climbed the stairs up to the public gallery.

Large reinforcements of uniformed and plain-clothes police were on duty in the court, public gallery and in the streets surrounding the Old Bailey that day. Hundreds of people queued for admittance to the court and extra police had to be drafted in to regulate the crowds.

Spot, wearing an expensively cut, brown double-breasted suit, was led into Number One court by two guards before sitting hunched, hands in lap, in the dock. Occasionally, Rita brushed down her tight black suit and strolled slowly along the balcony of the public gallery, glancing down at her husband. Her two detective bodyguards remained close by at all times. Back in her seat, Rita's head sunk on her chest and she twisted a lace handkerchief nervously. Tucked in the palm of one hand was a string of coloured beads.

The prosecution based its case on the evidence provided by Tommy Falco and Johnny Rice. The defence depended on statements by Spot and his wife that he was asleep at his flat in Hyde Park Mansions at the time of the alleged attack.

The set-up allegation against Jack Spot was repeated over and over again at the Old Bailey. But no one would say who the 'Mr X' was behind it. The police didn't want Billy Hill's name revealed in court because they feared that it could be used as a lever to get the case thrown out for legal reasons. In any case, most witnesses were too scared to utter his name.

Spot craned his head to see Falco walk in through a side door to the court looking neither left nor right, his face strained as though he was steeling himself for his ordeal. In the witness box, Falco half-turned to the judge, holding his arm awkwardly as though in pain. But when he realised the judge wasn't watching, his head turned and he stared across the court at Jack Spot, straight into his eyes.

Falco described himself as a 'commission agent' before shooting another glance at Spot. He admitted to the court having known Spot for 'maybe seven or eight years. I used to rent a club from him.' But he denied they were ever friends. He then took a deep breath before describing the 'attack': 'He came along and I saw something shining in the air and he brought it down on my arm. I gathered what was going on and brought my left arm up. I felt a pain in my arm, saw blood and grabbed hold of my wrist.'

'Did Comer say anything?' asked Prosecutor Ronnie Seaton.

Falco replied: 'Yeah. He did. He said: "This one's for Albert".'

Prosecutor Seaton glanced at the jury for a moment as though encouraging them to make a special note of this reply.

Next, Falco admitted his friendship with Albert Dimes. As Spot heard mention of Dimes' name, he placed his elbows on the dock rail and rested his forehead in his hands. As he later recalled: 'I forgot the courtroom, forgot that my liberty was involved, and forgot even that Falco was telling the judge of a criminal court that I had attacked him murderously and slashed his arm open to the bone. I could think only of Dimes, his narrowed eyes and his mocking face. Because Dimes was the symbol of all my misery. Dimes and those three minutes of madness.'

Tommy Falco then insisted to the court he never even wanted the police involved in the case. He said: 'I don't like putting people away. I would not do it to my worst enemy. I was afraid of what might happen afterwards if I put him away.'

Then the judge interrupted: 'I see how it goes on. One man slashes another and the other man says, "I will not put him down, my worst enemy, but I will slash him back." There is very little sense in it is there?'

Falco didn't respond. But then he wasn't the brightest of villains; at one stage he had to ask a QC to use 'less big words'. Falco then identified a blood-soaked jacket and shirt as those he was wearing at the time of the attack.

Falco denied seeing Scarface Rossi at Peter Mario's restaurant, in Gerrard Street, when Hill was planning the alleged set-up. Spot's defence counsel Victor Durand, QC, suggested Billy Hill had been in the restaurant and had said to *Sunday People* reporter Duncan Webb: 'I want you to have a go at Spot this week.' Falco again insisted he never saw Hill or Webb in the restaurant. Falco also denied that Billy Hill was his guv'nor. 'We're just friends,' he said.

Victor Durand then turned away from Falco and gestured to his junior who handed him a slip of paper. 'I want you to listen to these names,' he said, before reeling off Rice, Blythe, Warren, Fraser, Dennis and at least half a dozen other Hill associates. Falco admitted knowing them all. His eyes then darted around until they locked on Spot once more.

When main witness Johnny Rice took the stand he was asked about a suggestion that he and others had put their heads together to bring the charge against Spot. Rice replied: 'I would not risk the lives of my children, my wife and myself to do a thing like that.' Jack Spot listened intently to Johnny Rice's evidence. He still genuinely feared he was about to cop a lengthy prison sentence for a crime he hadn't committed.

ʃ   ʃ   ʃ

The following day, 17 July, Billy Hill was a surprise witness in the Falco slashing case. He strode, pale-faced, bespectacled and wearing a neat, double-breasted, blue serge suit, into the court. His Cockney accent and the way he leaned heavily on the edge of the witness box added to his casual demeanour.

As he prepared to be questioned, he shot a swift and mocking glance at Spot. Then he rattled off the oath like an old hand. As he gave the Bible back to the clerk of the court, he tugged at his own coat lapels gently. Hill told the court he was a clerk by profession and that he had known Spot since 1947 and Scarface Russo since about 1940.

'Did you ever embark on any scheme with Russo?' asked prosecutor Seaton.

'Na,' interrupted Hill confidently.

'You must wait for the question before giving answers,' the judge told Hill, who didn't even look up.

'I've seen the newspapers,' said Hill with a smirk.

Seaton then asked if Hill had ever spoken to Glasgow-based Scarface Russo about receiving a knife wound. Hill denied it, naturally.

But Hill's confidence was shaken by the first question from Spot's QC, Victor Durand. 'Do you know what I mean by the word "straight"?' Durand asked as he rose to begin a fifteen-minute examination. Hill quietly replied 'a straight line' as he slouched even more on the witness box. Then with the booming voice of a Sergeant Major, Mr Durand demanded: 'Do you mind standing up STRAIGHT in this court?' Hill sprang smartly to attention, smoothing down his jacket, and waited for the next question. He admitted knowing both Fraser and Warren, who had been convicted of attacking Spot, and that Rice was a business partner of his.

Durand then asked him: 'What title do you take for yourself, if not a kingdom or a dukedom?' Hill drew himself up, looked challengingly around the court at the judge, the jury and the public. Then he said loudly and clearly: 'I am the boss of the underworld.'

Hill made that boast for Spot's benefit. He didn't care about the assembled press. He simply wanted to make sure that Spot got the message. Spot later admitted thinking to himself: 'It's all yours, Billy. I'm not disputing the throne any longer. I'm finished now.' Many in the public gallery that day muttered and sneered because Hill had dared to utter those words in the highest court in the land. But others had a sneaking admiration for a man who had the nerve to make such a statement.

During the lunch recess, Spot was taken down to the cell below the courts, which was an escape from the irritation of looking at the smarmy, intimidating faces in the public gallery. An hour later, it was Albert Dimes' turn in the witness box. He denied that he was angry with Spot and Rita and described himself as a 'nonentity'. His testimony added little else to the case. Scotland Yard's Detective Inspector Mannings then admitted to the court that his officers had not kept a continuous watch on the Spot's home throughout the night of the alleged knife attack on Falco.

A few minutes later, the court was adjourned for the day and Spot was taken back to Brixton Prison in a Black Maria with postcard-sized, barred windows, to stop any press photographers from snatching a shot of the one-time king of the underworld.

The following day, defence witness Victor 'Johnny' Russo – a.k.a. Scarface – told the court how Billy Hill had offered him £500 to be slashed outside the Astor Club. Prosecutor Seaton asked Russo: 'Why did you change your mind?'

'I mix with a lot of crooked people,' explained Russo. 'And forever, people would be pointing at me and saying, "He's the man that got Spot done." I have never been accused of doing anything like that before, and it's just not worth the money.'

Then came Russo's prison cellmate Bill Kennedy, known as 'the Duke'. He told the court: 'He [Russo] said he was going to say the whole thing was a set-up, and mentioned the names of Rice, Hill and Dimes as some of those responsible for the set-up.' Either Russo was lying or Billy Hill had managed to purchase the services of Kennedy as a key witness.

Summing up, Spot's counsel Victor Durand made it clear to the court what he thought of his own client, Jack Spot. 'He's on a rung of a ladder that is a mile below the rung of decent society,' said Durand. He then, however, pointed out that being a crook didn't make Spot guilty of the charges he faced.

Mr Justice Streatfield advised the jury to reflect on the probability of the story of Spot lying in wait. The judge said: 'How in the world would Comer know that these two men [Falco and Rice] were going to that club, one only for the second time in his life? How would he know when they were coming out? How would he know they were going to walk away in that direction?

'Let us assume he was lurking there. What does he see? Not Falco by himself, rather a little fellow, but accompanied by that giant Rice. Do you think that a man with a razor is going to lurk there and have a slash at the little one and hope to get away with it? It may be that the slashing is done quickly, but does that man slash the smaller of the two men when he can be caught by that big, burly man Rice the next second?'

Then Mr Justice Streatfield made a comment that one newspaper, the *Daily Mirror*, thought of sufficient importance to splash across both its front and back pages the following day. 'Unhappily, in London at any rate, if not in other places in this country, there has for some little time been something like gang warfare going on – and heartily sick of it all respectable people are becoming. People slash one another, by way of revenge, with razors, and everyone is getting fed up with it. These scenes that we have seen, or heard of, are a disgrace to modern life in this great city. We only wish something could happen to stamp it out – as assuredly it will be, because common sense prevails in the end and law and order will be relied on.'

The judge continued: 'Some people might think judges attained their positions in almost pitiful ignorance of the affairs of the world in general. However that may be, that does not go for the jury. You may think that the very existence of gang warfare as I have called it might be a factor which lends colour to the possibilities that this in truth was a frame-up.'

Then the judge sent out the jury. Twenty minutes later, at 3.11 p.m. on 18 July 1956, the ten men and two women returned to find Jack Spot not guilty. There was a small ripple of applause from the public gallery. Others glared in anger. For the second time in twelve months, Spot had been found not guilty and discharged. He gave a slight bow to the judge, smiled with relief and stepped out of the dock.

Jack Spot tried to slip quietly through the door at the back of the court, but a crowd had gathered and reporters were trying to thrust their way through to get a quote. Uniformed police ushered Spot along a corridor to the lift at the end of the Old Bailey building and took him to a downstairs back exit. Spot hailed a taxi and went straight home to Rita. Behind him, he noticed about two hundred people sweeping towards the Old Bailey, trying to catch a glimpse of the notorious gangsters.

Also outside the Old Bailey was Billy Hill, still fuming over one counsel's description of him as a 'miserable little character'. He told reporters, 'If I'm a miserable little character, then why do the police watch me night and day?' Hill admitted that Warren and Fraser were 'two of my boys' and said that, despite Rita's evidence sending them to jail, he had taken no part in any attempt to 'frame' her husband. Many present rolled their eyes in disbelief.

23
CERTAIN FORCES

Spot came out of the trial a changed man. Gone was the mindless bravado. In its place was a more reflective character, fuelled by thoughts provoked through his sessions with his psychiatrist. Spot himself commented on his new status:

'The press made me. They built me up into a famous name. And, having done it, they waited patiently for my first slip. And when it came they sprang like a pack of ravenous wolves. They'd built me up to destroy me. They ruthlessly tore me to pieces and toppled me from my throne within the space of a few late-night specials. I've been treated like a monster, like a merciless, cold-blooded criminal. But I'm not like that at all, really. That wild beast stuff is newspaper talk. I'm like any other man. I've got the best wife any man could have, and two wonderful kids. Would my family stop with me if I was a monster? Would I worry about my wife and kids the way I do if I was merciless and inhuman? I'm not bad the way they say I am. Not inside. Not really bad. And what little bad there is inside me isn't my fault, really. That's what the psychiatrist said anyway.'

§ § §

At home, Rita was relieved, dazed and bewildered by her husband's acquittal. 'But I'm sure of one thing: it's going to be a new life for Jack and me from now on,' Rita told one reporter. 'We just want the chance to live the way I used to dream about when I was a little girl in Dublin.'

After the trial, there were public calls for Hill and his men to be prosecuted for perjury, but the police feared the case would never stand up properly in court. Hill began spending more time in Spain, but publication of yet another version of his life story, in the *Sunday People* (through Duncan Webb, naturally), meant he had to remain in London in the weeks following the trial because he was contracted to help publicise the articles. Hill would rather have been sunning himself in the Mediterranean because he knew the Krays would not be pleased having him around. They didn't want to be reminded of his power and influence in the underworld. They saw him purely in an 'advisory capacity' and they certainly didn't want him treading on their toes.

By now, the twins were rumoured to have thrown down the gauntlet to some Islington rivals by heading to north London in a van, armed to the teeth with guns and knives, intent on a showdown. But no one had risen to the bait. The Krays proudly informed Billy Hill about the incident. The last thing Hill wanted was all-out bloodshed, but he knew that, in the long term, he could do nothing to stop the Krays and their mob from heading into the West End. Hill started tipping the twins off about various businesses ripe for protection and even told them about some potential robbery targets. Hill was blatantly feeding such information to the Krays to try and keep them off his back.

Hill and Spot's earlier power had come from their skills in avoiding too much violence. Many of their biggest battles were never actually fought. More than anything else, they were both skilful fixers. And they went out of their way not to offend the police. They also prided themselves on keeping their men in order. But the Krays didn't appreciate such subtleties. The Krays weren't going to promote a 'sensible understanding' with the police because their attitude was, 'Coppers is dirt.'

For years, Spot and Hill had taken the protection money, as well as their cut on gambling and the loot from countless armed blaggings, and they had used their power base for one main purpose: the survival of the status quo. They had often acted more like businessmen, drawing their profits from a discrete monopoly and only becoming dangerous if they felt their empire was being threatened. Both Spot and Hill knew the odds were against them surviving once the big split occurred and that was why Hill had swallowed his pride and now backed the Krays.

When the twins disappeared from their mum's home, Fort Vallance, rumours swept London that they'd been killed in a gangland execution sponsored by their numerous enemies. Then it was claimed that the twins had fled the country and were living it up in the Bahamas on a wedge of cash paid out by Billy Hill to get them off his turf. Hill laughed at this because nothing could have been further from the truth.

The twins re-emerged unscathed a few days later when they set upon a rival gang in Clerkenwell. Ronnie Kray saw their smooth victory as a sign for the future and convinced himself that no one would now be able to prevent their takeover of the West End.

ƒ   *ƒ*   *ƒ*

Shortly after the end of the latest trial, Jack Spot once again tried to contact Hill. 'He talked about owing me £500 and asked if he could call and pay it,' Hill later recalled. Jack Spot never denied offering Hill the £500; he claimed it was the money Hill had wasted on trying to get him framed. But Spot said that never – 'even over my dead body' – did he want to be friends with Hill again.

Over in Soho, a couple of reporters caught up with Hill at one of his clubs and asked him if he would now make his peace with Jack Spot. 'I am a powerful man,' Hill said, 'and I don't have to make peace with anyone.' He said he was fed up of being wrongly blamed for major crimes committed in London, even though he and Spot had shared the spoils of many of the capital's most lucrative robberies. Hill also made a point of referring to a £100,000 Hatton Garden diamond snatch that had occurred just a few days earlier, complaining, 'They even say I did that.' He then, however, couldn't resist discussing the 'brilliant team' involved in that robbery. 'It was a job well done,' he boasted. 'Someone must have studied and imitated my own methods.' The underworld had little doubt that Hill still had his finger in a lot of pies. 'Planning. That's the secret. Pull off the unexpected. That fuddles the police,' said Hill, while still insisting he was now a reformed character.

*   *   *

A few days after his acquittal, Spot and twenty-seven-year-old Rita decided they should hold a belated celebration. Champagne corks popped and Scarface Russo was the guest of honour at Hyde Park Mansions. Spot even promised to drop him some cash the next day as a special thank you for his evidence in court. Russo recalled: 'Rita cried when she talked to me. She was so grateful for what I had done.'

Rita still insisted her husband was quitting the underworld once all the fuss had died down. Spot nodded in agreement when Rita spoke of it, but did he really mean it? Nearly all their money had gone on legal costs and other expenses and Rita knew they'd have to start all over again. She still intended to open a little business far away from London. Rita's dream remained a normal family life without having to constantly look over her shoulder. But others present at that party sensed that Rita's patience with her husband was beginning to run out. Nevertheless, she insisted that she loved her husband and was prepared to do anything for him: 'They can say what they like about Jack, but he is the only man in the world for me.'

Rita also made a point of saying she knew who was behind the threats to her and her family. 'I know they will stop at nothing,' she declared. 'I am not afraid of rats like that, but sometimes I worry about what they might do to our daughters.' In contrast,

Spot tried to play down the entire incident: 'It was a frame-up that didn't work. All I want to do is forget it and start life afresh away from all this rotten business.' He was talking, naturally, of steering clear of Billy Hill as he still didn't fully appreciate that the Kray twins were now busy in the shadows, manipulating the London underworld.

Meanwhile, two Scotland Yard detectives moved into Spot's mansion flat with instructions to answer every caller as well as continuing to escort Spot and his wife wherever they went. Even if Spot had wanted to pull off a few crimes, he wasn't going to get the chance while they were in residence.

*   *   *

The day after the party, Scarface Russo – standing in the pouring rain at a kiosk outside Madame Tussaud's in Marylebone – phoned Spot to remind him about the £100 cash Spot had promised him. Ten minutes later, Rita's sister Carmel appeared wearing a two-piece suit. Russo, with his coat collar turned up, partially hiding the vivid razor scars on his face, got into the back of a waiting car with her. For ten minutes they talked. Then Russo emerged clutching an envelope filled with twenty five-pound notes. It was a sign of the times that Jack Spot now had to use his wife's sister to carry out his errands. Russo himself later insisted to one reporter: 'There's nothing crooked about it. Jack was grateful for what I did. I only did my duty. It's a present to buy the kids something – and to cover my expenses for the three weeks I was waiting for the trial to come up.'

Within twenty-four hours, Russo was on a train back to Scotland to run his caff at Coatbridge, near Glasgow. Before his departure, he insisted to newsmen that he was not frightened of returning to London. 'I can come back to London again anytime. A man can be crooked and still have some decent instincts. When I saw people toasting the arrest of Jack Spot in Soho clubs I was sickened. I went to the police and told them all I knew.'

'Am I in danger?' Russo's scars rippled as his lips twisted into a grin. 'I tell you, if I'm killed, Billy Hill will be dead within the next twenty-four hours.' Russo was happy to discuss the gangs that 'plagued the capital'. He went on: 'It's time people got the idea that things in London are even worse than they imagine. If Spot had been convicted there would have been real trouble. I know fifty men who would have been quite happy to mix it with the mob from the other side and start a real war. I heard four men threw revolvers into the Thames when they heard the verdict.'

*   *   *

Spot and Rita made a very public display of getting daughters Rachel, aged four, and Marion, aged sixteen months, christened a few weeks after his acquittal of the Falco attack. Two policemen remained on duty outside Hyde Park Mansions. Another detective accompanied Spot's children, holding the hand of Rachel at the service at Our Lady of the Rosary, Marylebone Road. Afterwards, Spot told newsmen: 'My wife promised the priest that if I got off she would have the kiddies christened. She is a Roman Catholic and very religious.' He laughed when asked if he'd converted to Catholicism.

On 20 August 1956, Jack Spot and Rita spent more than an hour at Scotland Yard being questioned by Detective Superintendent Daws, who was investigating all aspects of the Falco case. The following day one Fleet Street paper reported that a man known as 'Big Brain' was at the top of the list of six names submitted to the Director of Public Prosecutions in connection with the plot to frame Spot. Many believed this was Billy Hill's new codename at the Yard. Spot continued to state that 'certain forces' were to blame for all his troubles. 'I'll never get away from them. They'll do me up again sometime.'

He considered opening a bar called 'Jack Spot's' on the basis that the public would fall over themselves to be served a beer by Jack Spot. But he dropped the idea after concluding that a lot of his old enemies might not like him publicising himself so brazenly. The only other alternative was to hit the real world and get himself a 'normal' job. He was forty-four years old with no specific skills, no references and, in his own words, 'nothing to commend me'. But Spot believed going straight was the only option available. He knew the cops would laugh behind his back, not to mention his old friends and foes in Soho. 'It would give Billy Hill a laugh too. But the more I thought about it, the more I saw it as the only answer to my problems. It'd even give me and Rita a little happiness,' he explained.

Was Jack Spot finally serious about walking away from a life of crime? Rita and the kids undoubtedly took priority over everything else. Forget the fast cars, fast women, gambling joints and racetrack dust-ups: Jack Spot needed a normal, stress-free life as a regular guy.

ƒ   ƒ   ƒ

Jack Spot still got a measure of respect in the outside world. A novelist called Madame Raymonde Marchard announced she was writing a play based on Jack Spot's exploits. Spot was naturally most flattered. Then further publicity came through a spate of petty libel writs between Spot, Billy Hill and Johnny Rice. As one journalist explained at the time: 'It was farcical. They were all threatening to sue each other for defamation. Yet everyone knew they were villains.' Eventually all three men dropped their actions when they realised the only people who'd win out of it all were the fat-cat lawyers charging vast hourly rates for their services.

Billy Hill continued spin-doctoring his own image by giving an interview to the *Sunday Express* insisting he was glad Jack Spot had got off the previous month. 'I'm real glad. No one should go to prison. I know what prisons are – I've spent sixteen of my forty-five years in them.' Bizarrely, Hill had insisted on being interviewed as he drove a green Jaguar with Albert Dimes sitting alongside him. 'Jack Spot hates me. I do not hate Jack Spot. He has sworn that he is my enemy,' said Hill, as he sailed right past the entrance to Spot's home at Hyde Park Mansions. Then he was asked if he'd make peace with his rival. 'Make peace with that villain? Never. If I go to him he'll believe that's a sign of weakness.'

Then, after coolly asking the Express reporter to 'gimme light' for his cigarette, Hill continued: 'I'm staying right here. I've done no wrong, no wrong at all. Perjury? I've nothing to fear. All this talk going on that I framed Jack Spot to get even for what his wife has been saying is nonsense. I don't think the police believe this and I don't think they will charge me. What would I want to frame that oaf for? They say I offered Russo £500 to have his arm slashed and swear in court that Spot did it. Give Russo a monick? If I gave Russo my apple core I'd miss it.'

Then Albert Dimes' chipped in: 'Get this. I'm a bookmaker. I'm an ordinary man. Ever since that fight I was involved in with Spot last year I've been called a gangster. Nonsense, lies.'

§   §   §

On 24 August 1956, Spot's old pal Sonny the Yank – the alleged merchant seaman from Stepney – was released from prison after serving almost a year for conspiracy in the Reverend Basil Andrews case. As Sonny walked out of Wandsworth Jail, a senior prison officer called from the doorway: 'This time, Sonny, make sure you catch that boat!'

Sonny was still fuming because he'd taken a fall for Jack Spot and had got absolutely nothing in return. Spot hadn't paid Sonny's family a retainer while he was inside, which destroyed any loyalty that might have remained between the two men. Spot knew Sonny was angry with him but there was nothing he could do about it because he didn't have the money to keep his own family afloat, let alone Sonny's or anyone else's.

Then a taxi arrived outside Wandsworth nick, containing Sonny's wife and daughter. Sonny hugged them warmly and he went back to Stepney for breakfast and a Turkish bath. That night the Krays laid on a special 'welcome home' party for Sonny, just to make sure he never returned to Jack Spot. He swore he'd never talk to Spot ever again.

24

BETWEEN THE LINES

In October 1956, Rita became an official pin-up for the Post Office when she was named one of the three most beautiful women in the news that year by the Union of Post Office Workers' journal. The two other women were Queen Soraya of Iraq and Drussilla Demetriades, a Cypriot whose fiancé had been killed by terrorists. Rita told a reporter who broke the news to her: 'At last I seem to be in good company.'

The trial of Billy Boy Blythe, Battles Rossi and Ginger Dennis – all accused of taking part in that attack on Spot and Rita outside their home – opened at the Old Bailey on 8 October before Mr Justice Cassels. Dodgy brief Patrick Marrinan, QC, was once again defending one of Hill's team.

Rita took the stand as key witness and immediately told the court: 'Blythe was bent over my husband and sort of digging things into him and Rossi came up and had a few whacks at my husband.' Rita's evidence was interpreted across the underworld as Jack Spot still hiding behind the skirt of his pretty young wife. Many villains reckoned he was so dominated by her that he'd simply not been able to prevent her giving evidence against some of London's most dangerous men.

On 16 October 1956, Blythe, Rossi and Dennis were convicted of unlawfully wounding Jack Spot. Blythe got five years and the other two were sentenced to four years each. Mr Justice Cassels stressed to the defendants. 'If men like you get tough with other people you will have to realise that the law can get tough with you.' Blythe was dragged away shouting, 'It's a mockery of justice.' Rossi and Dennis looked stunned. At the back of the court, officers mingled with members of the public in case of trouble.

Rita, dressed in a dove-grey dress over a navy-blue blouse, was held back by her police escorts in the court for nearly half an hour until the public had all departed. Outside, other detectives sat amongst the crowd waiting for Rita to appear. Finally, as the onlookers started to disperse, a police car drew up and Rita – surrounded by bodyguards – ran out of the main entrance to be bundled into a squad car that drove off at high speed. Fifteen detectives in plain clothes had been involved that day in her protection.

The mounting costs of a round-the-clock guard on Rita sparked a public outcry. One newspaper calculated how much it was costing per day to protect her, and Scotland Yard was unable to say when the guard would be dropped. Rita was still believed to be in danger from her husband's underworld associates. Anyone who called at Hyde Park Mansions to see Spot or Rita got a two-man police escort up to the front door.

ƒ   ƒ   ƒ

Just after the end of the Blythe, Dennis and Rossi trial, Spot's first wife, Mollie, emerged from the shadows to speak to the *Sunday Dispatch* newspaper. She lived just a couple of miles from Spot's West End home in the upstairs room of a boarding house. Most of the public hadn't even realised Spot was previously married. Mollie told the *Dispatch*: 'Those years leave a mark in any life. They ruined my health. I was a pretty and healthy girl when I married Jackie. I could tell of the years we spent together, where we went and whom we knew – I knew them all. I can fill in the gaps in the public story of Jack's life. But, though I don't think he would harm me, there are always his friends . . . and I've got to be careful.'

Mollie insisted she'd tried her hardest to 'make Jackie a better man'. She said she'd given him excessive freedom because she genuinely thought it would help him. But now she was reading in newspapers about his glamorous life with a pretty, new, young wife. 'I got no financial settlement. I have no money. I had thought Jackie would have been more of a gentleman.' She revealed that Spot had only occasionally given her money towards his son's upkeep. 'I have had a hard time, but when I divorced Jackie in law I divorced him from my heart.' Mollie pleaded with the *Sunday Dispatch*: 'Whatever you do, don't disclose this address.'

Spot told friends he felt bad about Mollie and his son when he read the interview. Rita had long since forbidden him from talking about them at home. As far as she was concerned, they didn't exist, which made Spot's efforts to be a responsible father to his only son even trickier. He'd only visited Mollie a handful of times over the previous twenty years. Now he was almost as broke as she, so there was little or no chance of him offering any financial support. Spot later claimed that Mollie had prevented him from seeing more of his son but it was impossible – as in many domestic disputes – to tell who was speaking the truth.

Meanwhile, the Krays suffered their first-ever setback when Ronnie was given a three-year jail sentence for his role in the bayoneting and stabbing of a man called Terry Martin. Ronnie was convinced by Billy Hill that Jack Spot had played a part in fingering him for the crime. Hill claimed Spot had become increasingly suspicious about the role the Krays had played in his own demise. The twins said they were outraged and swore that, if Spot ever tried to make a comeback, they'd break his legs. But they were shrewd enough to realise that Hill's claims needed to be taken with a pinch of salt.

Billy Hill knew that Spot had little more than his fat cigar to put between himself and the Krays. Five years earlier and he and Spot would have seen off the Krays and their tearaways with ease. Now, young as the twins were, they'd openly challenged the toughest criminals in London and Hill knew that Ronnie's jail sentence would only fuel the climate of fear.

The twins considered Jack Spot to be a phoney and Hill nothing more than their consultant. They believed their power base would expand rapidly because by the mid-1950s crime had outgrown the race gangs. But the one person who still didn't seem to fully appreciate the danger the Krays presented was Jack Spot.

♪   ♪   ♪

After the court case, reporter Duncan Webb, naturally encouraged by Billy Hill, set about putting the final twist of the knife into Jack Spot (figuratively speaking of course). He wrote an article for the *Sunday People* reminding readers of various questionable aspects of Spot's background and even encouraging the Home Secretary to have Spot investigated. Webb claimed that MPs wanted to know whether there was any truth in Spot's alleged boast that 'the police relied on me to clean-up the West End and certain racecourses'.

Billy Hill was quoted in the Webb article: 'One reason why Spot's now so unpopular in the underworld is because crooks are convinced he's a stool pigeon for the police. They are certain he has given information which has got more than one person gaoled.' Hill knew only too well that the best way to damage Spot was to label him a grass. Spot always denied ever helping the police and there is no evidence to suggest anything to the contrary. Once again, Jack Spot had been well and truly stitched up by Hill and an article written by Webb in the *Sunday People*.

♪   ♪   ♪

On 1 February 1957, Jack Spot collapsed after a heavy meal at Hyde Park Mansions and was rushed to St Mary's Hospital, Paddington. Fleet Street were tipped off about Spot's hospital drama and door-stepped him at St Mary's for quotes. Naturally, the one-time king of the underworld put his own spin on what happened. 'I got drunk,' he told reporters the following day. 'You could have knocked me down with a feather when I woke up this morning and found myself in St Mary's Hospital, Paddington. The last time I was there was when I had nearly two hundred stitches after being attacked.'

Spot claimed his sister-in-law had found him, passed out drunk in his own bed. He explained: 'She's never seen me like that before so she thought I was ill and called an ambulance . . . I went on the loose with some pals who were with me in the army. We had a few bottles of champagne. That's it fellas. That's all that happened.' Then he added with a smile: 'Of course it wouldn't have happened if my wife was around. Rita was away but she had a good laugh about it when I told her.'

Spot believed the story of his collapse was given to the press by some of his old enemies in Soho. He told one hack: 'Some people must be dancing, thinking I'm very ill. I'm sorry to disappoint them.' But the pressure on Spot was increasing from all sides. He'd started hearing whispers about the Kray twins and how they considered him to be 'dead meat'. At home, Rita and her family continued to press him about quitting London but he could barely afford to live at Hyde Park Mansions so what chance did he have away from his few remaining criminal enterprises?

Spot couldn't even afford to continue seeing his Harley Street psychiatrist, leaving a lot of his personal problems unsolved. His expensive Havana cigars were a thing of the past and his suits were starting to need replacing. He'd been squeezed out, but the very thing his psychiatrist had warned him about – his perceived invincibility – had, until now, prevented him from fully appreciating the seriousness of his situation.

*   *   *

A few days later, Jack Spot applied to Westminster City Council for a street-trader's licence to become a barrow boy in Victoria, central London. When one reporter rang up to verify the facts Spot growled: 'Load of rubbish. Why don't you people leave me alone?' In fact it was completely true, but Spot was worried his application might be rejected if the council realised who he was.

The pitch was in Churton Street, near a new market at the back of Warwick Way, Victoria. It was another attempt by Spot to earn an honest wage but, once news of his application got out, he knew he wouldn't be granted the licence. 'I can see no reason why I shouldn't earn a living, even as a barrow boy,' Spot told an associate. 'I'm up for bankruptcy proceedings and I have no money after the expenses of the legal cases, when I was injured and brought near death twice.' Just as Spot predicted, the licence application was turned down. All that earlier talk of opening a business 'far away from London' and renting a house in Sussex had been dropped. Even running a caff now seemed a distant dream.

Shortly afterwards, Spot's ego once again got the better of him when he agreed to have his picture painted for an exhibition at London's Royal Academy. Spot was highly amused and told one reporter: 'I've forgotten the name of the artist but they tell me the guy can get £2000 for a picture. Can you beat that?' Then he added: 'Imagine me being hung up there in the Royal Academy. Still I suppose it's better than being hung in Pentonville.'

In February 1957, Spot attended the London Bankruptcy Court and insisted on using the name John Colmore in the hope that Fleet Street wouldn't get a sniff of his appearance. But a pack of newshounds turned up to hear Spot deny to the court that he owned twenty handmade suits. He claimed he only had three suits, three pairs of shoes and two overcoats and 'a few ties'. Sole claimant was crime reporter Duncan Webb who wanted £1031 18s. 8d., which he said was still unpaid from the assault case back in 1954.

Spot admitted liabilities of £1321 and assets of £125. He claimed his wife owned the furniture in the flat, worth about £100. Spot told the hearing: 'I would have been better off in prison for three years then being beaten up by twenty-five men and being here today.' Spot said that in 1950 he had £2000 in Post Office savings. But, since then, he hadn't managed to save a penny. He claimed that, of the £2000, half had gone to bookmakers and half to pay for his son from his first marriage to go to boarding school. Spot did admit receiving £3200 for Sunday newspaper articles. But he'd splashed out much more than that on four solicitors' firms during his criminal proceedings. He also conceded having bookmaking pitches which he let out, but claimed he made just £4 a week from them.

The Official Receiver said Spot's annual income-tax return to April 1955 showed a profit of £600 but he could show no tax returns for the following financial year. Spot was then offically declared bankrupt and told by the court that eviction from his £5 10s. a week flat at Hyde Park Mansions would have to take place immediately. As a registered bankrupt, he could not hold the flat lease, although his solicitors did manage to arrange for a forty-eight-hour reprieve.

Outside the court, Rita insisted to reporters that they were on the breadline: 'People think we're millionaires. But we need three bedrooms and we can't afford the prices, let alone the key money. If the bailiffs come – well it's too bad. I've given up looking for a new place. Let them come. We've been in and out of jail. Being thrown out of a flat is nothing.'

Two days later, Rita and her daughter Rachel arrived home after horse riding in Hyde Park, just as the bailiffs were being let in by two policemen on duty outside the mansion block. Rita told one reporter waiting outside: 'My Jack is down in Surrey seeing a friend who might be able to find us somewhere to live within our means. We are in this jam because our defence in the courts cost so much.' A few minutes later, the bailiffs emerged with a sofa, two armchairs and a transistor radio plus a few boxes of books and cutlery. Spot's long and colourful reign at Hyde Park Mansions was over.

*   *   *

In his hour of dire financial need, Jack Spot turned to his old friend Vic Sims at the *Sunday Chronicle* who agreed to run an updated version of the paper's earlier serialisation of Spot's life story. The article introduced him thus: Jack Spot is not a criminal: he is purely and simply a fighter.

The *Sunday Chronicle* went on to project Spot as the hero of the East End: a man who had fought his way to the top. The paper even fed its readers a misconception about the origins of the name 'Spot': 'Down in Fieldgate Street, Whitechapel, the locals would say, when one of the big bruisers started insulting customers of a cafe: "That tearaway is asking for trouble." Then the shout would go up: "Jack's on the spot." And, within a few seconds, the bruiser would be on the floor.'

Jack Spot wasn't bothered about any inaccuracies. His main priority was the thousand-pound fee the paper agreed to pay provided he put his name to the series of articles. Even Rita's diamonds were no longer around to pawn, as she'd sold them off to help Spot's legal defence on his last court appearance. Spot now wanted to make a completely new start. He'd heard some of the rumours about what the Krays were planning once Ronnie got out of prison. Britain was a non-starter, so he decided to try abroad. Spot decided he'd travel alone to Quebec, Canada, to check it out before sending for Rita and the kids.

On 27 August 1957, Spot left Liverpool on the Greek-registered liner *Columbia*, under his own name. After saying farewell to her husband, Rita headed for Dublin. She didn't disclose Spot's plans to anyone while she stayed at her sister, Sadie's, top-storey flat on the rundown council estate. When one local reporter came knocking she told him: 'If I talked about Jack's plans, you can bet someone would step in and ruin them. In the last two years we have had enough. All we want is to be allowed to live in peace and bring up our children decently. We don't want people telling our daughters that they are Jack Spot's children. We don't want them to know anything about the past.'

While Jack Spot enjoyed a champagne-and-caviar lifestyle aboard the *Columbia*, Fleet Street was talking to Canadian immigration officials after receiving dozens of anonymous calls telling them that Spot had fled to Canada. On 4 September, Spot arrived in Quebec and was immediately detained. He told immigration officers that he was in Canada to visit a sick brother. Spot argued loudly with them as they hauled him off the liner: 'You can't do this to me. I've never done anything wrong.' Then he turned to a bunch of reporters on the quayside, shrugged his shoulders and said: 'What's the use? These people have it in for me anyway.' One immigration official told pressmen that a permit granting him temporary admission might be granted if Spot could show the necessity for visiting his 'sick brother in Winnipeg'. But there was no evidence he even existed. Until then, he was to be held by the authorities.

On the way to jail in Quebec, the head of immigration told Spot: 'You won't be seeing much of this country, bud.' He then kindly ordered his driver to make a detour around the city while he showed Spot some historical landmarks. Spot was held in a smaller cell than he'd ever been in Britain. Then he was taken to see the prison governor, who turned out to be a boxing fan. Spot and the governor were soon engaged in a discussion on the sport, and, 'from then on, things were not so bad', explained Spot.

Spot later pointed out he could easily have sneaked into Canada if he'd really wanted to. 'False passport, quick flight over, and I would have been in the clear,' he said. 'But I played it straight and look what happens. I am pushed around by a lot of immigration fellows and tossed in jail and, to add insult to injury, all I read in the papers is how bad this fellow Spot is.' Spot was officially deported from Canada the following day and boarded the *Skaubryn*, bound for Southampton. Immigration officials escorted him aboard the liner and he was kept in a locked cabin until the ship was out of territorial waters.

Five days later in Southampton, Rita, wearing a black-and-white hat and full-length, dark-brown fur coat, got up at dawn in her Southampton hotel to make the five-mile journey by tug to meet Spot as the *Skaubryn* anchored off the Isle of Wight. Spot, pale-faced, slipped back the catch of his steerage class cabin door to kiss Rita and grab his baggage. Once on the tug, he sipped tea with his wife and talked of his Canadian adventures, saying, 'A fine lark this, isn't it?'

Once on the train to London, Rita snapped down the window blind to keep out prying eyes from their second-class compartment. On arrival back at London's Waterloo Station, Spot told reporters: 'My holiday cost me £200 for nothing.' He insisted the Canadians had got it all wrong when they claimed he was visiting a sick brother. 'I haven't got a brother in Canada. I never said I had.' He also said that the Canadians had received anonymous letters stating that Spot intended to open illegal betting shops throughout the country.

Minutes later, a dark-blue, Mark II Jaguar arrived at Waterloo for Spot and Rita. Spot supervised the loading of his luggage into the boot and then they roared off into the early evening London traffic. The car had been sent by Reggie Kray as a 'welcome home' gesture'. Spot was too exhausted from his journey to question the wisdom in accepting such a 'gift'. One of the Krays oldest associates later explained: 'Reggie just wanted to remind Spot that things had changed, and he and Ronnie were now calling the shots. Reggie visited Ronnie in prison a few days later and they had a right laugh about it.' This time Jack Spot probably did get the message.

ƒ   ƒ   ƒ

Back in London, Spot and his family moved into a shabby, one-bedroom flat in the East End, near where Spot had been brought up, and right in the middle of the Krays' territory. But he had no choice in the matter. Spot was so desperate for money that he started hawking around an idea for an autobiographical book about his criminal career. Most of the big publishers instantly turned him down on the basis that he'd told everything to the newspapers already. But then Spot approached a smaller publisher called Alexander Moring, who suggested that a pulp-fiction writer called Steve Francis could be the perfect ghostwriter for such a project. Moring believed a more dramatic, fiction-style approach would work for the book. Spot signed a deal with Moring for £1000 with the promise of lots more cash to come if it was a best seller.

Francis and Spot spent hour after hour and day after day in each other's company, reliving Jack Spot's life, digging deep into his past. Francis wanted to analyse and uncover the truth and, as far as was possible, try to understand the events of Jack Spot's life. Francis believed there were a number of fundamental reasons that sparked Spot's declining role in the underworld: 'His downfall was not caused by authority, it was caused by his own inordinate pride, a touch of persecution mania and an unwillingness to admit he could be bested.'

Francis bled Spot dry of facts, making him relive his experiences, tripping him up with his own contradictory statements, checking and rechecking the real facts that Spot seemed reluctant to admit. Francis later admitted: 'It is doubtful whether many other books have been written suffering from so many handicaps as this one. From beginning to end, writing it was a tiptoe journey across broken glass.'

Francis struggled to find the right formula for the book because he was more used to writing fiction. The publishers warned Spot it would take at least six months for Francis to produce the first draft once the series of interviews were completed. 'I'd listened to Jack Spot's voice until merely the echo of it threatened to drive me round the bend,' Francis later recalled. 'I'd absorbed so much of Jack Spot, I could almost think in the way Jack Spot himself thought, so that's what gave me my angle.'

Francis faced one headache that he, as a novelist, had never encountered before: legal problems. As he later explained: 'If Jack Spot had lived a hundred years ago, there would be no such problem. I could have given places, dates, times and names and all other evidence of every crime he had committed. But Jack Spot still lived – and so did those who associated with him.' Francis was particularly disturbed by a number of anonymous threats he received.

Francis's big dilemma was telling the difference between fact and fiction. He later explained: 'Much of the information I possessed I couldn't substantiate. To substantiate it I needed facts, figures and dates. And this substantiating information was impossible to obtain from Jack Spot. Wild horses wouldn't drag it from him.'

When word got out that Spot was supposedly telling the *whole* story, many associates let it be known they would not tolerate their real names being published. Spot himself was also obsessed with pointing out repeatedly in the book that he was not a police grass. Even the introduction had to state: 'The underworld has a code which is rigidly enforced. No criminal dares to squeal upon another. Jack Spot hasn't and wouldn't break that code. He *daren't* break it!' So here was a warts-and-all book by Jack Spot, but it gave little away about his time in the underworld because he didn't want other villains to think he was a grass.

To make matters worse for Spot, it emerged that the book would not be completed and published for at least a year, leaving him penniless until then. Spot was forced to sign on the dole but found it a humiliating experience to queue up for his weekly allowance of £4 6s. He needed to pull something out of the hat – and fast – if he was going to survive.

25

HIGHBALLING

On 16 January 1958, Spot returned to the bankruptcy court to be discharged from his debts and, again, insisted on being referred to as John Colmore. He arrived with Rita on his arm, wearing a fur coat, which didn't seem a wise thing to wear under the circumstances. The couple sat together gloomily on a bench outside the courtroom while the application was heard. Spot insisted he hadn't worked since the original bankruptcy hearing and claimed a 'relative' had lent him the £113 it cost to travel to see his 'sick brother' in Canada.

Crime reporter Duncan Webb told the court he still hadn't received his compensation money from the attack three years ago. Webb opposed the application for a discharge, but he'd failed to lodge an earlier formal complaint because he'd been out of the country on an assignment. The Registrar threw out Webb's application, much to Spot's relief. When the couple were told the discharge had been granted, subject to a six-month suspension, both their faces lit up. Others, such as the electric and gas company plus Rita's favourite riding stable in Hyde Park were all left out of pocket by the decision.

Leaning on Spot's arm as they emerged from the hearing, Rita told waiting reporters: 'All Jack is interested in now is his home and children.' Spot smiled broadly and told the press: 'I've been living on the dole for months. Now I can start life all over again.' Brandishing an umbrella he then announced: 'Don't call me Spot any more. My name's Colmore. John Colmore. I know nothing about business. Sure, I know something about the racing game, but I've finished with that. Don't worry, I'll find something to do.' Then Rita chipped in: 'We've lost our home. Everything. Why don't you write about Billy Hill? They say he's a criminal.' Jack Spot winced as he heard his wife utter that name.

Rita still considered herself a quiet, simple Dublin girl thrust into the underworld spotlight. She blamed Spot's inability to find a 'straight' job on underworld look-out men who shadowed his every move. She claimed that, every time he applied for a job, 'someone put the knife in and made sure Jack's background became known'. The couple's efforts to open a business, such as a shop, pub or restaurant in Ireland, had all failed, claimed Rita, for this same reason. Spot's applications for jobs as a chauffeur and a lorry driver in London were also turned down. 'The underworld doesn't like letting go of anyone, so it set about to destroy us,' she told one reporter.

Rita was already doing her bit by working as a waitress in a restaurant near their tiny East End flat. She wanted to learn more about the catering trade, and still harboured dreams of opening a caff or restaurant. 'We won't make a fortune, but maybe we'll find peace of mind,' she explained: 'Only a woman could appreciate what it has been like. Seven years of marriage to my man have made me grow up quickly. I am still only twenty-eight. It was hard for me to stand up before the world in courts and at the Old Bailey, but I did it for my husband and my children.'

But, behind her loyal outburst, Rita now felt resentful towards her husband because the 'normal' life they had talked about so often simply wasn't materialising. She told one friend: 'If Jack had listened to me years ago we wouldn't have been in this position today, thrown out of our home and penniless.'

In June 1958, Rita reluctantly agreed to front a nightclub, called the Highball, in London's Lancaster Gate. 'It was the only way I knew how to make some dough,' Jack Spot later explained, claiming Rita used money from newspaper articles to finance the club. The third person behind the enterprise was Mrs Kaszia Hinga, who'd been connected to many London nightclubs since before the war. She believed that Spot's name was still worth exploiting.

Spot publicised the Highball by giving groups of Fleet Street reporters guided tours through the Regency-style lounge with its reproduction Louis XV furniture. Many of them sniggered when they spotted a jukebox in the far corner of the room. Spot believed he could run the club without treading on anyone else's toes. He even told one friendly hack: 'We've not had any trouble here and we aren't lookin' for it. We just want a peaceful club among our friends.' However Spot also loudly boasted to the visiting journalists that he expected the club to be a runaway success. 'We're limiting membership to our friends,' he said. 'A chain on the front door is supposed to keep out any unwelcome visitors.'

The Krays and Billy Hill were outraged when they heard Spot was involved in another club, even if his wife was supposed to be the owner. The Krays were the new club kings of the West End and the last thing they wanted was Jack Spot getting in their way. Mad Frankie Fraser later confirmed that the Highball was a real bone of contention. He explained: 'The club had to go. Spot and his wife had broken the code of conduct, time and again, by going to the police. If you go to the police like Spot and his wife done, then you pay the consequences.'

ℱ   ℱ   ℱ

Within two months of its opening, there were problems at the Highball. The first incident occurred in August 1958, when two men entered the club, picked up a metal bar stool and smashed a customer called Peter Edwards over the head with it. The two men then ran out to a van where a third thug handed out weapons, including crowbars. They used these to smash open the ground-floor door of the club. The men were all screaming, 'Jack Spot, Jack Spot, the fucker. We're going to do him up.'

The police arrived just as the heavies were running off and a battle ensued. Meat porters John Main, of Islington, John Harris, of Camberwell, and Benjamin Harris, also from Camberwell, all ended up at Bow Street magistrates court. They were accused of causing grievous bodily harm to Peter Edwards and to PC Peter Long, with intent to resist arrest, and with assaulting another policeman.

The initial GBH charges were dropped when victim Peter Edwards refused to give evidence against the three men. Prosecutor Richard du Cann explained: 'He is a seaman employed by the Norwegian Merchant Navy and since this arrest he has gone back to sea and is, in the words of the song, on a slow boat to China.'

A few weeks later, Rita left the Highball in the charge of her doorman whilst she went to a party at a nearby flat. Three hours later, just after closing time, a mob of burly men entered the building through the basement. They poured paraffin over the bar stools and chairs, stacked all the tables in the middle of the dance floor and then set light to them before scrambling out through the basement door. Minutes later, the alarm was raised by a cleaning lady. She jumped in a taxi and fetched Jack and Rita, who arrived to find the premises ablaze. One of Spot's few remaining pals told reporters: 'Someone's trying to get at Jack. It's gang warfare.'

Later that morning, Scotland Yard issued a statement saying they feared that the blaze was an attack by a rival mob and that it might provoke fresh outbreaks of gang warfare. Spot defiantly told journalists that he'd reopen the Highball and call it the Silver Slinger.

Then Jack Spot heard on the criminal grapevine that Billy Hill had opened a bank account with £5000 in it, to set Mad Frankie Fraser up again once he got released. Since being sentenced for the chiv attack on Spot and Rita, Fraser had been certified insane and transferred to Broadmoor Mental Hospital. Spot was told that Fraser was being primed by Hill to finish off Spot once he got out. Perhaps it really was time to leave the underworld behind.

After the fire at the Highball Club, Spot and Rita sent their two young daughters to Torquay 'for their own safety' and finally conceded defeat by dropping all plans to reopen the club. Desperate for money, Spot gave an interview to *Illustrated* magazine and projected himself with a new image: 'I am a Jew and that's one thing I am proud of. My wife is Roman Catholic and there have been rumours that I will change my religion. Not true. I will die a Jew.'

Spot desperately tried to give the impression that fighting oppression was his number-one priority. He even began taking credit for an improvement in the anti-Semitic attitude of many Britons. And, for the first time, Spot insisted that crime definitely did not pay. 'I have read that crime is on the increase in Britain, especially among teenagers. My advice to them, by one who knows, is to go out to work.'

Spot believed there was a Fleet Street conspiracy to blacken his name. 'My enemies won't stop hounding me and neither will the sensational newspapers who are still trying to make me out to be another Al Capone. Just look at what I've got to live for: my wife Rita, whom the Union of Post Office Workers journal rightly described as one of the three most beautiful women in the world, and my little daughters, Ray and May. I don't run around with Tom, Dick or Billy any more. I'm a family man. I stay home most nights with the wife and kids.'

By the autumn of 1958, Jack Spot's star may have faded but he still had a remarkable ability to capture headlines. More than one thousand articles had been written about him over the previous ten years. 'I bet not many people have had this amount of stuff written about them,' he boasted to one old lag. And he had a point: Bertrand Russell and Sophia Loren were way behind Spot on the cuttings count.

It seemed now that even Spot's once most loyal henchmen had started taking a pop at him in the press. One-time heavyweight protector Johnny Carter gave an interview to the *Star* newspaper and said he'd been a bodyguard to Spot. Carter's fury was fuelled by Spot's failure to pay him his salary any more. On reading Carter's interview, Spot was so angry he immediately telephoned the *Star* to tell them: 'Why can't you leave my name out of things? Someone's always having a go at me.' Then he raised his voice further and shouted: 'What a lot of fuckin' nonsense. Carter never worked for me. Anyway, I've no time for small-timers.' Spot completely denied ever meeting Carter until the *Star* pointed out that it had a photograph of him together with Carter.

ƒ   ƒ   ƒ

Jack Spot – Man of a Thousand Cuts was finally published in December 1958. Previous books by author Steve Francis's nom de plume 'Hank Janson' boasted sales of thirteen million and it was hoped at least some of his readers would be interested in Spot. But Francis, who dictated his Janson novels onto a tape recorder and then sent the tapes off to his publisher, had struggled to give the book a proper voice. In trying to immerse himself in Spot's character, Francis had written a book that couldn't make up its mind whether it was fact or fiction.

Spot was infuriated. He'd wanted to publish the autobiography to make some much-needed cash and put the record straight about certain events in the past. Steve Francis had wanted it to read like one of his Hank Janson novels, which meant it ignored many issues close to Spot's heart.

Spot later admitted that his relationship with Steve Francis was often fraught with tension. 'He ain't a bad bloke. But he had a way of saying things that sometimes got right up my snout. And sometimes I knew he was deliberately goading me. There were even one or two occasions when I felt the red rage glowing deep down inside me and my fingers began to twitch.' The book – with its tacky fiction-style cover – was not a great success. Worst of all, the publishers wouldn't even splash out for a celebrity-filled launch party like the one Billy Hill had been given. Spot made no more than a few hundred pounds from royalties on the book.

By the beginning of 1959, Jack Spot had truly hit rock bottom. He was once again virtually penniless and still living in that run-down East End flat with Rita and the kids. Spot even admitted to one pal that he was surprised Rita hadn't deserted him. 'She could have made a clean break from me, gone far away and lived quietly,' he said.

Then Rita finally persuaded Spot to move to Dublin and they hoped things would start to look up. Initially, Spot was treated as a celebrity which was perfect since he was desperate not to lapse into obscurity. He even made a few bob as a bookie's runner on courses in Dublin and Cork.

Back in London, the Krays – lacking the steady training of Spot and Hill – were steaming through the underworld like runaway Chieftan Tanks. They wanted control of every important manor in the capital. The twins liked everyone to know that they wouldn't tolerate disloyalty. A lot of people got cut, and the word went out: don't mess with the Krays. The Krays ignored the fact that Spot and Hill's power had come from their ability to avoid violence. They weren't politicians who negotiated their way out of aggravation; they thrived on confrontation. Violence and fear were like a drug to the Krays and they needed very regular fixes. If they needed to knock someone off to prove a point then so be it. As Ronnie later explained: 'We weren't playing kids' games any more.'

New 'industries' sprang up for gangsters like the Krays. In 1960, the Jockey Club decided to introduce proper betting shops to every high street, effectively wiping out the illegal gambling dens and street-corner bookies who'd been so much a part of Jack Spot and Billy Hill's reign. As the big credit bookmakers prepared for the legalisation of off-course betting, the smaller bookmakers and their protectors were being squeezed out of the picture. A favourite racket for the new generation of gangsters was protection of the newly opened betting shops. Then there were the one-armed bandits (fruit machines), which began being installed in shops and clubs across the capital. A new criminal era was dawning and gangsters like Billy Hill and Jack Spot were yesterday's men.

ƒ   ƒ   ƒ

Now living in Dublin, Jack Spot struggled to make ends meet. In the summer of 1960, he told Rita he needed to return to London to find work. The couple agreed they would be reunited once Spot had found a safe, secure home for Rita and their daughters.

Spot, now calling himself John Colmore, eventually got himself a job running a small furniture business off Gloucester Road, Kensington, in West London, and moved into a shabby two-room flat above the shop. But when he asked Rita to join him, it quickly became clear she was not happy. 'Jack had missed London desperately while Rita hated the place and never really wanted to set foot there ever again,' explained one associate who knew Spot during this period. 'Jack later reckoned that she'd let him go to London 'cause she thought he'd not find a job and then come back to her in Dublin.'

Spot was heartbroken by Rita's refusal to travel to London and begged her to reconsider. According to one of her relatives in Dublin, that was when she made the decision to end their marriage. 'Rita was always her own woman. It was that strength which Jack had relied upon for long, but now she'd decided there was more to life than a crummy flat in West London.' Rita told Spot she wanted to give the girls a new life away from any of the reminders of the London underworld. Spot knew the strength of Rita's maternal instincts and knew there was little he could do to prevent the estrangement from his beloved family.

In Dublin, one of Rita's oldest friends was emigrating to the USA and she heard that the Americans were particularly welcoming to Irish applications for a Green Card. In 1961, Rita and their two daughters turned up in New York, where they stayed with friends.

Shortly afterwards, she met a man and moved down to Florida where she got a job running a restaurant. At last one of her dreams had come true.

Back in London, Jack Spot accepted that his marriage was over and filed for divorce. At first he tried to keep in touch with the children, but transatlantic phone calls were incredibly expensive and he'd never been much of a letter writer. Eventually, contact between them became rare. Spot always looked back on the split from Rita as the best and worst decision of his life. He claimed he granted a non-contested divorce, to 'allow Rita to start her life again away from all the danger that I'd created'. But in reality he had little choice.

Now he'd lost everything: his wife and his children. He kept photos of them all on his mantlepiece as a reminder of the good old days when he was king of the underworld. And, with more time on his hands than he'd ever had before, he started working out how the Krays had been so instrumental in his downfall. By the time he'd put all the pieces of the jigsaw together, it was too late to do anything except wait until the day came when he could get his revenge. Before, Spot had always blamed Hill for his demise, but he now saw that the Krays were behind it all. They'd wriggled their way into his life while dealing with Hill behind his back throughout. They'd manipulated the underworld to ensure that they would ultimately be the only victors.

26

RETIRING UNGRACEFULLY

In the good old days, Jack Spot had owned Soho and bought £100 dinners at the finest restaurants. Now 'John Colmore' walked everywhere and received few visitors in his flat in Gloucester Road: 'because it is so humble and in a bit of a mess like me.' But he hadn't completely walked away from his previous life of crime. Spot developed a neat sideline in stolen meat, which he got from a couple of West London contacts who worked in Cadby Hall, the headquarters of J. Lyons, in Hammersmith. Spot specialised in supplying local restaurants, which helped supplement his low wages from the furniture shop.

But Spot's skills as a criminal were not what they used to be and, in January 1962, he was caught and nicked by the local constabulary. On 6 February, he admitted handling thirty shillings' worth of meat from Cadby Hall. He gave his name to West London Magistrates as 'John Colmore, a forty-nine-year-old butcher of Romford Street, Whitechapel,' and pleaded guilty to stealing the meat. Spot told the court: 'I'm sorry this has happened. I lost my job because of it. I have to look for another.' In fact he was still running that furniture shop in the Gloucester Road. The police disclosed to the court that, under the name of Comer, he had at least five convictions, including grievous bodily harm. But Magistrate Mr Seymour Collins, told Spot: 'As so many years have passed without any convictions, I will fine you £12 instead of sending you to prison.'

ʃ   ʃ   ʃ

The following month, Spot's fame seemed about to provide him with some much-needed extra cash. The *Sunday Express* got a snap of him at the lounge at London's Heathrow Airport in the company of film producer Michael Goodman and an actress named Patricia Kilcarrif. Spot and his new friends were about to board a plane to Dublin where Goodman was scouting locations to film *The Jack Spot Story*, described as a ninety-minute film based on real events. Spot proudly claimed he was an advisor on the production. When asked if he'd ever done any filming before, Spot quipped: 'Only at Scotland Yard. They took me front-face and side-face.'

Spot once again mentioned his 'crime doesn't pay' theme, which he hoped would be the moral of the film. He even explained to one reporter: 'The idea of this project is to prevent crime. All I've got to show for my big-shot gangster days are three hundred stitches and a marked face. The only people who know that there is nothing in crime in the long run are people like me. The average crime film makes me and all the other villains laugh: they are rubbish. For the truth – even though it makes us look past mugs – is that we could not possibly win.'

Spot believed that much of the film would revolve around the period when he was king of the underworld. 'I am reconstructing many leading crimes, often with the people who committed them.' Producer Michael Goodman's other 'advisors' included London Airport robber Sam Ross. Ross explained: 'I've had something like thirty years in gaol and I've been mixed up with the biggest villains of the past twenty years. Now I have quit. My children go to good schools. I've made fortunes and I've lost them, and the whole business frankly hasn't been worth the candle.'

Producer Goodman boasted that he expected to make a million pounds from *The Jack Spot Story*. He described the project as 'the gangster film to end all gangster films. It lifts the lid off gambling, the rackets – the lot.' But, within days, tensions flared up between big-talking Goodman and his criminal 'advisors' and Spot quit the production. Goodman explained: 'There were so many arguments in my flat about it, that I have brought in an independent writer to rewrite it.' The film never actually saw the light of day.

Over in Spain, Billy Hill had deliberately cut down the number of his regular visits to London to remain at his Marbella home on a more permanent basis. Hill was the only one who got out with a bag full of loot. He considered Spot and many others to be part of a bygone era. He'd gradually retreated from London quietly to avoid any problems with the Krays, but that didn't stop him entertaining them at his whitewashed hacienda whenever they felt the need to soak up the sunshine.

ℐ   ℐ   ℐ

In August 1963, the Great Train Robbery changed the face of British crime. Jack Spot – already completely off the crime scene – dearly wished he'd been involved in the most audacious British crime of the twentieth century. And Billy Hill would no doubt have loved a piece of the action. But none of them even had a whiff of it.

Just a few weeks after the robbery, Spot was interviewed by a young film-maker called John Irvin who was researching a new Spot film project. Irvin visited Spot at his flat in Gloucester Road, Kensington, and remembers it as an impersonal home: 'It was like something out of the 1920s. Everything was very dingy and dark. He had drapes and net curtains up. Spot kept going on about wanting the world to know that crime didn't pay and how that was the message he wanted to put across.' Spot still wore crisp shirts and well-pressed slacks but they 'looked a little bit ragged'. He still had photos of Rita and the girls adorning every shelf and every side table in his flat. 'You couldn't miss them,' said Irvin.

Spot was full of disdain for the Krays. 'They're a wild, stupid bunch with no respect,' Spot told Irvin. 'I should have stopped them right from the start.' It was soon apparent to him that Spot was trying to rewrite history in a bizarre way. 'He looked on himself as some kind of Robin Hood,' said Irvin. 'And he was trying to use us to project that image.'

At the same interview, sound recordist Oein McCann was shocked by Spot's physical state. 'I couldn't believe he was only in his early fifties. He looked a lot like Lew Grade in many ways and he seemed like a broken man. He was all hunched up and seemed smaller than the six-foot tall man we'd been expecting to meet. He was sunken into his jacket. No neck. His shoulders seemed to go up to his ears.'

Spot offered the two men huge doorstep ham sandwiches and brown bottles of woodpecker cider with rubber twist tops. He then agreed to accompany the film team on a tour of his old East End haunts. 'He was terrified,' McCann later recalled. 'Every time we drove past certain places or stopped at traffic lights, he slumped down in the car so no one could see him. We passed one oyster stall in Whitechapel and Spot had tears welling up in his eyes because he was so surprised that it was still there. It was a sorry sight to behold.'

After three hours of touring his old manor, Spot begged the film team to take him home. 'He was exhausted, mentally and physically. He'd obviously found it very difficult going back to all those old haunts,' explained McCann. McCann also noticed that Spot never asked his guests any questions about themselves. 'We were just faces to him. Nothing more. He'd just say: "What d'you want to know?" That was it. He was a very sad figure, lacking in any basic curiosity. His only interest seemed to be in the past and all the power and fear.'

The film company dropped the project after concluding that 'he wasn't trying hard enough to tell us everything'. McCann recalled: 'We'd seen this as a potential movie project – the story of a gangster in fifties London but his view was far too one-sided. It would never have worked.'

§   §   §

In October 1963, Spot was paid £200 for a TV appearance on the programme *The Braden Beat*. On air, Spot claimed that crime in Britain was now under the control of the American Mafia. Scotland Yard totally rubbished his outburst, saying it was simply Spot's way of getting some much-needed headlines. But Spot insisted he was speaking the truth. He even later told Fleet Street crime reporter Norman Lucas: 'I know the identities of the men who work for the Mafia in London. I know I'm sticking my neck out by revealing the truth about the Mafia's control of the underworld in Britain. But if hired thugs are sent to beat me up, they will be publicly admitting guilt. I don't care what happens to me in the future.'

Spot reckoned that one-armed bandits, or fruit machines, were the Mafia's biggest source of income. He also alleged they controlled betting shops, amusement arcades, casinos and racecourse bookies. He claimed that two Mafia men moved to London after his own demise as king of the underworld. Spot claimed he couldn't name the two 'Mafia men' because he was afraid they might sue him for libel.

He explained to Norman Lucas: 'One of them pretends to be a respectable citizen and claims he's left his days of thuggery behind. The other is a man everybody knows as a bookie who will stop at nothing. He is a man born of Italian parentage who was interned during the war.' The two men sounded more like Billy Hill and Albert Dimes than a couple of New York dons. In reality, Spot was having one last dig at his oldest enemies, but he didn't have the courage to identify them.

Scotland Yard responded by saying: 'We know the men. We are satisfied they have no connection with the Mafia and, at present, their activities are within the law.'

ʃ　　ʃ　　ʃ

By the beginning of 1966, Soho had turned into a much uglier place than it had been in Jack Spot's heyday. Dirty bookshops were everywhere and 'near-beer' joints, clip joints and cinemas showing pornographic films attracted the oddest types and a few tourists wanting to see the naughty bits of London. One of the commonest scams was the blue film racket, in which a smooth-talking spiv would stand outside a doorway and invite punters in to see a dirty movie. After taking their money, the customers were then directed upstairs, to an empty floor, while the spiv moved on to another doorway.

Prostitution as well as strip clubs and champagne bars were controlled by criminals such as Jimmy Humphreys and the Mason brothers, as well as by two of Spot's contemporaries, the notorious vice barons Silver and Mifsud. The Krays, just like Spot and Hill before them, had steered clear of vice.

Scotland Yard detective 'Nipper' Read tracked Jack Spot down to his flat on the Gloucester Road, to ask him about the Krays' activities in the spring of 1966. Read claimed at the time: 'Spot was down on his luck and knew nothing. In fact he was rather hoping to capitalise on the interest in the Krays with another story in the newspapers about old times.' In fact, Read's statement was a deliberate smokescreen. Spot went out of his way to help the police with their inquiries because he now knew that the Krays had been instrumental in his own downfall and he was out for revenge. But he wanted to be certain nobody knew he was helping the police with their inquiries. After years of denying being a grass, he'd finally gone over to the other side. 'I don't reckon Spotty ever grassed anyone up except the Krays. He just couldn't forgive them for helping bring him down,' one old East End villain admitted.

Spot was particularly furious after Read told him that Billy Hill had entertained the twins at his newly acquired villa in Tangiers, Morocco, after Ronnie had killed mobster George Cornell in the Blind Beggar in March 1966. Now it all made sense to Spot. 'Hill and those Kray nutters conspired to kick me out of London,' he later told one acquaintance.

Spot furnished Nipper Read with stacks of information on the Krays' contacts and associates. He even pointed the finger at Ronnie Kray over the death of a bookmaker in 1957. 'Spotty was out for revenge and he had little to lose,' explained an old lag who knew him throughout the sixties. 'He blamed the Krays for encouraging Billy Hill to have him done over.'

Read later recalled: 'Spot had clearly been through hard times. But there was still the well-cut suit and the smart brown fedora. He still talked a good fight, asserting that he had taught the twins "all they know".' Spot even admitted to Read: 'You know what did it for me, Nipper? The papers. All that "king of the underworld" thing. It was the worst day's work I ever did. Nobody even knew me before that and then suddenly everybody's trying to put one on me. That was my mistake, Nipper: publicity.'

A few months later, detectives led by Nipper Read swooped and arrested the Krays, plus many members of their firm. The twins later got life sentences for the murders of villains George Cornell and Jack 'The Hat' McVitie.

With those other underworld danger men, the Richardson's, locked up as well, there was now an opening for a new gang in the capital. How Jack Spot must have wished he was twenty years younger. Instead, he continued working in a variety of menial jobs for the following ten years. A handful of girlfriends came and went but he admitted to one pal that he still missed Rita and his daughters desperately. In 1975, Spot tried to organise a trip to Florida to see his daughters after getting a Christmas card from them. But his application for a visa was turned down because of his criminal record.

Those who met Spot during this period say that he continued to age at an alarmingly fast rate. By the late 1970s, he looked at least ten years older than sixty-five years. One East End villain bumped into Spot when he was sitting on the top deck of a bus travelling up Kensington High Street. 'At first, Spotty completely denied who he was,' the villain later recalled. 'Then I sat down next to him and asked him about Rita and the girls and he looked heartbroken. He felt so bad about Rita, the girls and even some of the blokes he'd chivved down the years, I reckon it was the guilt that aged him so much.'

In October 1984, Jack Spot turned up at a charity boxing match at the Elephant and Castle, in south-east London. He was now seventy-two years old, but still immensely proud of the past. 'Three hundred stitches I've had. The doctors ran out of thread so I put them in touch with my tailor,' he told one reporter who recognised him.

It was more than twenty years since he'd last attended a boxing match. The only visible sign of his violent past was the deep razor slash scar running from the side of his lips down over his chin. Spot was still perfectly turned out in a dark business suit and carrying a rolled umbrella. He boasted to another reporter he encountered that he'd met the Duke of Norfolk at the races the previous Saturday. 'He gave me a great reception. Of course I knew the old Duke well. He always held me responsible for solving the problems of bookmakers welshing.'

Eighteen months later, Spot gave his last full interview to a newspaper, the *Evening Standard*. He admitted having many regrets about his life of crime: 'I never wanted all that. My Rita never wanted it. Bad for me. Bad for her. Bad for the kids.' When he was asked what he was doing now, his eyes narrowed, 'Nothing'. Then he put his own spin on his downfall. 'They came at me with choppers and knives and always mob-handed. Not one man in my whole life. No one ever came to Jack Spot and said, "Come on, let's have a fight."' Spot refused to be drawn on the subject of Billy Hill throughout the interview.

Then on 19 July 1988, Jack Spot – still a very dapper-looking character in a neat grey suit, matching grey homburg hat and a neatly rolled black umbrella – turned up at the Frank Bruno versus Tim Witherspoon World Heavyweight Championship weigh-in. Few noticed him and at first no one seemed to recognise him, even though his name might have rung a few, unsettling bells. When one veteran Fleet Street reporter finally recognised Spot, he asked him how he was. 'Bit of arthritis, but can't grumble,' responded Spot, raising his hat in a polite salute before shuffling off into the distance.

Less than a year later, Jack Spot's arthritis got so bad that he had to be admitted into a National Health-funded nursing home in Eastbourne, Sussex. He told many of his fellow residents that he was a 'retired butcher'. In 1993, Rita and his two grown-up daughters paid him a visit in Eastbourne. He was barely able to recognise them because of his rapidly failing health. In the winter of 1996, Jack Spot died of natural causes at the nursing home. He was eighty-four years old. Not one newspaper carried a reference to his death.

EPILOGUE

BILLY HILL maintained a reasonable lifestyle throughout the sixties, even making occasional guest appearances at some of the Krays' clubs, unlike Jack Spot. Hill also grabbed a few more head-lines, thanks to his friendships with upmarket socialite Lady Docker, evil property landlord Peter Rachman and Profumo girl Mandy Rice-Davies. But most of the time he kept a low profile at his sunshine home – steering clear of the ruthless sixties gangsters who'd taken over his turf.

In the early seventies, Hill returned to England and ran an upmarket nightclub in the respectable commuter-belt town of Sun-ningdale, Berkshire. Then, in 1976, he split up with long-time love Gypsy Riley and took up with a black nightclub singer. When his girlfriend committed suicide a couple of years later, Hill shut himself away in his flat in Moscow Road, just a stone's throw from where Spot had once lived at Hyde Park Mansions. He was racked with remorse and blamed himself because he'd left her after a row and returned home the following day to find her body.

Hill died on New Year's Day 1984 at the age of seventy-four. Jack Spot described him as 'the richest man in the graveyard' and former love Gypsy arranged the funeral. None of his old under-world cronies were informed until after the cremation service. Hill had arranged for his last lover's twelve-year-old son to inherit his entire fortune. Hill also made a settlement with Gypsy, whom he'd lived with throughout his heyday. Part of the deal was that she should look after the twelve-year-old boy.

Mad Frankie Fraser later recalled: 'Bill was a very smart man, not sharp but a classy dresser. He neither stood out or not. You could take him in any company and he wouldn't let you down.' The Krays sent their condolences from their cells. Without Billy Hill their reign of terror would never have got off the ground.

ALBERT DIMES and FRANKIE FRASER continued their careers in crime. In the early sixties, they joined the Richardsons in South London. Dimes abandoned the racetrack for the even more lucrative business of supplying fruit machines to nightclubs. He became friendly with Hollywood star Stanley Baker and, through him, was introduced to movie director Joseph Losey. Dimes worked as an advisor on Losey's 1960 movie *The Criminal* in which Baker played the leading character – a combination of Dimes, Hill and Jack Spot. Dimes always reckoned he never fully recovered his health following the 'fight that never was' in Soho with Spot. He died of cancer at his home in River Street, Islington, in 1972, at the age of fifty-seven.

FRANKIE FRASER first went to prison when he was aged thirteen and spent thirty-two of his next forty years in jail. He was thirty-nine in 1962 when he emerged from his seven-year sentence for cutting Jack Spot at Albert Dimes' behest. On his release, Dimes and Billy Hill gave Fraser a party at the Pigalle Club in Piccadilly, with Shirley Bassey and Winifred Attwill, the ragtime pianist, as guests of honour. Then, in 1967, he was convicted as one of the Richardson's 'torturers'. Various prison clashes meant he eventually served the full nineteen-year sentence. He was finally released in April 1985. In August 1991, Fraser was gunned down outside Turnmill's nightclub, in the Farringdon area of London. Naturally he refused to identify his assailant to police. Today, Fraser makes a living by hosting bus tours around the East End of London, where he proudly points out the scenes of notorious local crimes. He also occasionally pops up in Christmas pantos.

BILLY BLYTHE died, aged thirty-nine, on the operating table of Walton prison hospital in Liverpool, after a stomach operation in February 1957. Hill and other friends arranged a lavish funeral at Kensal Green cemetery, where Reverend Basil Andrews had been the curate just a few years earlier.

TEDDY MACHIN, the chiv-man, was one of many Jack Spot accused of turning Hill against him – was severely wounded when two shotgun blasts were fired through the window of his home in Canning Town in 1970. Later it emerged that Machin, by then sixty years old, had upset the son of one of his numerous female lovers.

JOHNNY RICE was sentenced to twelve months' imprisonment in May 1957 for receiving stolen car logbooks, obtaining books of petrol coupons under false pretences and stealing motorcycle registration books. He refused to squeal on the others involved with him in the racket – including Billy Hill.

AGGIE HILL, Billy Hill's ex-wife, prospered well following Hill's decision to quit London for Spain. Her only setback came when Selwyn Cooney, the manager of her New Cabinet Club in Gerrard Street, was murdered in 1960 by Jimmy Nash, whose brother Johnny reckoned he was on his way to becoming the new boss of the underworld (although the Krays no doubt disagreed). In the 1970s, Aggie moved to Jersey where she opened a nightclub and became a wealthy and respected member of the community.

PATRICK MARRINAN, QC, continued to rub the police up the wrong way. Scotland Yard's legendary Tommy Butler – later head of the Flying Squad – had Marrinan's phone tapped in the middle of 1957 because of concerns about the lawyer's close ties to Hill and other mobsters. Marrinan was disbarred on evidence provided through those phone taps and moved back to Ireland to try and start a new life.

DUNCAN WEBB continued his one-man journalistic crusade against crime. Bizarrely, he got a papal dispensation to marry killer Donald Hume's wife, Cynthia, in September 1958. Two weeks later he died at the age of forty-one – from war wounds rather than from any injuries caused by London's most notorious criminals. Just before he died, he provided police with evidence which secured the acquittal of Ian Gordon, a young airman who had been convicted of the murder of a woman he was courting.

SUPERINTENDENT HERBERT SPARKS, head of the CID at West End Central from 1954–58 went on to head the Flying Squad in 1959. He retired in 1961 and wrote his life story the following year, but ended up being successfully sued for libel by a man he falsely accused of being an armed robber. Sparks died in 1991.

MOISHA BLUEBALL got heavily involved with the Krays as they emerged onto the West End scene. Spot later claimed that Moisha 'taught them everything they knew'. But Moisha never got the appreciation he deserved and died impoverished and frightened in the mid-1960s. He and Spot never spoke again after he was jailed for the conspiracy involving Reverend Basil Andrews.

SONNY THE YANK turned his back on crime and became a restaurateur in West London. He disowned Spot and managed to go straight, enjoying a long and healthy life away from the underworld.

REVEREND BASIL ANDREWS settled in Oxford following the perjury trial. He claimed to anyone who'd listen that he'd given up the demon drink, as well as gambling and women. A newspaper reporter eventually found him living on a church pension of £5 a week and counting every penny. 'Meals must be of the most economical sort. Bread and cheese for lunch; a cheap but hot meal at night. Only very occasionally can I afford a drink.' Andrews insisted he'd found peace at last.

CHRIS GLINSKI, witness to the 'fight that never was', continued to live on the fringes of the underworld and re-emerged into the criminal limelight as a witness against Mad Frankie Fraser at his 'torture' trial in 1967.

ROSE HEILBRON, Spot's counsel in the Battle of Frith Street trial, became the first woman to be appointed a High Court judge. Her daughter, also a QC, practises in London today.

CHIEF SUPERINTENDENT TED GREENO retired in 1958 and wrote a highly acclaimed book about his police experiences.

DETECTIVE NIPPER READ, having finally brought the Krays to justice virtually single-handedly in the mid-sixties retired gracefully and went on to write a best-selling autobiography about his own fight against crime.

GLOSSARY

backhander	bribe
bang to rights	caught red-handed
bang up	to imprison
bent	crooked
bird	prison sentence
blag	wages snatch, robbery etc
bogey	a police detective
brass	prostitute
case	check out
chalk money	a blackmailing system imposed on race-course bookies who paid out protection to gangs to avoid having their stands wrecked
chiv	a taped-up razor for cutting, not stabbing
cop	receive a sentence
cozzer	policeman
DCI	Detective Chief Inspector
DCS	Detective Chief Superintendent
DI	Detective Inspector
dippers	pickpockets
drum	a flat or house
faces	renowned criminals
factory	police station
fence	criminal who sells stolen goods
finger	accuse

fitted up	framed
folding money	banknotes
frummers	Orthodox Jews
grass	informer
guv'nor	senior policeman/gang boss
have one's collar felt	to be arrested
hook	thief
iron	homosexual (iron-hoof = poof)
jack	£5
jump up	stealing from lorries
manor	territory of a villain or policeman
minder	bodyguard/trouble-shooter
monkey	£500
Mr Wood	policeman's truncheon
old lag	long-tcrm prisoner
peter	prison, police cell or safe
piker	unreliable person/gypsy
pitch or stand money	extortion racket on bookies at a racecourse
ponce	plmp
pony	£25
porridge	prison
rubber	drinking or gambling club
run-in	secret location for unloading and storing stolen goods
scam	deception
screaming	informing to the police
screw	prison officer
screwsman	burglar or safe-breaker
shillelagh	Irish stick used in fights
shooter	gun
slag	small-time crook
snout	informer/tobacco
spieler	gambling club
spiv	a man who earns his money doing an honest day's work for a bookie

sponge	money demanded by thugs for damping bookies' sponges for a fee at racecourses
stretch	prison sentence
stripe	cut someone's face with a chiv
swallow	accept a situation without protest
sweeny todd	the Flying Squad
tealeaf	thief
team	regular gang of criminals
tearaway	small-time but generally violent and reckless criminal
tom	prostitute
tomfoolery	jewellery
tooled up	to be equipped with weapons for a crime
top hats	uniformed police
top man	tic-tac men at racecourses
turned over	premises raided by police
verbals	report of 'off-the-record' remarks made by villain to police
villain	crook of some standing
welsher	pulling a fast one at a racecourse
wide	aware of how the world *knows*, of the codes of the underworld
workman	someone employed in a drinking club or spieler

BIBLIOGRAPHY

Born Fighter (1990) by R. Kray, Arrow
Cherrill of the Yard (1953) by F. Cherrill, Harrap
Cloak Without Dagger (1956) by P. Sillitoe, Pan Books
Crime Reporter (1956) by D. Webb, Fleetway
Deadline for Crime (1955) by D. Webb, Muller
Elephant Boys (2000) by B. McDonald, Mainstream
Inside the CID (1957) by P. Beveridge, Evans Brothers
Jack Spot, Man of a Thousand Cuts (1959) by H. Janson, Alexander
   Moring
London After Dark (1954) by R. Fabian, Naldrett Press
Mad Frankie (1994) by F. Fraser with J. Morton, Warner
Mad Frank's Diary (2000) by F. Fraser and J. Morton, Virgin
Nipper (1988) by L. Read with J. Morton
Smash 'n' Grab (1993) by R. Murphy, Faber and Faber
Soho (1956) by A. Tietjen, Allan Wingate
The Profession of Violence (1972) by J. Pearson, HarperCollins
The Underworld (1953) by J. Phelan, Harrap
Tough Guys Don't Cry (1983) by J. Cannon, Magnus Books
War on the Underworld (1960) by E. Greeno, John Long

INDEX